Faluba / Morvay

CONVERSATION GUIDEBOOK
English-Catalan-Spanish

English version by Darryl James Clark
Revision by John Matthews, lecturer
at the Escola Universitària de
Traductors i Intèrprets
(EUTI)

[EDICIONS DE LA MAGRANA]

Kálmán Faluba and Károly Morvay are lecturers in Catalan and Spanish at the University of Budapest.

This edition has been made possible thanks to the help of the Departament de Cultura de la Generalitat de Catalunya.

First edition: May 1992
Second edition: Juli 1994
Third edition: July 1995
Fourth edition: July 1996
Fifth edition: September 1997
Sixth edition: June 1998
Seventh edition: November 1999

Edicions de la Magrana, SA
Pàdua, 83 - 08006 Barcelona
Tel. 93 4173000. Fax: 93 4170106
E-mail: magrana@magrana.es
Internet: http://www.magrana.es

Printed by Novagràfik, Puigcerdà, 127 - 08019 Barcelona
ISBN: 84-7410-590-0
Legal Deposit: B. 47.817 - 1999

TABLE OF CONTENTS

LETTER FROM THE PUBLISHER

Dear friend,

Perhaps you are planning to visit Barcelona, or maybe you are already here. Whichever the case may be, you'll make good use of this book which includes texts in the two languages that are spoken here: Catalan and Spanish. In Barcelona you will indeed hear people speak Catalan, one of the seven Romance languages spoken in Europe and, therefore, a language germane to French or Italian. Today Catalan is legally considered to be Catalonia's own language and is official along with Castilian or Spanish. Barcelona is the capital of Catalonia, which includes the cities of Barcelona, Figueres, Tarragona, Girona, Lleida, Vielha, etc., etc.. A country with such essential sites to visit as the Costa Brava, Montserrat, the Sagrada Familia, the Pyrenees, the Picasso, Dalí, Miró, and Tàpies museums, the Museum of Romanesque Art, etc. Catalonia is a nationality within Spain: it has its own autonomous government, its own Parliament and its own political institutions. Likewise, the Balearic Isles and Valencia, where Catalan is also spoken, have a similar political organization.

Catalan is a language spoken by over ten million inhabitants in a territory that extends from French Catalonia (the region of Rosselló) to Alacant, to the south of Valencia. To the east, Catalan is also spoken in the Balearic Isles and to the west, it is spoken right up to the boundary with Aragón. Each region, however, speaks it with its own variations, as occurs with any other language in any other country. Gaudí spoke Catalan as did Miró, Dalí, Pau Casals, etc. Picasso also spoke Catalan, although he was born in Malaga, because he learned it while living in Barcelona.

If you wish to practice Catalan, you will have easy access to newspapers, magazines and books, two T.V. channels that broadcast exclusively in Catalan and another that does so partially; diverse radio stations, both commercial and classical music stations.

Likewise, most signs and signals are in Catalan: businesses, public administration centers, street signs and names, etc. Don't be alarmed: they are easy to comprehend and most of them have the Spanish translation alongside. Therefore, the use of Catalan needn't be an insurmountable obstacle during your visit.

I sincerely hope this guide will be of great assistance to you. We have created it with that idea in mind. And we will gratefully accept all suggestions and recommendations you might have to offer.

Edicions de la Magrana
Apartat de Correus 9487
08080 Barcelona

0.2 INSTRUCTIONS FOR THE USE OF THIS CONVERSATION GUIDE

Our guide consists of four main units. The first - which follows the preface and these instructions - presents the phonetic characteristics of Catalan and Spanish. The second and longest unit, which opens with basic rudiments of grammar, includes materials arranged in thirteen sections. The third unit is a a trilingual vocabulary list, and the fourth, an index.

The phrases and words generally appear in three columns, in English, Catalan and Spanish respectively. On a few occasions we have deviated from this succession, providing for situations in which we must help the tourist confronted with written texts. On these occasions the first column will be in Catalan. The section «Avisos» («Notices»), of exceptional nature, has only two columns: in the left column there are phrases and words both in Catalan and Spanish.

The unit dedicated to pronunciation first discusses the phonetic characteristics of Catalan and afterwards those of Spanish. In addition to the main practical rules that aim at assuring a correct reading, we offer the user the Catalan version of a text and the Spanish version of the same text, plus a series of diverse phrases in both languages with their respective transcriptions.

The section entitled Grammar is not a theoretical treatise on the system of the two languages, but an illustration of some of their features, such as the different forms of the articles, pronouns, possessives, demonstratives, etc. You will also find information on conjugation, for example the regular forms of the present indicative, as well as the irregular forms of the verbs ser, estar, tenir (to be, to be, to have)/ tener, voler (to have, to want)/ querer and haver (to want, to have) in the same tense. At any rate, the user who desires a more complete view of Spanish or Catalan conjugation, will have to refer to other sources, which are easy to find in each language.

Under the title of «Common words and phrases», we have gathered together all types of material that could be necessary for concrete communicative acts, more or less independently of the subject. This same section contains expressions for social life, formulas which help to establish an initial contact.

The main part of our guide is composed of simple recurrent phrases arranged thematically. With the aid of the list of vocabulary, these phrases can be completed and/or modified. We frequently include variants of a same phrase, with interchangeable elements. These are separated with a slanted line. If there are more than two variants, or if the modification involves entire word groups, the elements to be interchanged are placed apart in a new line. We point out optional constructions or words with suffixal parentheses.

In order to facilitate the use of this guide, we've included an extensive index at the end of the guide.

The vocabulary that brings this book to a close contains the essential indications relating to the gender (and, exceptionally, to the number) of the nouns. We indicate the gender wherever it is not recognizable through the application of a few simple rules. Normally, we shall consider nouns ending in «a» to be feminine, and the rest to be masculine. Those which don't follow this rule are indicated with an «m» (masculine) or an «f» (feminine): día m (day), estació f (station, season). There are Catalan and Spanish nouns which are only (or preferably) used in the plural. This is pointed out with the abbreviations m pl and f pl. We also offer the feminine forms of adjectives, whenever they differ from the masculine ones.

0.3 PRONUNCIATION

THE PRONUNCIATION OF CATALAN

Rules of stress

Some monosyllables are stressed: dur [dú] hard; got [gót] glass; dors [dórs] back.

A few monosyllables (prepositions, pronouns and articles) are not stressed: amb [am] with; de [da] of; en [an] in.

Polysyllables are pronounced according to these rules:

1. The penultimate syllable is stressed in words ending in:A vowel (except for diphthongs), a vowel + /s/ (except for diphthongs, /en/ or /in/ : metro [métru] subway/underground; diversos [divérsus] diverse; valen [bálan] they cost.

2. The final syllable is stressed of words ending in: A diphthong or a diphthong + /s/, groups of consonants, /an/, /on/, /un/ and other consonants except /s/, and /n/ after /e/ and /i/: arreu [arréw] everywhere; creus [kréws] cross; interessant [intarasán] interesting; ciutat [siuwtát] city.

3. In all cases contrary to rule 1 and 2, the stress is shown with a written accent mark. Words with the stress on the antepenultimate syllable always carry a written accent: anglès [anglás] English; americà [amariká] American; pàgina [pajina] page.

Sometimes a written accent is placed to differentiate between two identically spelled words: si [sí] if; sí [sí] yes; be [bé] sheep; bé [bé] well (adv.).

Catalan vowels

Catalan vowels have different values, depending on position and accent. In general, Catalan vowels are much more tense than English vowels, the position of the mouth remaining the same throughout the pronunciation of the vowel.

vowel	phonetic symbol	explanation
a	[á]	Stressed /a/ is an open vowel between the English /a/ in rat and father: pare [pára] father; mitjà [midjá] medium; ànec [ának] duck.
	[a]	Unstressed /a/ has a neutral sound like the English /a/ and /e/ in sugar and never: casa [káza] house; afecta

		[afékta] it affects; Barcelona [Barselóna] Barcelona.
e		Stressed /e/ has two sounds: [e] Open /e/ like in English sell: pel [pel] hair; terra [terra] land; vostè [busté] you (polite pronoun).
	[é]	Closed /e/ is like the /a/ in English say, but without any glide at the end: cent [sén] one hundred; nét [nét] grandson; festa [fésta] party.
	[a]	Unstressed /e/ sounds the same as unstressed /a/, exept before an /a/, where it sounds the same as a closed /e/: cine [sína] cinema; veure [béwra] to see; but: teatre [teátra] theater.
i	[ee]	The Catalan /i/ is like the English /ee/ in seen. When stressed it is somewhat longer: vi [bee] wine; línia [leenya] line; difícil [difeesil] difficult.
	[y]	The unstressed /i/ between two vowels is like the English /y/ in yet: noia [noya] girl.
o		Stressed /o/ has two sounds:
	[ou]	Open /o/ is like the English /ou/ in cough: transport [transpourt] transport; lògica [loujika] logic; obra [oubra] work.
	[ó]	Closed /o/ is like the English /o/ in rope without the final /w/ sound: sóc [sók] I am; catorze [katórza]; fourteen; boca [bóka].
	[oo]	Unstressed /o/ is somewhat like the

		English /oo/ in foot: obrir [oovrí] to open; ferro [férroo] iron; orella [ooreya] ear.
u	[oo]	Stressed or unstressed, the Catalan /u/ sounds like the English /oo/ in foot, as in the Catalan unstressed /o: número [noomeru] number; dur [doo] hard; puc [pook] I can.
[w]		Between two vowels Catalan /u/ is like the English /w/ in want: escriuen [eskríwan] they write; beuen [béwan] they drink.

Catalan diphthongs

The first vowel in Catalan diphthongs has its regular value (stressed or unstressed) and the second /i/ or /u/ is transcribed as a semiconsonant. So mai [máy] (never) and vuit [buyt] (eight) are monosyllables and aire [áy-ra] (air) and boira [bóy-ra] (fog) are two syllable words. If /i/ and /u/ are not part of a diphthong along with the preceding vowel, these letters are marked with an accent or a diaeresis: veí [ba-í] neighbor; llengües [yéngwas] languages.

diphthong	phonetic symbol	explanation
ai	[áy]	Like English /y/ in sky: aire [áyra].
au	[áw]	Like /ou/ in English loud: pau [páw] peace.
ei	[éy]	Like /ey/ in English they: servei [servéy] service.
eu	[ew]	Combination of Catalan closed /e/ and /u/: seu [séw] his/hers/yours.
iu	[iw]	Like /u/ in English unit: ciutat [siwtát] city.

oi	[óy]	Like /oy/ in English boy: boyra [bóyra] fog.
ou	[ów]	Like /ew/ in English sew: sou [sów] you are (pl.).
ui	[wí]	Like the English we: vuit [bwít] eight.
ua	[wá]	Like /wa/ in English watch: quatre [kwátra] four.
üe	[wa]	Like /wa/ in English was: llengües [yéngwas] languages.
üi	[wí]	Like the English we: argüir [argwí] to argue.
uo	[wó]	Like /wo/ in English won't: quotidià [kwotidyá] daily.

Catalan consonants

consonants	phonetic symbol	explanation
1. b		There are five different pronunciations depending on position:
	[b]	Like /b/ in English boy in initial position or after /m/: Barcelona [barselóna]; també [també] also.
	[p]	At the end of a word or before an unvoiced consonant, sounds like /p/ in English pound: árab [árap] arab; absorbir [apsurpí] to absorb.
	[bb]	The sound is double when between a stressed vowel and /l/: oblidar [oobblidá] to forget; doble [dobbla] double.
	[ ]	After /m/ in final position, /b/ is silent: amb [am] with; tomb [tóm] turn.

	[b]	In all other positions /b/ is much softer than in English. Pronounced with the lips slightly open, like when blowing out a candle: autobús [awtobús] bus/coach; descobrir [daskubrí] to discover.
2. c		There are five different pronunciations depending on position:
	[s]	Followed by /e/ or /i/, it is pronounced somewhat like the /c/ in English city: cent [sen] one hundred; ciutat [siwtat] city.
	[k]	In most other positions the /c/ is pronounced as English /k/ or hard /c/ : com [kom] how; cultura [kultúra] culture.
	[kk]	The /k/ sound is doubled when between a stressed vowel and /l/: espectacle [aspaktákla] show; article [artíkkla] article.
	[g]	Before a voiced consonant, /c/ sounds like /g/ in English glow: anècdota [anégdoota] anecdote.
	[ ]	After /n/ in final position, /c/ is silent and the /n/ is pronounced like /ng/ in English wrong: cinc [sing] five; banc [báng] bank.
3. ç	[s]	The ç sounds like /c/ in English city: plaça [plása] square; cançó [kansó] song.
4. d		The /d/ has four different sounds depending on position.
	[d]	In an initial position or after /l/, /m/, /n/ or a plosive, the Catalan /d/ is

similar to the English /d/ in don't, but placing the tip of the tongue against the back of the front teeth: dir [dí] to say; falda [fálda] skirt.

[t] In a final position or before an unvoiced consonant, similar to /t/ in English store: verd [bert] green; adquirir [atkirí] to acquire.

[th] In most other positions, the Catalan /d/ is similar to the English /th/ in that: cada [kátha] each; parada [parátha] stop (as in bus stop).

[ ] Silent in final position after /l/ and /n/ and in the group /rds/: perds [pers] you lose; dividend [dividén] dividend.

5. f [f] Like English /f/ in from: fama [fáma] fame; telefèric [teleférik] cable car.

6. g This letter has seven distinct pronunciations depending on position.

[g] In an initial position before /a/, /o/, /u/, /l/, /r/ or after /n/, Catalan /g/ sounds like the English hard /g/ in go: gat [gát] cat; gota [gota] drop. The /u/ is silent in /gue/ and /gui/ unless it is marked with a diaeresis: guerra [gerra] war; guisar [gisá] to cook argüir [argwí] to argue.

[g] When not in an initial position, nor preceded by /n/, /g/ followed by /a/, /o/, /u/, /l/ or /r/ is like English /g/ in rug but softer: pagar [pagár] to pay; aguantar [agwantá] to endure.

	[gg]	Usually double when between a stressed vowel and /l/: segle [séggla] century; regla [rrégla] ruler.
	[j]	Before /e/ and /i/, Catalan /g/ sounds like the /s/ in English division: gener [jené] January; girar [jirá] to turn.
	[tch]	In the endings /aig/, /eig/, /oig/ and /uig/, sounds like English /tch/ in itch: maig [mátch] May; veig [bétch] I see.
	[k]	In a final position, except in the above mentioned cases, sounds like /c/ in English cat: llarg [yárk] long; cástic [kástik] punishment.
	[ ]	After /n/ in final position, /g/ is silent and the /n/ is pronounced as in English wrong: sang [sáng] blood; fang [fáng] mud.
7. h	[ ]	Catalan /h/ is always silent: herba [érba] grass; hora [ora] hour.
8. j	[j]	Similar to the English /s/ in measure: jo [jó] I; menjar [manjá] to eat.
9. k	[k]	Used only in words of foreign origen: kiwi [kíwi] kiwi.
10. l		Two different sounds depending on position.
	[l]	In an initial position, after a consonant or between vowels, Catalan /l/ is like English /l/ in like: línia [línya] ine; parlo [párloo] I speak; hola [ola] hello.

[l] Betweeen a vowel and a consonant, or in a final position, Catalan /l/ is like English /l/ in little, drawing back the tongue while saying it: el [el] he; alga [álga] seaweed.

11. l.l [ll] Double /l/ with a dot is pronounced double: novel_la [nuvella] novel; satèlit [satéllit] satellite.

12. ll [y] This letter has one sound. It is similar to the English /li/ in million, or the /y/ in yet. It is pronounced placing tip of tongue against lower teeth: lliure [yíwra] free; coll [cóy] neck.

13. m [m] Like the English /m/ in more: més [més] more; impedir [impadí] to impede.

14. n Three different pronunciations depending on position.

[n] Before a vowel and in any other position excluding those listed below, is like n/ in English son: nom [nóm] name; ànec [ának] duck; donant [dunán] donor.

[ng] Before /c/, /qu/ or /g/, sounds like / ng/ in English wrong: cinc [síng] five; anglès [anglés] English; enquesta [engkésta] inquiry.

[m] Before /f/ or /v/, sounds like an /m/: enfocar [amfocá] to focus; enviar [ambiá] to envy.

15. ny [ni] The group /ny/ sounds somewhat like the /ni/ in English onion: Espanya [aspánia] Spain; company [kumpán] companion.

16. p		Two different sounds depending on position.
	[p]	In most positions sounds similar to English /p/in poor but less plosive: pare [pára] father; comprar [cumprá] to buy.
	[ ]	Silent after /m/ when final or between /m/ and another consonant except /l/ and /r/: camp [kám] camp; temps [téms] time.
17. qu	[k]	Before /e/ or /i/, sounds like /k/ in English kite: enquesta [ankésta] inquiry; adquirir [athkirí] to acquire.
18. qü, qu	[kw]	Catalan /qu/ before /e/ or /i/ and /qu/ before /a/ or /o/ sounds like English /qu/ in quick: quatre [kwátra] four; qüestió [kwastió] question.
19. r		Catalan /r/ and /rr/ are different from the English /r/ and, execpt at the end of words, are rolled with one flap or various flaps depending on position, with the tip of the tongue vibrating against the upper palate.
	[r]	Pronounced with one flap of the tip of the tongue against the hard palate: partir [partí] to depart; cara [kára] face. Also at the end of some words: car [kár] expensive; pur [púr] puro; amor [amór] love.
	[rr]	Pronounced with several flaps of the tip of the tongue against the hard palate when at the beginning of a word or after l/, /m/, /n/ or /s/: roda [rrotha]wheel; enregistrar [anrre-jistrá] to register; carrer [karré] street.

	[ ]	Silent at the end of infinitives and many nouns: cantar [kantá] to sing; carrer [karré] street; dur [dú] hard.
20. s		Two different pronunciations depending on position.
	[s]	In an initial position, within a word except when between vowels or before a voiced consonant and at the end of a word sounds like English /s/ in son or /ss/in class, but shorter: set [sét] seven; mosca [móska] fly; dos [dós] two.
	[z]	Between vowels or before a voiced consonant, this letter is pronounced like the short and soft /s/ in nose: casa [káza] house; validesa [bali-déza] validity; desmai [dazmáy] faint.
21. ss	[s]	Only between vowels and sounds like [s]: possibilitat [posibilitát] possibility.
22. t		Three different pronunciations depending on position.
	[t]	In most positions Catalan /t/ is like the English /t/ in take, pronounced placing the tip of the tongue against the back of the upper teeth: trencat [trankát] broken ;manat [manát] handful; tots [tóts] all.
	[d]	Before a voiced consonant, sounds like English /d/ in lead: viatge [biádja] trip ;metge [médja] doctor; mitjà [midjá] medium.
	[ ]	Silent after /l/ or /n/ when final and in the group /rts/: molt [mól] much/

very; bevent [bevén] drinking; dimarts [dimárs] Tuesday.
In the groups /tl/, /tll/ and /tm/, the Catalan /t/ is usually added to its neighbour, resulting in a double consonant: bitllet [biyyét] ticket; setmana [sammána] week.

23. v		Two different pronunciations depending on position.
	[b]	In initial position or after /n/, sounds like /b/ in English boy: vida [bítha]; vagó [bagó] coach (train); enviar [ambiá] to send.
	[v]	In all other positions, /v/ is much softer than in English, and is pronouced with the lips slightly open, like when blowing out a candle: diversos [divérsus] diverse; servir [serví] to serve.
24. w	[b], [v]	Not part of the Catalan alphabet. Used only in foreign words and pronounced as a /b/ or /v/: wàter [báter]; watt [bát] watt.
25. x		Four different pronunciations depending on position.
	[sh]	In an initial position or after a consonant, sounds like /sh/ in English shy: xarxa [shársha] net; xàfec [sháfak] shower. It is also pronounced this way when preceded by a vowel + /i/. The /i/ is silent except after /gu/: baixar [bayshá] to go down; això [aysh ó] that; guix [gísh] plaster.
	[ks]	After a stressed vowel, sounds like /x/ in English box; taxi [táksi] taxi; fix [fíks] fixed; firm.

	[gz]	Before a stressed vowel, sounds like the /ggs/ in English eggs: exàmen [agzáman] exam; exòtic [agzótik] exotic.
	[tch]	The group /tx/ between vowels or at the end of a word sounds like /tch/ in English itch: cotxe [cótcha] car; despatx [daspátch] office.
26. y		Used only in words of foreign origen. Sounds like an /i/ would in the same position: yacht [yat].
27. z	[z]	Pronounced like /z/ in English zero: catorze [katórza] fourteen; zero [zeru] zero.

Illustrational text

Descobreixi Barcelona Transports Municipals de Barcelona li porporciona la possibilitat de descobrir al seu aire la ciutat de Barcelona posant al seu servei diversos mitjans de transport que l'acostaran al més característic i interessant de la ciutat.	dazkubréyshi barselóna transports munisipáls da barselóna li prupursyóna la pusivilitat da dazkuvrí al séw áyra la siwtát da barselóna pusán al séw servéy divérsus mitjáns da transport ka lakostarán al més karaktarístik i intarasán da la siwtát.
Per això haurà d'adquirir un bitllet amb validesa per a un o mig dia (a partir de les catorze hores) que li permetrà utilitzar lliurement i sense límit de viatges els cinc mitjans: l'autobús línia cent, el tramvia blau, el funicular de Montjuïc i el funicular del Tibidabo.	par ayshó awrá dathkirí un biyyét am balithésa par a un o mita dia (a partí da las katórza) horas) ka li parmetrá utilitzá yiwramén i sénsa límit da byátjas als síng mitjáns: lawtovús línya sén, al trambía blaw, al funikulá da monjuwík i al funikulá dal tivithávoo.

Amb el bitllet que vostè ad- quireixi podrà pujar i baixar a qualsevol de les parades i tantes vegades com ho desitgi.	ám al biyyét ka busté ad- kireyshi puthrá pujá i bayshá a kwalsavól da las parádas i tántas vagádas kóm oo dasítji.

Translation of illustrational text
Discover Barcelona

Municipal Transports of Barcelona provides you with the possibility of discovering the city of Barcelona at your leisure, placing at your disposal diverse means of transport that will take you to the most characteristic and interesting sites in the city.

To do so you must purchase a ticket valid for a whole day or half a day (starting at two o'clock p.m.) which will allow you to freely use, without any limit of trips, the five different means: the bus number one hundred, the Blue Streetcar/tram, the Montjuïc funicular railway, the Montjuïc cable car and the Tibidabo funicular railway.

With the ticket you purchase, you can get off and on at any of the different stops as many times as you like.

THE PRONUNCIATION OF SPANISH

Rules of stress

In words with no written accent, the stress position is indicated by the word ending according to these rules:
1. Words ending in a consonant, except for /n/ or /s/, have the stress on the last syllable: Madrid (Madrid); venir (to come); eficaz (efficient).
2. Words ending in a vowel or in /n/ or /s/ have the stress on the penultimate syllable: casa (house); usan (they use); niños (children).

Words with the stress indicated by a written accent are:
1. Words ending in a vowel or in /n/ or /s/ with the stress on the last syllable: café (coffee); irán (they will go); anís (anise).
2. Words ending in a consonant (except /n/ or /s/) with the stress on the penultimate syllable: árbol (tree); ángel (angel).
3. All words with the stress on the antepenultimate syllable: pétalo (petal); cándido (candid).

Spanish vowels
Spanish vowels always have the same value. Compared with English, the pronunciation of Spanish vowels is much more tense, the position of the mouth remaining the same throughout the pronunciation of the vowel.

vowel	phonetic symbol	explanation
a	[a]	The Spanish /a/ is an open vowel, similar to the English /a/ in father or /o/ in son, but more open and frontal: arte [árte] art; mesa [mésa] table; amor [amór] love.
e	[e]	The Spanish /e/ is more closed than the English /e/ in men. Similar to the first /e/ in element. Without diphthongal glide: era [éra] it was; queso [késo] cheese; café [kafé] coffee.
i	[i]	The Spanish /i/ is similar but not as long as the /ee/ in seen and not as

		open as the /i/ in sit: isla [izla] island; idea [ithéa] idea; casi [kási] almost.
o	[o]	The Spanish /o/ is not like English /o/ in pot It is similar to the English /ou/ in bought but shorter. It's very similar to the French /eau/ in beau. Without diphthongal glide [ou]: ola [óla] wave; roca [róka] rock; oler [olér] to smell.
u	[u]	The Spanish /u/ is similar to English /oo/ in boot, but not as long: uno [úno] one; luna [lúna] moon; usar [usár] to use.

Observation:
Every letter is pronounced in Spanish except for the inaspirate /h/ as in hola [óla] hello, and the /u/ in the groups /qu/, /gue/, /qui/, which is silent unless it bears a diaeresis: guerra [gerra] war, vergüenza [bergwéntha] shame.

Spanish Diphthongs
In the Spanish falling diphthongs (ai, au, ei, eu, oi, ou) the second element (i, u) is louder and more prominent than in English.

diphthong	phonetic symbol	explanation
ai	[ai]	Like /i/ in the English bite: aire [áire] air; ayer [aiér] yesterday.
au	[au]	Like /ou/ in the English round: auto [áuto] car.
ei	[ei]	Like /ei/ in the English they. The first ey element is more closed than in English: seis [séis] six; rey [réi] king.
eu	[eu]	Combination of the Spanish /e/ and /u/: deuda [déutha] debt.
oi	[oi]	Like /oy/ in the English boy. The

		first oy vowel is more closed than in English: Oír [oír] to hear; soy [sói] I am.
ou	[ou]	Like /o/ in the English know. The first vowel is more closed than in English: bou [bóu] ox.
ia	[ya]	Like /ya/ in English yard: playa [pláya] ya beach; criar [kriyár] to raise.
ie	[ye]	Like /ye/ in English yes. The second element is more closed than in English: cien [thyén] one hundred.
io	[yo]	Like /yo/ in English yogurt. The second yo vowel is more closed: proporción [proporthyión] proportion; cayó [kayó] he/she fell.
ua	[wa]	Combination of Spanish /a/ and /u/: cuatro [kwátro] four.
ue	[we]	Like /we/ in English west: fue [fwé] it was.
uo	[wo]	Like /wo/ in English won't: antiguo [antígwo] old.
iu	[yu]	Like /u/ in English unit: yute [yúta] jute; ciudad [thyuthath] city.
ui	[wi]	Like /wee/ in English weed: fuí [fwí] I was, I went.

Consonants

consonants	phonetic symbol	explanation
1. b		There is no difference between /b/ and /v/ when spoken. Similar to the English /b/. The English /v/ doesn't

		exist in spoken Spanish. There are two different pronunciations depending on position.
	[b]	1. Like the English /b/ in initial positon or after /m/ or /n/: bueno [bweno] good; ver [ber] to see; hombre [ómbre] man; también [también] also; enviar [enbiár] to send.
	[v]	2. In any other positon the /b/ and /v/ are softer than in English. Pronounced with the lips slightly open, like when blowing out a candle: árbol [árvol] tree; deber [devér] duty; autobús [autovús] bus /coach.
2. c		Two different pronunciations depending on position.
	[th]	Followed by /e/ or /i/, it is pronounced like the English /th/ in think: Barcelona [Bárthelona]; ciudad [thyutháth] city; cien [thyén] one hundred. In some regions of Spain this /c/ is pronounced like an /s/.
	[k]	Followed by /a/, /o/, /u/ or a consonant it is pronounced as /k/ or hard /c/: catalán [katalán] Catalan; funicular [funikulár] funicular; casa [kása] house.
3. ch	[tch]	Like the English /ch/ in church; coche [kótche] car; chocolate [tchokoláte] chocolate; ancho [ántcho] wide.
4. d		The /d/ has two different pronunciations depending on position.
	[d]	In an initial positon and after /l/ or /n/, the Spanish /d/ is similar to the

		English, but placing the tip of the tongue against the back of the upper front teeth: día [día] day; falda [fálda] andar [andár] to walk.
	[th]	In any other position the Spanish /d/ is similar to the English /th/ in that: madre [máthre] mother; medio [méthyo] half. At the end of a word, the /th/ sound of the Spanish /d/ is much softer: Madrid [Mathríth] Madrid; ciudad [thyutháth].
5. f	[f]	Like an English /f/: foto [fóto] photo; fama [fáma] fame.
6. g		This letter has three distinct pronunciations depending on position.
	[g]	Before /a/, /o/, /u/, when initial in a breath group or after n, the Spanish / g/ is like the English hard /g/ in go: pagar [pagár] to pay; gato [gáto] cat; gorra [górra] cap; gusto [gústo] taste. The /u/ is silent in /gue/ and /gui/ unless it carries a diaeresis: guerra [gérra] war;guisar [gisár] to cook. güira [gwíra] calabash.
	[x]	The Spanish /g/ before /e/ and /i/ has the same sound as the Spanish /j/, which has a hard gutteral sound as in the Scottish loch. It's much stronger than the English /h/: gente [xénte] people; gitano [xitáno] gipsy.
	[g]	In all other positions the Spanish /g/ is similar to the hard /g/, but the tongue doesn't make full contact with the soft palate, and the air going through the narrow passage makes

		some friction: siglo [síglo] century; alegre [alégre] happy.
7. h		This letter is not pronounced in Spanish and has no phonetic symbol: hora [óra] hour; hola [óla] hello.
8. j	[h]	Similar to the English /h/ but much stronger. It has a gutteral sound like /ch/ in Scottish loch: viaje [byáhe] trip; julio [húlyo] July.
9. k	[k]	Like English /k/ in key, and used only in words of foreign origen: kilómetro [kilómetro] kilometer; kiosco [kyósco] kiosc.
10. l	[l]	Like English /l/ in like: línea [línea] line; caldo [káltho] broth; papel [papél] paper.
11. ll	[y]	This letter has one sound. It is similar to the English /li/ in million, or the /y/ in yet. It is pronounced placing the tip of the tongue against the lower teeth: llamar [yamár] to call; billete [biyéte] ticket.
12. m	[m]	Like the English /m/: motor [motór] motor; amo [ámo] owner; empezar [empethár] to begin.
13. n		The Spanish /n/ has three pronunciations depending on position.
	[n]	Like the English /n/, but said with the tip of the tongue against the back of the upper teeth: nada [nátha] nothing; mundo [múntho] world; enfermo [enférmo] sick.
	[ng]	Before hard /c/ and /g/ and before /j/ and /qu/ the Spanish /n/ is similar to

		the English /n/ in song: hongo [óngo] mushroom; banco [bángko] bank.
	[m]	Before /p/, /b/, /v/, /f/ and /m/, the Spanish /n/ is like an /m/: invitar [imbitár] to invite; informar [imformár] to inform; inmenso [iménso] immense.
14. ñ	[ny]	This sound is similar to the English /ni/ and /ny/ in onion and canyon, though somewhat different. The middle of the tongue is raised to touch the hard palate blocking the mouth passage. The ai passes through the nose: año [ányo] year; España [espánya] Spain; Cataluña [katalúnya] Catalonia.
15. p	[p]	Like the English /p/ but not as plosive and without aspiration: padre [páthre] father; cuerpo [kwérpo] body; comprar [komprár] to buy.
16. q	[k]	Used only in combinations of /que/ and /qui/. The /u/ is silent, and the sound is like the /k/ or hard /c/: aquí [akí] here; queso [késo] cheese; quitar [kitár] to remove.
17. r		The Spanish /r/ and /rr/ are different from the English /r/ and are always pronounced, rolled with one flap or various flaps depending on position, with the tip of the tongue vibrating against the upper palate.
	[r]	This letter is pronounced with one flap of the tip of the tongue against the hard palate. When at the end of a word: dar [dar] to give; mujer [muhér] woman. When within a word

		and not preceded by /n/, /l/ or /s/: tren [tren] train; hervir [ervír] to boil.
	[rr]	This letter is pronounced with several flaps of the tip of the tongue against the hard palate. When there is a double /rr/: perro [pérro] dog; error [errór] error. When there is a single /r/ at the beginning of a word: reir [rreír] to laugh; rana [rrána] frog. When there is a single /r/ preceded by /n/, /l/ or /s/ within a word: alrededor [alrrethethór] around; honra [ónrra] honor; Israel [Izrraél] Israel.
18. s		This letter has two pronunciations depending on position.
	[s]	When initial, intervocalic, final and before a voiceless consonant (c, f, j, k, p, q, t) it is similar to English /s/ in son or /ss/ in class, but its sound is much shorter: subir [suvír] to go up; cosa [kósa] thing; tos [tós] cough; España [espánya] Spain.
	[z]	The Spanish /s/ is pronounced like the short soft English /s/ in nose when before a voiced consonant (b, d, g, l, m, n, r, v): isla [ízla] island; cosmos [kózmos] cosmos; desván [dezván] attic; esbozo [ezvótho] sketch.
19. t	[t]	The Spanish /t/ is like the English /t/ in stop, placing the tip of the tongue against the back of the upper teeth: tomar [tomár] to take; todo [tótho] all; tonto [tónto] fool.
20. v		See consonant /b/.

21. w		Not part of the Spanish alphabet. Used only in foreign words.
	[b] or [v]	Pronounced like Spanish /b/ or /v/: water [báter] toilet; watio [bátyo] watt.
	[w]	Like English /w/ in foreign words: whiskey [wíski]; week-end [wíkend] weekend.
22. x		Two pronunciations depending on position.
	[gs]	Pronounced like /gs/ when initial or final: xilófono [gsilófono] xylophone; silex [sílegs] silex.
	[ks]	Before a consonant it is pronounced like English /ks/ in drinks though the /k/ is barely audible before consonants: examen [eksámen] exam; excusar [ekskusár] to excuse; explicar [e(k)splikár] to explain.
23. y		Three pronunciations depending on position.
	[i]	Like the Spanish vowel /i/ when between consonants and when meaning «and»: subir y bajar [suvr i bahr] to go up and to go down.
	[dy]	When /y/ is at the beginning of a sylable preceded by /n/ or /l/, it has a sound similar to the English /j/ in jump, but not so strong: inyección [indyekthión] injection; el yate [el dyáte] the yacht.
	[j]	In the Spanish diphtongs /ya/, /ye/, /yo/ and /yu/ it is pronounced like the /y/ in English yes: yaguar [jágwar]

jaguar; yeso [jéso] plaster; yodo [jótho] iodine.

24. z	[th]	Similar to the English /th/ in think : utilizar [utilithár] to use; zapato [thapáto] shoe.

Illustrational text

You will find the translation of the following text after the Catalan version of the same.

Descubra Barcelona Transportes Municipales de Barcelona le proporciona la posibilidad de descubrir a su aire la ciudad de Barcelona poniendo a su servicio diferentes medios de transporte que le acercarán a lo más característico e interesante de la ciudad.	deskúvra barthelóna transpórtes munithipáles de barthelóna le proporthyóna la posivilithath de deskuvrír a su áire la thyutháth de barthelóna ponyéntho a su servíthyo diferéntes méthyos de transporte ke le atherkarán a lo mas karakterístiko e interesánte de la thyutháth.
Para ello deberá adquirir un billete con validez para uno o medio día (a partir de las catorce horas) que le permitirá utilizar libremente y sin límite de viajes los cinco medios: el autobús línea cien, el tranvía azul, el funicular de Montjuïc*, el teleférico de Monjuïc y el funicular de Tibidabo.	pára éyo deverá athkirír un biyéte kon balithéth pára úno o méthyo día (a partir de las katórthe óras) ke le permitirá utilithár livreménte i sin límite de byáhes los thínko méthyos: el autovús línea thién, el tranviya athúl, el funikulár de monjuík, el telefériko de monjuík i el funikulár de tivithávo.
Con el billete que usted adquiera podrá subir y apearse en cualquiera de sus paradas y tantas veces como lo desee.	kon el biyéte ke usteth athkyera pothrá suvir i apeárse en kwalkyéra de sus parathas i tántas béthes komo lo desée.

*Montjuïc - a Catalan placename meaning «Jewish Mountain». The /j/ is pronounced like English /j/ in jump and the /t/ is silent.

A few practice examples.

Please be so kind.	Faci el favor. [fázi el favó]	Haga el favor. [ága el favór]
Good morning, sir.	Bon dia, senyor. [bón dia, sanyó]	Buenos días, señor. [bwénos días, senyor]
Good-bye, madam.	Adéu, senyora. [adéw, sanyóra]	Adiós, señora. [athyós, senyora]
Thank you for your help, miss.	Gràcies per la seva ajuda, senyoreta. [grásias par la séva ajutha, sanyoríta].	Gracias por su ayuda, señorita. [gráthyas por su ajutha senyoríta]
I am American.	Sóc americà. [sok amariká]	Soy americano. [soi amerikáno]
I am English.	Sóc anglès. [sok anglés]	Soy inglés. [soi inglés]
My name is John Smith	Em dic John Smith. [am dík John Smith]	Me llamo John Smith. [me yámo John Smith]
I don't understand you.	No l'entenc. [no lanténk]	No le entiendo. [no le entyéntho]
Could you repeat what you said?	Vol repetir el que ha dit? [ból rrapatí al ka a dít]	¿Quiere repetir lo que ha dicho? [kyére rrepetír lo ke a ditcho?]
Please speak slowly.	Per favor, parli a poc a poc. [por fabó, párli a pók a pók]	Por favor, hable despacio. [por favór, ávle dezpáthyo]
Could you help me?	Vol ajudar-me? [ból ajuthár-ma ?]	¿Quiere ayudarme? [kyére ajuthárme?]
I need a room for three. nights.	Em cal una habitació per a tres nits. [am kál ún avitasyó par rés níts]	Necesito una habitación para tres noches. [nethesíto úna avitathió pára trés nótches] `
Where is there a telephone booth?	On hi ha una cabina telefònica? [ón i á úna kavína telefónika?]	¿Dónde hay una cabina telefónica. [dónthe áy úna kavína telefónika?]
Is it far from here?	Es lluny d'aquí? [as yuin dakí]	¿Está lejos de aquí? [está léhos de akí]
How much is it?	Quant costa?	¿Cuanto cuesta?

	[kwán kósta?]	[kwánto kwesta?]
Bring me a beer.	Porti'm una cervesa. [pórtim una servésa]	Tráigame una cerveza. [tráygame úna thervétha]
How much do I owe you?	Quant li dec? [kwán li déc?]	¿Cuánto le debo? [kwánto le dévo?]
We're travelling by car.	Viatgem amb cotxe. [Byadjém am kótcha]	Viajamos en coche. [byahámos en kotche]
We will arrive on May sixteenth.	Arribarem el setze de maig. [arrivarém al sédza da mátch]	Llegaremos el dieciséis de mayo. [yegarémos el dyethiséis de mayo]

1. **GRAMMAR**. GRAMÀTICA. *GRAMÁTICA*

1.1 **Prepositions**. Preposicions. *Preposiciones*

to Barcelona
a Barcelona
a Barcelona

in Barcelona
a Barcelona
en Barcelona

from Barcelona
de Barcelona
de Barcelona

to Peter's house
a casa d'en Pere
a casa de Pedro

at / in Peter's house
a casa d'en Pere
en casa de Pedro

from Peter's house
de casa d'en Pere
de casa de Pedro

next to / beside the cathedral; near the cathedral
al costat de la catedral; vora la catedral
al lado de la catedral; junto a la catedral

before the holidays
abans de les festes
antes de las fiestas

after arriving
després d'arribar
después de llegar

with rice
amb arròs
con arroz

still (of water)
sense gas
sin gas

in front of the building
davant l'edifici
delante del edificio

behind the tower
darrere la torre
detrás de la torre

during the trip
durant el viatge
durante el viaje

between the center and the hotel
entre el centre i l'hotel
entre el centro y el hotel

for Mary
per a la Maria
para María

accepted by everyone
acceptat per tothom
aceptado por todo el mundo

on / upon the table; on / over the table
sobre la taula; damunt la taula
sobre la mesa; encima de la mesa

under the bed
sota el llit
(de)bajo (de) la cama

around; about
al voltant de
alrededor de

since; from
des de
desde

towards
cap a
hacia

until; up to
fins a
hasta

according to
segons
según

1.2 **The definite article**. L'article definit. *El artículo definido*

the month
el mes
el mes

the months
els mesos
los meses

the year
l'any
el año

the years
els anys
los años

the week
la setmana
la semana

the weeks
les setmanes
las semanas

the season
l'estació
la estación

the seasons
les estacions
las estaciones

1.3 **Interrogatives**. Interrogatius. *Interrogativos*

How old is he / she / it? How old are you? (polite)
Quants anys té?
¿Cuántos años tiene?

How is he / she / it?; How are you? (polite)
Com està?
¿Cómo está?

Where is he / she / it?; Where are you? (polite)
On és?
¿Dónde está?

Where's he / she / coming from?; Where are you coming from?
D'on ve?
¿De dónde viene?

Where's he / she going?; Where are you going? (polite)
A on va?
¿Adónde va?

Who has seen it?
Qui ho ha vist?
¿Quién lo ha visto?

Who has he / she given it to?; Who have you given it to?
A qui l'ha donat?
¿A quién lo ha entregado?

Who does he / she want to visit?; Who do you want to visit?
A qui vol visitar?
¿A quién quiere visitar?

Who did he / she / you receive it from?
De qui l'ha rebut?
¿De quién lo ha recibido?

Who is he / she travelling with?; Who are you travelling with?
Amb qui viatja?
¿Con quién viaja?

How far does this train go?
Fins on va aquest tren?
¿Hasta dónde va este tren?

How long is he / she staying in Spain? How long are you staying in Spain?
Fins quan es queda a Espanya?
¿Hasta cuándo se queda en España?

Which (one) would he / she / you like?
Quin desitja?
¿Cuál desea?

Which of the two did he / she / you speak to?
Amb quin dels dos ha parlat?
¿Con cuál de los dos ha hablado?

How much gasoline / petrol do you want?
Quanta gasolina vol?
¿Cuánta gasolina quiere?

How much is it?
Quant costa? Quant val?
¿Cuánto cuesta? ¿Cuánto vale?

What is this / that?
Què és això?
¿Qué es esto?

Why is he / she leaving?; Why are you leaving?
Per què se'n va?
¿Por qué se va?

When can we see each other?
Quan podem veure'ns?
¿Cuándo podemos vernos?

What is he / she / it like?
Com és? De quina mena és?
¿Cómo es? ¿Qué?

What color is it?
De quin color és?
¿De qué color es?

What's his / her / your room like?
Com és la seva habitació?
¿Cómo es su habitación?

What type of room would he / she / you like?
Quina mena d'habitació desitja?
¿Qué habitación desea?

What does he / she want the cloth for? What do you want the cloth for?
Per a què vol la roba?
¿Para qué quiere la tela?

What would you / he / she like?
Què desitja?
¿Qué desea?

What would you like with your meat?
Amb què desitja la carn?
¿Con qué desea la carne?

1.4 **The personal pronouns.** Els pronoms personals. *Los pronombres personales*

Who? / Whom?
Qui?
¿Quién?

Who is it?
Qui és?
¿Quién es?

Me. It's me.
Jo. Soc jo.
Yo. Soy yo.

You. It's you.
Tu. Ets tu.
Tú. Eres tú.

Him. It's him
Ell. És ell.
Él. Es él.

Her. It's her.
Ella. És ella.
Ella. Es ella.

You. It's you. (polite)
Vostè. És vostè.
Usted. Es usted.

Us. It's us.
Nosaltres. Som nosaltres
Nosotros. Somos nosotros.
Nosotras. Somos nosotras.

You. It's you. pl
Vosaltres. Sou vosaltres.
Vosotros. Sois vosotros.
Vosotras. Sois vosotras.

Them. It's them. m
Ells. Són ells.
Ellos. Son ellos.

Them. It's them. f
Elles. Són elles.
Ellas. Son ellas.

You. It's you. pl (polite)
Vostès. Són vostès.
Ustedes. Son ustedes.

This man / gentleman.
Aquest senyor.
Este señor.

That woman / lady.
Aquella senyora.
Aquella señora.

These men / gentlemen.
Aquests senyors.
Estos señores.

Who should I speak to?
A qui caldria dirigir-se?
¿A quién habría que dirigirse?

To me.
A mi.
A mí

To you.
A tu.
A ti.

To him
A ell / ella.
A él / ella.

To you. (polite)
A vostè.
A usted.

To us.
A nosaltres.
A nosotros / nosotras.

To you. pl
A vosaltres.
A vosotros / vosotras.

To them.
A ells / elles.
A ellos / ellas.

To you. pl (polite)
A vostès.
A ustedes.

To this woman.
A aquesta senyora.
A esta señora.

To that man.
A aquell senyor.
A aquel señor.

To these women.
A aquestes senyores.
A estas señoras.

With whom do you / does he / she wish to speak?
Amb qui desitja parlar?
¿Con quién desea hablar?

With me.
Amb mi.
Conmigo.

With you.
Amb tu.
Contigo.

With him / her.
Amb ell / ella.
Con él / ella.

Who are they calling?
A qui criden?
¿A quién llaman?

Me. They are calling me.
A mi. Em criden a mi.
A mí. Me llaman a mí.

You. They are calling you.
A tu. Et criden a tu.
A ti. Te llaman a ti.

Him. They are calling him.
A ell. El criden a ell.
A él. Le llaman a él.

Her. They are calling her.
A ella. La criden a ella.
A ella. La llaman a ella.

You. They are calling you. (polite)
A vostè. El / la criden a vostè.
A usted. Le / la llaman a usted.

Us. They are calling us.
A nosaltres. Ens criden a nosaltres.
A nosotros. Nos llaman a nosotros.
A nosotras. Nos llaman a nosotras.

You. They are calling you. pl
A vosaltres. Us criden a vosaltres.
A vosotros. Os llaman a vosotros.
A vosotras. Os llaman a vosotras.

Them. They are calling them. m
A ells. Els criden a ells.
A ellos. Les llaman a ellos.

Them. They are calling them. f
A elles. Les criden a elles.
A ellas. Las llaman a ellas.

You. They are calling you. pl (polite)
A vostès. Els / les criden a vostès.
A ustedes. Les / las llaman a ustedes.

1.5 **The possessives.** Els possessius. *Los posesivos*

Whose is it?
De qui és?
¿De quién es?

Whose book is this?
De qui és aquest llibre?
¿De quién es este libro?

It's mine. It's my book.
És meu. És el meu llibre.
Es mío. Es mi libro.

It's yours. It's your book.
És teu. És el teu llibre.
Es tuyo. Es tu libro.

It's yours / his / hers. It's your / his /her book.
És seu. És el seu llibre.
Es suyo. Es su libro.

It's his / hers. It's his / her book.
És d'ell / d'ella. És el llibre d'ell / d'ella.
Es de él / ella. Es el libro de él / ella.

It's yours. It's your book. (polite)
És de vostè. És el llibre de vostè.
Es de usted. Es el libro de usted.

It's Mr. Smith's. It's Mr. Smith's book.
És del senyor Smith. És el llibre del senyor Smith.
Es del señor Smith. Es el libro del señor Smith.

It's ours. It's our book.
És nostre. És el nostre llibre.
Es nuestro. Es nuestro libro.

It's yours. It's your book. pl
És vostre. És el vostre llibre.
Es vuestro. Es vuestro libro.

It's theirs / yours (polite). It's their / your book.
És seu. És el seu llibre.
Es suyo. Es su libro.

It's theirs. It's their book. m / f
És d'ells / d'elles. És el llibre d'ells / d'elles.
Es de ellos / ellas. Es el libro de ellos / ellas.

It's yours. It's your book. pl (polite)
És de vostès. És el llibre de vostès.
Es de ustedes. Es el libro de ustedes.

Whose letter is this?
De qui és aquesta carta?
¿De quién es esta carta?

It's mine. It's my letter.
És meva. És la meva carta.
Es mía. Es mi carta.

It's yours. It's your letter.
És teva. És la teva carta.
Es tuya. Es tu carta.

It's his / hers / yours (polite). It's his / her / your letter.
És seva. És la seva carta.
Es suya. Es su carta.

My brother is tall.
El meu germà és alt.
Mi hermano es alto.

Your sister is nice.
La teva germana és simpàtica.
Tu hermana es simpática.

Our family is very large.
La nostra família és molt gran.
Nuestra familia es muy grande.

Our parents and yours don't know each other.
Els nostres pares i els vostres no es coneixen.
Nuestros padres y los vuestros no se conocen.

1.6 **The demonstratives.** Els demostratius. *Los demostrativos*

Which? What?
Quin? Què?
¿Cuál? ¿Qué?

This / that train.
Aquest / aqueix tren.
Este / ese tren.

This / that square.
Aquesta / aqueixa plaça.
Esta / esa plaza.

These / those tickets / bills / notes.
Aquests / aqueixos bitllets
Estos / esos billetes.

These / those houses.
Aquestes / aqueixes cases.
Estas / esas casas.

That boat / ship.
Aquell vaixell.
Aquel barco.

That trailer / caravan.
Aquella caravana.
Aquella caravana.

Those buildings.
Aquells edificis.
Aquellos edificios.

Those mountains.
Aquelles muntanyes.
Aquellas montañas.

What is this / that?
Què és això / allò?
¿Qué es esto / eso?

This / that is a conversation guide.
Això/ allò és una guia de conversa.
Esto / eso es una guía de conversación.

I don't like this / that.
Això / allò no m'agrada.
Esto / eso no me gusta.

1.7 **Description of persons. Comparison.**
Descripció de persones. Comparació.
Descripción de personas. Comparación.

Paul is one meter, eighty centimeters tall.
En Pau fa un metre vuitanta.
Pablo mide un metro ochenta.

Martha is one meter, sixty centimeters tall.
La Marta fa un metre seixanta.
Marta mide un metro sesenta.

Paul is much taller than Martha.
En Pau és molt més alt que la Marta.
Pablo es mucho más alto que Marta.

Martha is shorter than Paul.
La Marta és més baixa que en Pau.
Marta es más baja que Pablo.

Paul is very tall.
En Pau és molt alt.
Pablo es muy alto.

Charles is as tall as Joseph.
En Carles és tan alt com en Josep.
Carlos es tan alto como José.

Charles weighs eighty kilos, Joseph sixty-five.
En Carles pesa vuitanta quilos, en Josep seixanta-cinc.
Carlos pesa ochenta kilos, José sesenta y cinco.

Joseph is thinner than Charles.
En Josep és més prim que en Carles.
José es más delgado que Carlos.

Joseph is very thin.
En Josep és molt prim.
José es muy delgado.

Joseph is very, very thin.
En Josep és primíssim.
José es delgadísimo.

Joseph is too thin.
En Josep és massa prim.
José es demasiado delgado.

Joseph is not at all fat.
En Josep no és gens gras.
José no es nada gordo.

1.8 **Conjugation. Regular verbs.**
Conjugació. Verbs regulars.
Conjugación. Verbos regulares.

TO SPEAK | **I speak** | **you speak**
Parlar | parlo | parles
Hablar | *hablo* | *hablas*

he / she / speaks; you speak (polite)
parla
habla

we speak
parlem
hablamos

you speak
parleu
habláis

they speak; you speak (polite)
parlen
hablan

TO FEAR | **I fear** | **you fear**
témer | temo | tems
temer | *temo* | *temes*

he / she fears; you fear (polite)
tem
teme

we fear
temem
tememos

you fear
temeu
teméis

they fear; you fear (polite)
temen
temen

TO JOIN / UNITE | **I join** | **you join**
unir | uneixo | uneixes
unir | *uno* | *unes*

he / she joins; you join (polite)
uneix
une

we join
unim
unimos

you join
uniu
unís

they join; you join (polite)
uneixen
unen

1.9 **Conjugation. Irregular verbs.**
Conjugació. Verbs irregulars.
Conjugación. Verbos irregulares.

The verb of existence TO BE
(with permanent properties or with nouns)
El verb d'existència ésser / ser
(Amb propietats permanents o amb substantius)
El verbo de existencia ser
(Con propiedades permanentes o con sustantivos)

I am tall. I'm a dentist.
Sóc alt, -a. Sóc dentista.
Soy alto, -a. Soy dentista.

You are tall. You are a dentist.
Ets alt, -a. Ets dentista.
Eres alto, -a. Eres dentista.

He / she is tall. He / she is a dentist; You are tall; you are a dentist. (polite)
És alt, -a. És dentista.
Es alto, -a. Es dentista.

We are tall. We are dentists.
Som alts / altes. Som dentistes.
Somos altos, -as. Somos dentistas.

You are tall. You are dentists.
Sou alts / altes. Sou dentistes.
Sois altos, -as. Sois dentistas.

They / you (polite) are tall. They / you are dentists.
Són alts / altes. Són dentistes.
Son altos, -as. Son dentistas.

The verb of existence TO BE
(with acquired or temporary properties)
El verb d'existència estar
(Amb propietats adquirides o transitòries)
El verbo de existencia estar
(Con propiedades adquiridas o transitorias)

I'm tired. m / f
Estic cansat, -ada.
Estoy cansado, -a.

You're tired.
Estàs cansat, -ada.
Estás cansado, -a.

He / she is tired.; You're tired (polite)
Està cansat, -ada.
Está cansado, -a.

We're tired.
Estem cansats / cansades.
Estamos cansados, -adas.

You're tired.
Esteu cansats / cansades.
Estáis cansados, -adas.

They're tired; You're tired. (polite)
Estan cansats / cansades.
Están cansados, -adas.

The verb of possession TO HAVE
El verb de possesió tenir
El verbo de posesión tener

I have
tinc
tengo

you have
tens
tienes

he / she / it has; you have (polite)
té
tiene

we have
tenim
tenemos

you have
teniu
tenéis

they have; you have (polite)
tenen
tienen

1.10 **Quantitatives**
Quantitatius
Cuantitativos

You (polite) can stay here as long as you like.
Pot passar aquí tant de temps com vulgui.
Puede pasar aquí tanto tiempo como quiera.

This shop is open all day long.
Aquesta botiga està oberta tot el dia.
Esta tienda está abierta todo el día.

I'd like to buy some gifts.
Voldria comprar uns regals.
Quisiera comprar unos regalos.

I've bought enough gifts.
He comprat bastants / prou regals.
He comprado bastantes regalos.

I've got little money / I haven't got very much money.
Tinc pocs diners / No tinc gaires diners.
Tengo poco dinero.

Today is less sunny / sunnier than yesterday.
Avui fa menys / més sol que ahir.
Hoy hace menos / más sol que ayer.

We want to go to the beach every day.
Volem anar a la platja tots els dies.
Queremos ir a la playa todos los días.

Each / every room has a refrigerator.
Cada habitació té nevera.
Cada habitación tiene nevera.

We want to stay here a couple of days.
Volem passar aquí un parell de dies.
Queremos pasar aquí un par de días.

I understand everything.
Ho entenc tot.
Lo entiendo todo.

I don't understand anything.
No entenc res.
No entiendo nada.

I've got many / very many questions.
Tinc moltes / moltíssimes preguntes.
Tengo muchas / muchísimas preguntas.

1.11 Cardinal numbers
Numerals cardinals
Numerales cardinales

0 zero zero *cero*	**1 one** un, -a *uno / un, -a*	**2 two** dos, dues *dos*
3 three tres *tres*	**4 four** quatre *cuatro*	**5 five** cinc *cinco*
6 six sis seis	**7 seven** set siete	**8 eight** vuit ocho
9 nine nou *nueve*	**10 ten** deu *diez*	**11 eleven** onze *once*
12 twelve dotze doce	**13 thirteen** tretze trece	**14 fourteen** catorze catorce
15 fifteen quinze *quince*	**16 sixteen** setze *dieciséis*	**17 seventeen** disset *diecisiete*
18 eighteen divuit dieciocho	**19 nineteen** dinou diecinueve	**20 twenty** vint veinte
21 twenty-one vint-i-u(n), -una *veintiuno / veintiún, -a*	**22 twenty-two** vint-i-dos, -dues *veintidós*	**21 twenty-three** vint-i-tres *veintitrés*

24 twenty-four
vint-i-quatre
veinticuatro

31 thirty-one
trenta-u(n), -una
treinta y uno / un, -a

32 thirty-two
trenta-dos, -dues
treinta y dos

33 thirty-three
trenta-tres
treinta y tres

40 forty
quaranta
cuarenta

44 forty-four
quaranta-quatre
cuarenta y cuatro

50 fifty
cinquanta
cincuenta

60 sixty
seixanta
sesenta

70 seventy
setanta
setenta

80 eighty
vuitanta
ochenta

90 ninety
noranta
noventa

92 ninety-two
noranta-dos, -dues
noventa y dos

100 one hundred
cent
ciento / cien

101 one hundred and one
cent u(n), -a
ciento uno / un, -a

105 one hundred and five
cent cinc
ciento cinco

200 two hundred
dos-cents, dues-centes
doscientos, -as

234 two hundred and thirty-four
dos-cents trenta-quatre
doscientos treinta y cuatro

300 three hundred
tres-cents, -centes
trescientos, -as

345 three hundred and forty-five
tres-cents quaranta-cinc
trescientos cuarenta y cinco

400 four hundred
quatre-cents, -centes
cuatrocientos, -as

500 five hundred
cinc-cents, -centes
quinientos, -as

600 six hundred
sis-cents, -centes
seiscientos, -as

700 seven hundred
set-cents, -centes
setecientos, -as

800 eight hundred
vuit-cents, -centes
ochocientos, -as

900 nine hundred
nou-cents, -centes
novecientos, -as

1000 one thousand
mil
mil

1001 one thousand and five
mil u(n), -a
mil uno / un, -a

1241 one thousand two hundred and forty-one
mil dos-cents quaranta-u(n)
mil doscientas cuarenta y uno

1992 one thousand nine hundred and ninety two
mil nou-cents noranta-dos
mil novecientos noventa y dos

3000 three thousand
tres mil
tres mil

4624 four thousand six hundred and twenty-four
quatre mil sis-centes vint-i-quatre
cuatro mil seiscientos veinticuatro

one million
un milió
un millón

one billion; one milliard
mil milions
mil millones

1.12 **Ordinal numbers**
Numerals ordinals
Numerales ordinales

first
primer, -a
primer(o), -a

second
segon, -a
segundo, -a

third
tercer, -a
tercer (o), -a

fourth
quart, -a
cuarto, –a

fifth	**sixth**
cinquè, -ena	sisè, -ena
quinto, -a	*sexto, -a*
seventh	**eighth**
setè, -ena	vuitè, -ena
séptimo, -a	*octavo, -a*
ninth	**tenth**
novè, -ena	desè, -ena
noveno, -a	*décimo, -a*

1.13 **Fractional numbers**
Nombres trencats / fraccionaris
Números quebrados / fraccionarios

(one) half	**one / a third**	**one / a fourth**
mig, mitja; meitat f	un terç	un quart
medio, -a; mitad f	*un tercio*	un cuarto
one / a fifth	**one / a sixth**	**one / a tenth**
un cinquè	un sisè	un desè
un quinto	*un sexto*	*un décimo*
one / a tenth	**one / a hundredth**	**two thirds**
un desè	un centèssim	dos terços
un décimo	*un centésimo*	*dos tercios*
three fourths	**four fifths**	
tres quarts	quatre cinquens	
tres cuartos	*cuatro quintos*	

1.14 **What time is it? Excuse me, could you tell me the time?**
Quina hora és? Perdoni, pot dir-me l'hora?
¿Qué hora es? Perdone, ¿puede decirme la hora?

It's one (o'clock)	**It's two (o'clock) (approximately)**
És la una.	Són les dues (aproximadament).
Es la una	*Son las dos (aproximadamente).*

It's three / eight / eleven (o'clock) sharp.
Són les tres / vuit / onze (en punt).
Son las tres / ocho / once (en punto).

It's after nine.
Són les nou tocades.
Son las nueve pasadas.

It's a quarter past twelve.
És un quart d'una.
Son las doce y cuarto.

It's a quarter past one.
És un quart de dues.
Es la una y cuarto.

It's a quarter past three / four/ five.
És un quart de quatre / cinc / sis.
Son las tres / cuatro / cinco y cuarto.

It's half past twelve.
Són dos quarts d'una.
Son las doce y media.

It's half past one.
Són dos quarts de dues.
Es la una y media.

It's half past six / eight / eleven.
Són dos quarts de sis / vuit / onze.
Son las seis / ocho / once y media.

It's a quarter to one.
Són tres quarts d'una.
Es la una menos cuarto.

It's a quarter to two.
Són tres quarts de dues.
Son las dos menos cuarto.

It's a quarter to eight / ten / twelve.
Són tres quarts de vuit / deu / dotze.
Son las ocho / diez / doce menos cuarto.

It's ten (minutes) past one.
És la una i deu (minuts).
Es la una y diez minutos.

It's twenty-five (minutes) to seven.
Són dos quarts i cinc (minuts) de set.
Son las seis y treinta y cinco minutos.

It's ten (minutes) to eight.
Són les vuit menys deu (minuts); Són tres quarts i cinc de vuit.
Son las ocho menos diez (minutos).

It's twenty-five (minutes) past six.
Són dos quarts menys cinc (minuts) de set.
Son las seis y veinticinco (minutos).

It's twenty minutes to eight.
Són tres quarts menys cinc de vuit.
Son las ocho menos veinte (minutos).

It's noon / midday.
És migdia.
Es mediodía.

It's midnight.
És mitjanit.
Es medianoche.

1.15 **(At) What time?**
A quina hora?
¿A qué hora?

At one (o'clock).
A la una.
A la una.

At two (o'clock).
A les dues.
A las dos.

At three / eight / eleven (sharp).
A les tres / vuit / onze (en punt).
A las tres / ocho / once (en punto).

At ten (o'clock) in the morning.
A les deu del matí.
A las diez de la mañana.

At half past three in the afternoon.
A dos quarts de quatre de la tarda.
A las tres y media de la tarde.

At a quarter past ten at night.
A un quart d'onze del vespre.
A las diez y cuarto de la noche.

At half past two in the morning.
A (dos) quarts de tres de la matinada.
A las dos y media de la madrugada.

At twenty to six.
A tres quarts menys cinc de sis.
A las seis menos veinte.

At noon / midday.
Al migdia.
A mediodía.

At midnight.
A mitjanit.
A medianoche.

After eight.
Després de les vuit. A les vuit tocades.
Después de las ocho. A las ocho pasadas.

Around eleven (o'clock).
Cap a les onze.
A eso de las once.

Before seven (o'clock).
Abans de les set.
Antes de las siete.

In five minutes.
D'aquí a cinc minuts.
Dentro de cinco minutos.

1.16 **The date**
La data
La fecha

The Olympic Stadium in Barcelona was inaugurated on September 8th (eighth), 1989 (nineteen eighty-nine).
L'Estadi Olímpic de Barcelona va ser inaugurat el 8 (vuit) de setembre de 1989 (mil nou-cents vuitanta-nou).
El Estadio Olímpico de Barcelona fue inaugurado el 8 (ocho) de septiembre de 1989 (mil novecientos ochenta y nueve).

What's today's date?
A quin dia som avui?
¿A cuántos estamos?

Today is January 19th (nineteenth).
És el 19 (dinou) de gener.
Estamos a 19 (diecinueve) de enero.

When did you arrive?
Quan ha arribat vostè?
¿Cuándo ha llegado usted?

On December first.
El primer de desembre. L'u de desembre.
El primero de diciembre.

On November second.
El dos de novembre.
El dos de noviembre.

Between the seventh and the tenth of last month I was in Madrid.
Entre el set i el deu del mes passat vaig ser a Madrid.
Entre el siete y el diez del mes pasado estuve en Madrid.

From the twenty-fifth of next month on.
A partir del vint-i-cinc del mes que ve.
A partir del veinticinco del mes que viene.

At the beginning of the month.
Al començament del mes.
A comienzos de mes.

In the middle of August.
A mitjan agost.
A mediados de agosto.

At the end of July.
A finals de juliol.
A fines / finales de julio.

In nineteen ninety-two.
El mil nou-cents noranta-dos.
En mil novecientos noventa y dos.

1.17 **The days of the week**
Els dies de la setmana
Los días de la semana

Monday
dilluns
lunes

Tuesday
dimarts
martes

Wednesday
dimecres
miércoles

Thursday
dijous
jueves

Friday
divendres
viernes

Saturday
dissabte
sábado

Sunday
diumenge
domingo

1.18 **The months of the year**
Els mesos de l'any
Los meses del año

January
gener
enero

February
febrer
febrero

March
març
marzo

April
abril
abril

May
maig
mayo

June
juny
junio

July
juliol
julio

August
agost
agosto

September
setembre
septiembre

October
octubre
octubre

November
novembre
noviembre

December
desembre
diciembre

1.19 **Holidays**. Festes. *Fiestas*

January 1st, New Year's Day
1 de gener, Cap d'Any
1 de enero, Año Nuevo

January 6th, Epiphany
6 de gener, Reis
6 de Enero, Epifanía

March 19th, St. Joseph
19 de març, Sant Josep
19 de marzo, San José

Good Friday
Divendres Sant
Viernes Santo

Easter Monday
Dilluns de Pasqua
Lunes de Pascua

April 23rd, St. George
23 d'abril, Sant Jordi
23 de abril, San Jorge

May 1st, Day of the Worker
1 de maig, la Festa del Treball
1 de mayo, la Fiesta del Trabajo

May 15th, St. Isidore
15 de maig, Sant Isidre Llaurador
15 de mayo, San Isidoro Labrador

Whitsunday
Dilluns de Pentecosta
Lunes de Pentecostés

June 24th, St. John
24 de juny, Sant Joan
24 de junio, San Juan

July 25th, St. James
25 de juliol, Sant Jaume
25 de julio, Santiago Apóstol

August 15th, Assumption of the Virgin Mary
15 d'agost, Assumpció de la Verge Maria
15 de agosto, Asunción de la Virgen María

September 11th, National Day of Catalonia
11 de setembre, Diada de Catalunya
11 de septiembre, Fiesta Nacional de Catalunya

October 12th, Columbus Day
12 d'octubre, Dia de la Hispanitat; el Pilar
12 de octubre, Día de la Hispanidad

November 1st, All Saints' Day
1 de novembre, Tots Sants
1 de noviembre, Todos los Santos

December 6th, Constitution Day
6 de desembre, Dia de la Constitució
6 de diciembre, Día de la Constitución

December 8th, Immaculate Conception
8 de desembre, Immaculada Concepció
8 de diciembre, Inmaculada Concepción

December 25th, Christmas
25 de desembre, Nadal
25 de diciembre, Navidad

December 26th, Boxing Day
26 de desembre, Sant Esteve
26 de diciembre, San Esteban

2. COMMON WORDS AND PHRASES
PARAULES I FRASES FREQÜENTS
PALABRAS Y FRASES FRECUENTES

2.1 **Notices.** Avisos. *Avisos*

abierto — **open**
alquiler — **rent; rental; hiring**
aparcament; *aparcamiento* — **parking lot; car park**

ascensor; *ascensor* — **elevator; lift**
aseo(s) — **toilet(s); rest room(s)**
atenció!; *¡atención!* — **attention!; beware!**

caballeros	**gentlemen**
caixa; *caja*	**bank; cashier's desk**
cerrado	**closed**
compte!	**be careful! look out!**
consigna; *consigna*	**checkroom; left luggage**
¡cuidado!	**be careful!**
dones; *damas*	**ladies**
empenyeu; *empujar*	**push**
entrada; *entrada*	**entrance**
entrada lliure; *entrada libre*	**no obligation to buy**
Entri per l'altra porta;. *Entre por la otra puerta*	**please use the other door**
entreu	**enter!; entrance**
escales mecàniques; *escaleras mecánicas*	**escalator**
es lloga	**for rent**
estireu	**pull**
fora de servei; *fuera de servicio*	**out of service; out of order**
fumadors; *fumadores*	**smokers**
gratis; *gratis*	**free**
homes; *hombres*	**men**
horari; *horario*	**timetable; schedule**
informació; *información*	**information**
lavabo; *labavo*	**toilet; lavatory; washroom**
lliure; *libre*	**free; vacant; unoccupied**
mujeres	**women**
no fumadors; *no fumadores*	**non-smokers**
no fumeu; *no fumar*	**no smoking**
no funciona; *no funciona*	**out of order**
No s'admeten gossos; *No se admiten perros*	**dogs are not admitted**

obert	**open**
ocupat; *ocupado*	**occupied; engaged**
¡ojo!	**careful!; watch out!**
perill; *peligro*	**danger**
privat; *privado*	**private**
prohibit; *prohibido*	**prohibited; forbidden**
prohibit el pas; *prohibido el paso*	**no trespassing; no thoroughfare**
reservat; *reservado*	**reserved**
salida	**exit**
salida de emergencia	**emergency exit**
se alquila	**for rent; for hire; to let**
senyores; *señoras*	**women; ladies**
senyors; *señores*	**men; gentlemen**
silenci; *silencio*	**silence; keep quiet**
sortida	**exit**
sortida d'emergència	**emergency exit**
tancat	**closed**
taquilla	**ticket office; box office**
tirar	**pull**
Toqueu el timbre; *Toquen el timbre*	**ring the bell**
ull viu!	**careful!**

2.2 **Greetings**
Fórmules de salutació
Fórmulas de saludo

Upon meeting. En trobar-se. *Al encontrarse*

Hello!	**Good morning!**
Hola!	Bon dia!
¡Hola!	*¡Buenos días!*

Good afternoon / evening!
Bona tarda!
¡Buenas tardes!

Good night!
Bona nit!
¡Buenas noches!

Welcome!
Benvingut! m, Benvinguda! f
¡Bienvenido! m, ¡Bienvenida! f

Welcome ! pl
Benvinguts! m, Benvingudes! f Déu vos guard!
¡Bienvenidos! m, ¡Bienvenidas! f

Leave taking. En separar-se. *Al separarse*

So long! See you later!
A reveure!
¡Hasta la vista!

See you later / soon!
Fins aviat!
¡Hasta luego!

See you tomorrow!
Fins demà!
¡Hasta mañana!

See you on Friday!
Fins divendres!
¡Hasta el viernes!

Goodbye! farewell!
Adéu!
¡Adiós!

Goodbye! farewell!
Adéu-siau!
¡Adiós!

Have a good time! Have fun!
Passi-ho bé!
¡Que lo pase bien!

Have a good time! Have fun! pl
Passin-ho bé!
¡Que lo pasen bien!

Good night!
Bona nit!
¡Buenas noches!

Give my regards to your husband.
Records al seu marit.
Recuerdos a su marido.

2.3 **Forms of address.** Tractaments. *Tratamientos*

Sir! Mister!
Senyor!
¡Señor!

Mrs! Madam! Lady!
Senyora!
¡Senyora!

Young man / lady!
Jove!
¡Joven!

Miss!
Senyoreta!
¡Señorita!

Gentlemen!
Senyors!
¡Señores!

Ladies!
Senyores!
¡Señoras!

Ladies and gentlemen!
Senyores i senyors!
¡Señoras y señores!

Friend! Pal!
Amic!
¡Amigo!

Mr. Sala!
Senyor Sala!
¡Señor Sala!

Mrs. Sala!
Senyora Sala!
¡Señora Sala!

2.4 Beginning conversation
Entaulant una conversa
Entablando conversación

May I accompany you?
Puc acompanyar-lo / acompanyar-la?
¿Puedo acompañarle / acompañarla?

Excuse me for bothering you.
Perdoni la molèstia.
Perdone usted la molestia.

Excuse me, are you from here?
Perdoni, vostè és d'aquí?
Perdone, ¿usted es de aquí?

How are you?; How is everything?
Com va això?
¿Qué tal?

Please!; If you please!
Sisplau! Si us plau!
¡Por favor!

We know each other already, don't we?
Oi que ja ens coneixem?
Nosotros ya nos conocemos, ¿verdad?

May I? Do you mind?
Em permet?
¿Me permite?

What happened?
Què ha passat?
¿Qué ha pasado?

What's new?
Què hi ha de nou?
¿Qué hay de nuevo?

May I tell you something?
Puc dir-li una cosa?
¿Puedo decirle algo?

Do you like the program / show?
Li agrada el programa?
¿Le gusta el programa?

Did you know that...
Sap vostè que...
¿Sabe usted que...

2.5 **Introduction**. Presentació. *Presentación*

What's your name?
Com es diu vostè?
¿Cómo se llama usted?

My name is John Smith.
Em dic
Me llamo

My wife's name is Ann.
La meva dona es diu Anna.
Mi mujer se llama Ana.

This / That boy is my son.
Aquest noi és el nostre fill.
Este muchacho es nuestro hijo.

His name is Peter.
El seu nom és Pere.
Su nombre es Pedro.

I'm American.
Sóc americà.
Soy americano.

We are American.
Som americans.
Somos americanos.

I don't speak Catalan / Spanish well, but I do speak French.
No parlo bé el català, però conec el francés.
No hablo bien el español, pero hablo el francés.

Do you know my friend?
Coneix la meva amiga?
¿Conoce usted a mi amiga?

Do you know each other?; Have you met?
Vostès es coneixen?
¿Se conocen ustedes?

We know each other; We have met.
Ens coneixem.
Nos conocemos.

We don't know each other. We haven't met.
No ens coneixem.
No nos conocemos.

We only know each other by sight.
Només ens coneixem de vista.
Sólo nos conocemos de vista.

Allow me to introduce my friend.
Permeti'm que li presenti el meu amic.
Permítame que le presente a mi amigo.

Allow me to introduce my fiancée
Permetin-me que els presenti la meva promesa.
Permítanme que les presente a mi novia.

Pleased to meet you.
Encantat, -ada.
Encantado, -a.

The pleasure is mine.
El gust és meu.
El gusto es mío.

Pleased to meet you. How do you do?
Molt de gust.
Mucho gusto.

Here, this is my calling / visiting card.
Tingui, la meva targeta (de visita).
Tenga, mi tarjeta (de visita).

2.6 **How to ask for / offer something. Being polite.**
Com demanar / oferir alguna cosa? Fórmules de cortesia.
¿Cómo pedir / ofrecer algo? Fórmulas de cortesía.

Please!
Sisplau! Si us plau! Per favor!
¡Por favor!

Please help me.
Ajudi'm, faci el favor.
Ayúdeme, por favor.

I'd like to ask you (for) something.
Voldria demanar-li una cosa.
Quisiera pedirle algo.

Could / Can you help me?
Vol ajudar-me?
¿Quiere ayudarme?

I need some information.
Em cal una informació.
Necesito una información.

Could you lend me a pen?
Pot prestar-me un bolígraf?
¿Puede prestarme un bolígrafo?

Could you tell me the name of this street?
Pot dir-me el nom d'aquest carrer?
¿Puede decirme el nombre de esta calle?

What can I do for you?
En què puc ajudar-lo?
¿En qué puedo ayudarle?

I can accompany you.
Puc acompanyar-lo.
Puedo acompañarle.

If you need anything, just let me know.
Si li cal res, no deixi d'avisar-me.
Si necesita algo, no deje de avisarme.

May I smoke?
Puc fumar?
¿Puedo fumar?

May I sit down?
Em permet que segui?
¿Me permite que me siente?

You are very kind.
Vostè és molt amable.
Es usted muy amable.

With great pleasure!
Amb molt de gust.
¡Con mucho gusto!

Don't worry!
No pateixi!
¡Pierda usted cuidado!

You are free to do so.
És ben lliure de fer-ho.
Es usted muy dueño / dueña de hacerlo.

I am at your disposal.
Estic a la seva disposició.
Estoy a su disposición.

You can count on me.
Pot comptar amb mi.
Puede contar conmigo.

2.7 **Acceptance, refusal**
Acceptació, rebuig
Aceptación, rechazo

Of course (so)!
No cal dir!
¡Por supuesto!

It's a good idea!
És una bona idea!
¡Es una buena idea!

Thank you.
Gràcies.
Gracias.

No, thank you.
Gràcies, no.
No, gracias.

I am honoured.; It's an honour for me.
Em sento honrat / honrada.
Me siento honrado / honrada.

Don't bother.
No es molesti.
No se moleste.

No.
No.
No.

I don't want to.
No en vull.
No quiero.

I can't.
No puc.
No puedo.

I don't feel like it.
No en tinc ganes.
No tengo ganas.

I don't have time.
No tinc tamps.
No tengo tiempo.

Gladly. With pleasure.
Amb molt de gust.
Con mucho gusto.

All right!; Fine!
D'acord!
¡De acuerdo!; ¡Vale!

By no means!; No way!
De cap manera!
¡De ninguna manera!

Out of the question!; I wouldn't think of it!
Ni pensar-hi!
¡Ni hablar!

Naturally!; Of course!
Naturalment!
¡Naturalmente!

2.8 **Thanks, gratitude**. Agraïment. *Agradecimiento*

Thank you.
Gràcies. Mercès.
Gracias.

Thanks for your help.
Gràcies per la seva ajuda.
Gracias por su ayuda.

Thank you very much.
Moltes gràcies. Moltíssimes gràcies.
Muchas gracias. Muchísimas gracias.

You're welcome. Don't mention it.
De res. No s'ho val.
No hay de qué.

I thank you for your advice.
Li agraeixo el seu consell.
Le agradezco su consejo.

I'm very grateful to you.
Li estic molt agraït / agraïda.
Le estoy muy agradecido / agradecida.

Much obliged.
Li estic obligat / obligada.
Le estoy obligado / obligada.

2.9 **Liking, preference**
Grat, preferència
Agrado, preferencia

What do you think?
Què li'n sembla?
¿Qué le parece?

Do you like it?
Li agrada?
¿Le gusta?

Do you like them?
Li agraden?
¿Le gustan?

I like beer / ale.
M'agrada la cervesa.
Me gusta la cerveza.

I prefer beer to wine.
Prefereixo la cervesa al vi.
Prefiero la cerveza al vino.

I prefer meat.
Prefereixo la carn. M'estimo més la carn.
Prefiero la carne.

Which do you choose?
Quin tria?
¿Cuál escoge?

I like both (of them).
M'agraden tots dos.
Me gustan los dos.

I'm very happy.
Estic molt content / contenta.
Estoy muy contento / contenta.

I like it / him / her.
M'agrada.
Me gusta.

You like it / him / her.
T'agrada.
Te gusta.

He / She / likes it / him / her. You like it / him /her.
Li agrada.
Le gusta.

We like it / him / her.
Ens agrada.
Nos gusta.

You like it / him / her.
Us agrada.
Os gusta.

They like it / him / her. You like it / him / her.
Els agrada.
Les gusta.

2.10 Apology, sympathy
Excusa, llàstima
Excusa, lástima

Sorry. I beg your pardon.
Perdó.
Perdón.

Pardon me. Excuse me.
Perdoni'm. Disculpi'm.
Perdóneme. Discúlpeme.

What a shame / pity!
Quina llàstima!
¡Qué lástima!

I'm (very) sorry.
Ho sento (molt). Em sap (molt de) greu.
Lo siento (mucho).

It doesn't matter.
No hi fa res.
No importa.

It's not my fault.
No és culpa meva.
No es mi culpa.

Don't take it badly.
No s'ho prengui malament.
No lo tome a mal.

I'm sorry, but I can't do it.
Ho sento, però no puc fer-ho.
Lo siento, pero no puedo hacerlo.

Unfortunately.
Desgraciadament. Dissortadament.
Desgraciadamente.

2.11 **Affirmation, agreement**
Afirmació, acord
Afirmación, acuerdo

Yes.
Sí.
Sí.

That's right. That's how it is.
És així.
Es así.

Of course!; I should say so.
I tant! Ja ho crec que sí.
¡Desde luego! ¡Ya lo creo!

Indubitably. Certainly.
Indubtablement.
Indudablemente.

It's true. That's right
És veritat.
Es verdad.

I agree with you.
Estic d'acord amb vostè.
Estoy de acuerdo con usted.

It's a good idea.
És una bona idea.
Es una buena idea.

I have no objection. I don't mind.
No hi ha cap inconvenient.
No hay ningún inconveniente.

Of course (so)!
No cal dir!
¡Por supuesto!

Exactly.
Exactament.
Exacto.

Indeed. Exactly.
Efectivament.
Efectivamente.

Naturally. Of course.
Naturalment.
Naturalmente.

You're right.
Té raó.
Tiene usted razón.

All right. Very well. O.K.
Molt bé.
Está bien.

However / As you like.
Sigui con vostè vulgui
Sea como usted quiera.

All right. Fine.
D'acord.
De acuerdo. Vale.

Understood! It's clear.
Entesos! És clar.
¡Entendido! Está claro.

2.12 **Negation, disagreement**
Negació, desacord
Negación, desacuerdo

No.
No.
No.

By no means. No way.
De cap de les maneres.
De ninguna manera.

Out of the question! I wouldn't think of it!
Ni pensar-hi!
¡Ni hablar! ¡Ni pensarlo!

Far from it.
Ni de bon tros.
Ni mucho menos.

Nonsense! Rubbish!
Fugi!
¡Que va!

You are mistaken / wrong.
Vostè s'equivoca.
Usted se equivoca.

You are wrong.
Vostè no té raó.
Usted no tiene razón.

That's a lie!
(És una) mentida!
¡(Es una) mentira!

I'm against it.
Estic en contra.
Estoy en contra.

I don't agree.
No hi estic d'acord.
No estoy de acuerdo.

I don't know.
No ho sé.
No lo sé.

(I have) no idea.
No en tinc ni idea.
Ni idea.

Nothing.
Res.
Nada.

No one. Nobody.
Ningú.
Nadie.

2.13 **Doubt, hypothesis, probability**
Dubte, hipòtesi, probabilitat
Duda, hipótesis, probabilidad

It depends.
(Això) depèn.
Depende.

They / You must be strangers.
Deuen ser estrangers.
Serán extranjeros.

I suppose (so).
Suposo.
Supongo.

I doubt it.
Ho dubto.
Lo dudo.

Who knows!
Qui ho sap!
¡Quién sabe!

It's impossible. It can't be.
És impossible. No pot ser.
Es imposible. No puede ser.

I don't think so.
No ho crec.
No lo creo.

Maybe. Perhaps.
Potser.
Quizás. Tal vez.

Probably.
Probablement.
Probablemente.

For sure. Probably.
Segurament.
Seguramente.

Maybe. Perhaps.
Qui sap si.
A lo mejor.

It's / That's incredible.
És increïble.
Es increíble.

It's not likely / probable.
És poc probable.
Es poco probable.

It's possible. Maybe.
És possible. Pot ser.
Es posible. Puede ser.

We'll see.
Ja ho veurem.
Ya veremos.

You don't say!
No m'ho digui!
¡No me lo diga usted!

It's probable.
És probable.
Es probable.

It's unlikely.
És improbable.
Es improbable.

2.14 Intention, plans
Intenció, plans
Intención, planes

I want to stay / lodge in Figueres.
Vull allotjar-me a Figueres.
Quiero alojarme en Figueres.

I intend to visit Girona.
Tinc la intenció de visitar Girona.
Tengo la intención de visitar Gerona.

I plan to leave on Tuesday.
Penso sortir dimarts.
Pienso salir el martes.

What do you want to do?
Què vol fer?
¿Qué quiere hacer?

What are your plans for tomorrow?
Quin pla té per demà?
¿Qué plan tiene para mañana?

I'd like to go shopping.
Voldria sortir a compar.
Quisiera hacer unas compras.

If you like, we could have dinner / supper together.
Si li sembla, podríem sopar plegats.
Si le parece, podríamos cenar juntos.

I want.
Vull.
Quiero.

You want.
Vols.
Quieres.

He / She wants.; You want.
Vol.
Quiere.

We want.
Volem.
Queremos.

You want.
Voleu.
Queréis.

They want
Volen.
Quieren.

2.15 Obligation, necessity
Obligació, necessitat
Obligación, necesidad

I have to exchange money.
He de canviar diners.
Tengo que cambiar dinero.

You have to wait a while.
Ha d'esperar una mica.
Tiene que esperar un poco.

You / they must fill out / in this card.
Han d'omplir aquesta fitxa.
Tienen que llenar esta ficha.

We have to speak.
Hem de parlar.
Tenemos que hablar.

I should go.
Hauria d'anar-me'n.
Tendría que irme.

I / He / She / You shouldn't smoke so much.
No hauria de fumar tant.
No debería fumar tanto.

One has to be careful.
Cal anar amb compte.
Hay que ir con cuidado.

One doesn't have to be afraid.
No cal tenir por.
No hay que tener miedo.

It's necessary.
Cal.
Es necesario.

It's not necessary.
No cal.
No es necesario.

I need two fifty peseta stamps.
Em calen dos segells de cinquanta pessetes.
Me hacen falta dos sellos de cincuenta pesetas.

We need gasoline / petrol.
Ens cal gasolina.
Nos hace falta gasolina.

We don't need anything.
No ens falta res.
No nos falta nada.

I have to
he / haig de
tengo que

you have to
has de
tienes que

he / she / it has to; you have to
ha de
tiene que

we have to
hem de
tenemos que

you have to
heu de
tenéis que

they / you have to
han de
tienen que

2.16 **Surprise, exclamation**
Sorpresa, exclamació
Sorpresa, exclamación

You don't say!
Què diu, ara?
¡No me diga!

Ouch! Oh dear!
Ai!
¡Ay!

What a surprise!
Quina sorpresa!
¡Qué sorpresa!

Don't tell me!
No m'ho digui!
¡No me lo diga!

I can't believe it!
No m'ho puc creure!
¡No me lo puedo creer!

Are you sure?
Vol dir?
¿Está usted seguro / segura?

Well! How strange!
Caram! Carai!
¡Caramba!

That's / It's incredible!
És increïble!
¡Es increible!

That's / It's impossible!
És impossible!
¡Es imposible!

How lovely / pretty!
Que bonic!
¡Qué bonito!

That's / It's unbelievable!
Sembla mentida!
¡Parece mentira!

Help!
Socors! Auxili!
¡Socorro!

Damn! Well!
Ostres!
¡Ostras!

2.17 Congratulations, wishes, condolence
Felicitacions, vots, compassió
Felicitaciones, votos, compasión

Congratulations! Best wishes!
Per molts anys!
¡Felicidades!

Cheers!
Salut!
¡Salud!

Happy New Year!
Bon any! Feliç any nou! Feliç cap d'any!
¡Feliz año nuevo!

To your health!
A la teva / seva salut!
¡A tu / su salud!

Congratulations!
Enhorabona!
¡Enhorabuenra!

Enjoy your meal!
Bon profit! Que aprofiti!
¡Que aproveche!

Have fun! Have a good time!
Que es diverteixi!
¡Que se divierta!

Have fun! Have a good time! pl
Que es diverteixin!
¡Que se diviertan!

Have a good trip!
Bon viatge!
¡Buen viaje!

Happy holidays!
Bones festes!
¡Felices fiestas!

Merry Christmas!
Bon Nadal! Bones festes de Nadal!
¡Felices Navidades! ¡Felices Pascuas!

(I hope you) Get better soon.
Que es posi bo aviat.
Que usted mejore pronto.

My deepest sympathy.
El meu condol més sincer.
Mi más sentido pésame.

When is the funeral?
Quan serà l'enterrament?
¿Cuándo será el entierro?

I wish you much luck.
Li / els desitjo molta sort.
Le / les deseo mucha suerte.

My very best wishes! Congratulations!
Moltes felicitats!
¡Muchas felicidades!

The same to you!
Igualment!
¡Igualmente!

3. PERSONAL DETAILS
DADES PERSONALS
DATOS PERSONALES

Surname(s); Last name(s)
Cognom(s)
Apellido(s)

First name
Nom
Nombre

Nationality
Nacionalitat
Nacionalidad

Country, place and date of birth
País, lloc i data de naixement
País, lugar y fecha de nacimiento

Profession
Professió
Profesión

Address
Domicili
Domicilio

Passport number
Número de passaport
Número de pasaporte

3.1 **Name and surname(s) / Last name(s)**
Nom i cognom(s)
Nombre y apellido(s)

What's his / her / your name?
Com es / se diu?
¿Cómo se llama?

What's this man's name?
Com es diu aquest senyor?
¿Cómo se llama este señor?

Your surname / last name, please.
El seu cognom, sisplau.
Su apellido, por favor.

What's your name?
Com et dius?
¿Cómo te llamas?

What's your name?
Quin és el teu nom?
¿Cuál es tu nombre?

My name is Peter.
Em dic Peter.
Me llamo Peter.

Is that his / her / your first or last name?
Aquest és el seu / teu nom o el seu / teu cognom?
¿Este es su / tu nombre o su / tu apellido?

That is my Christian name.
Aquest és el meu nom de pila.
Este es mi nombre de pila.

How do you spell / pronounce your name?
Com s'escriu / es pronuncia el teu nom?
¿Cómo se escribe / se pronuncia tu nombre?

What was your mother's name?
Com es deia la teva mare?
¿Cómo se llamaba tu madre?

Is it a typical American / English / Catalan / Spanish name?
És un nom típicament americà / anglès / català / castellà?
¿Es un nombre típicamente americano / inglés / catalán / español?

3.2 **Family**
Família
Familia

Your marital status?
El seu estat civil?
¿Su estado civil?

I'm married.
Sóc casat / casada.
Soy casado / casada.

Without being indiscreet, are you married?
Si no és una indiscreció, vostè és casat / casada?
Si no es una indiscreción, ¿está usted casado / casada?

No. I'm still single.
No, sóc solter / soltera encara.
No, soy soltero / soltera todavía.

I have a fiancé / fiancée
Ja tinc promès / promesa.
Ya tengo novio / novia.

I've been married for one year.
Sóc casat / casada des de fa un any.
Estoy casado / casada desde hace un año.

I'm going to get married next year.
Em casaré l'any vinent.
Me casaré el año que viene.

I got married last year.
Em vaig casar l'any passat.
Me casé el año pasado.

I've gotten a divorce from my husband.
M'he divorciat del meu marit.
Me he divorciado de mi marido.

I'm divorced.
Sóc divorciat / divorciada.
Soy divorciado / divorciada.

I'm a widow / widower.
Sóc vídua (viuda) / vidu (viudo).
Soy viuda / viudo.

My husband / wife is no longer alive. (He / she is dead).
El meu marit / La meva dona ja no viu. (Ha mort.)
Mi marido / mujer ya no vive. (Ha muerto.)

He / She died three years ago.
Va morir fa tres anys.
Murió hace tres años.

Do you have children?
Té fills?
¿Tiene hijos?

Do you have children? pl
Teniu fills?
¿Tienen hijos?

No I / we don't.
No, no en tinc / tenim.
No tengo. No tenemos.

Yes, we do.
Sí, que en tenim.
Sí que tenemos

How many children do you have?
Quants fills teniu?
¿Cuántos hijos tienen?

Our first child was born this year.
El nostre primer fill ha nascut aquest any.
Nuestro primer hijo nació este año.

Is it a boy or a girl?
És un nen o una nena?
¿Es un niño o una niña?

It's a girl.
És una nena.
Es una niña.

We have two sons.
Nosaltres tenim dos fills.
Nosotros tenemos dos hijos.

I have two daughters.
Tinc dues filles.
Tengo dos hijas.

I also have grandchildren.
També tinc néts.
Tengo también nietos.

Are your parents / grandparents still alive?
Els seus pares / avis viuen encara?
¿Sus padres / abuelos viven todavía?

Yes, thank God.
Sí, gràcies a Déu.
Sí, gracias a Dios.

My father isn't alive, but my mother is.
El meu pare ja no és viu, però la meva mare, sí.
Mi padre ya no vive, pero mi madre, sí.

Do you have brothers and sisters?
Té germans?
¿Tiene hermanos?

No I don't.
No en tinc.
No tengo.

I have two brothers / sisters.
Tinc dos germans. Tinc dues germanes.
Tengo dos hermanos / hermanas.

I have many relatives.
Tinc molts parents.
Tengo muchos parientes.

We are a large family
Som una família nombrosa.
Somos una familia numerosa.

3.3 **Age.** L'edat. *La edad*

How old are you? How old is he / she / it / are you?
Quants anys tens / té?
¿Cuántos años tienes / tiene?

I'm thirty (years old).
Tinc trenta anys.
Tengo trenta años.

He / She / It is 40 years old.
Té 40 anys d'edat.
Tiene 40 años de edad.

And how old is your brother?
I quants anys té el teu germà?
¿Y cuántos años tiene tu hermano?

He hasn't turned 20 yet.
Encara no ha fet els 20 anys.
Todavía no ha cumplido 20 años.

How old are you?
Quina edat té?
¿Qué edad tiene?

I have just turned seventy.
Acabo de complir els setanta.
Acabo de cumplir los setenta.

That's impossible! You look much younger.
No pot ser! Sembla molt més jove.
¡No puede ser! Parece mucho más joven.

How old is your grandson / granddaughter?
Quina edat té el seu nét / la seva néta?
¿Qué edad tiene su nieto / nieta?

He / She turned eight today.
Avui ha fet vuit anys.
Hoy ha cumplido ocho años.

He / She is still a boy / girl.
És un nen / una nena encara.
Es un niño / una niña todavía.

My friend's birthday is today. (Today is his birthday).
El meu amic també fa avui anys. (Avui celebra el seu aniversari del naixement.)
Mi amigo también cumple hoy años. (Hoy celebra su cumpleaños.)

My parents are getting on in age.
Els meus pares ja són grans.
Mis padres tienen ya una cierta edad.

They are old.
Són vells.
Son viejos.

3.4 **Level of education.**
Nivell d'instrucció.
Nivel de instrucción.

Studies. Education
Estudis. Educació
Estudios. Educación

elementary
elementals
elementales

secondary
mitjans
medios

higher
superiors
superiores

university.
universitaris.
universitarios.

My grandson goes to nursery school.
El meu nét va al parvulari.
Mi nieto va al parvulario.

My daughter already works.
La meva filla ja treballa.
Mi hija ya trabaja.

My son is still studying
El meu fill encara estudia.
Mi hijo todavía está estudiando.

He attends university / college.
Va a la universitat.
Va a la universidad.

What year is he in?
En quin any / curs està?
¿En qué año / curso está?

He's a freshman / sophmore / junior.
Està en el primer / segon / tercer any / curs.
Está en el primer / segundo / tercer año / curso.

My son is younger.
El meu fill és més jove.
Mi hijo es más joven.

He's in primary school.
Va a l'escola primària.
Va a la escuela primaria.

He's in high school.
Va a l'institut.
Va al instituto.

What grade is he in?
A quina classe va?
¿A qué clase va?

He's in first / second grade.
Està en la primera / segona classe.
Está en la primera / segunda clase.

He goes to a vocational training school.
Va a una escola professional.
Va a una escuela profesional.

My daughter is in upper high school this year. ("Batxillerat" denotes the entire period of secondary education).
La meva filla aquest any fa el batxillerat.
Mi hija esta año hace el bachillerato.

She studies a lot / hard.
Estudia molt / bé.
Estudia mucho / bien.

My son wants to be a doctor.
El meu fill voldria ser metge.
Mi hijo quisiera ser médico.

He'd like to go to college / university.
Voldria anar a la universitat.
Quisiera ir a la universidad.

He has to take the entrance examination.
Ha de fer l'examen de selectivitat.
Tiene que hacer el examen de selectividad.

His / Her friend enrolled in the Law School.
La seva amiga es va matricular a la Facultat de Dret.
Su amiga se matriculó en la Facultad de Derecho.

My friend studies Spanish philology / has a bachelor's degree in Spanish.
El meu amic estudia filologia / llicenciatura espanyola.
Mi amigo estudia filología / licenciatura española.

He has exams now.
Ara té exàmens.
Ahora tiene exámenes.

He successfully passed all his exams.
Va fer tots els exàmens amb èxit.
Hizo / Pasó todos los exámenes con éxito.

He still has a few exams to take.
Li manquen encara uns exàmens.
Le faltan todavía unos exámenes.

He has to resit one of his exams.
Ha de repetir un dels exàmens.
Tiene que repetir uno de los exámenes.

He finishes / graduates this year.
Acaba / Es gradua aquest any.
Acaba / Se gradua este año.

He's writing his master's thesis.
Està escrivint la tesina.
Está escribiendo la tesina.

He's writing a doctoral thesis.
Escriu una tesis doctoral.
Escribe una tesis doctoral.

He doesn't have a job yet.
Encara no té feina.
Todavía no tiene trabajo.

He's a qualified engineer.
És enginyer diplomat.
Es ingeniero diplomado.

3.5 **Profession. Job.**
Professió. Treball.
Profesión. Trabajo.

Where do you work?
On treballa vostè?
¿Dónde trabaja usted?

I work at a factory / store / school.
Treballo en una fàbrica / botiga / escola.
Trabajo en una fábrica / tienda / escuela.

I work at home.
Treballo a casa.
Trabajo en casa.

I'm a housewife.
Sóc mestressa de casa.
Soy ama de casa / Mis labores.

I don't work. I'm retired / a pensioner.
Ja no treballo. Sóc jubilat / jubilada / pensionat / pensionada.
Ya no trabajo. Soy jubilado / jubilada / pensionado / pensionada.

I'm still studying.
Encara estudio.
Estoy estudiando todavía.

I don't have a job.
No tinc feina.
No tengo trabajo.

I'm unemployed.
Sóc parat / parada. Estic en atur.
Soy parado / parada.

What's your profession?
Quina és la seva professió?
¿Cuál es su profesión?

What do you do?
A què es dedica?
¿A qué se dedica?

I'm a professor, but I work in journalism.
Sóc professor, però em dedico al periodisme.
Soy profesor, pero me dedico al periodismo.

We are colleagues.
Som col.legues.
Somos colegas.

My husband works too much.
El meu marit treballa massa.
Mi marido trabaja demasiado.

He's worked since he was eighteen.
Treballa des de l'edat de divuit anys.
Trabaja desde la edad de dieciocho años.

Are you / Is he happy with your / his job?
Està content del seu treball?
¿Está contento de su trabajo?

Do you / Does he earn much?
Guanya molt?
¿Gana mucho?

Do they pay him well?
Li paguen bé?
¿Le pagan bien?

What's the average wage here?
Quin és el seu salari mitjà aquí?
¿Cuál es el salario medio aquí?

How much does a high school teacher earn / make?
Quant guanya / cobra un professor d'institut?
¿Cuánto gana / cobra un profesor de instituto?

How many vacation days do you have?
Quants dies de vacances té?
¿Cuántos días de vacaciones tiene?

One month.
Un mes.
Un mes.

We are off on Saturday.
Els dissabtes fem festa.
Los sábados hacemos fiesta.

3.6 Geographic names
Noms geogràfics
Nombres geográficos

I'm a foreigner.
Sóc estranger / estrangera.
Soy extranjero / extranjera.

Excuse me, are you from here?
Perdoni, vostè és d'aquí?
Perdone, ¿usted es de aquí?

Where are you from?
D'on és / són?
¿De dónde es / son?

We are from New York.
Som de Nova York.
Somos de Nueva York.

What country / city are you from?
Vostè, de quin país / quina ciutat és?
¿Usted de qué país / ciudad es?

These young people aren't from Europe.
Aquests joves no són d'Europa.
Estos jóvenes no son de Europa.

I'm Catalan.
Sóc català / catalana.
Soy catalán / catalana.

What's the capital of England?
Quina és la capital d'Anglaterra?
¿Cuál es la capital de Inglaterra?

The capital of England is London.
La capital d'Anglaterra és Londres.
La capital de Inglaterra es Londres.

What's the name of your (native) city?
Com es diu la seva ciutat (natal)?
¿Cómo se llama su ciudad (natal)?

What nationality are you?
Quina és la teva nacionalitat?
¿Cuál es tu nacionalidad?

I'm French.
Sóc francès.
Soy francés.

What region / area of Spain are you from?
De quina regió / comarca d'Espanya és vostè?
¿De qué región / comarca de España es usted?

I'm a native of Mallorca.
Sóc natural de Mallorca.
Soy natural de Mallorca.

Where do you live?
On vius?
¿Dónde vives?

I live in Barcelona now.
Ara visc a Barcelona.
Ahora vivo en Barcelona.

I'll give you my address.
Et / li dono la meva adreça.
Te / le doy mi dirección.

4. **LANGUAGES. KNOWLEDGE OF LANGUAGES**
LLENGÜES. CONEIXEMENT DE LLENGÜES
LENGUAS. CONOCIMIENTO DE LENGUAS

Excuse me, I'm a foreigner and I don't speak Catalan / Spanish.
Perdoni, sóc estranger i no parlo català / castellà.
Perdone, soy extranjero y no hablo catalán / castellano (español)

Do you speak English, French or German?
Parla anglès, francès o alemany?
¿Habla usted inglés, francés o alemán?

I speak Italian fairly well.
Parlo bastant / prou bé l'italià.
Hablo bastante bien el italiano.

I speak a little French
Parlo una mica el francès.
Hablo un poco francés.

And can you also read / write (in) this language?
I llegeix / escriu també en aquesta llengua?
¿Y lee / escribe también en esta lengua?

Spanish is not a difficult language.
El castellà no és una llengua difícil.
El español no es una lengua difícil.

Catalan pronunciation is not easy.
La pronúncia catalana no és fàcil.
La pronunciación catalana no es fácil.

Do you understand me?
Vostè em comprèn? M'entens?
¿Me entiende usted? ¿Me entiendes?

I understand you.
El / La comprenc.
Le / La entiendo.

I don't understand you.
No et comprenc.
No te entiendo.

I don't understand. What did you say?
No l'entenc. Què diu?
No le entiendo. ¿Qué dice?

What did you say? What?
Què dius? Què? Com?
¿Qué dices? ¿Qué? ¿Cómo?

Please speak a little more slowly.
Parli una mica més a poc a poc, sisplau.
Hable un poco más despacio, por favor.

The Catalan speak very quickly / fast.
Els catalans parlen molt ràpidament.
Los catalanes hablan muy rápido.

Please repeat it / that.
Repeteixi-ho, sisplau.
Repítalo, por favor.

Could you repeat it / that?
Podries repetir-ho?
¿Podrías repetirlo?

What does this word / sentence mean?
Què significa aquesta paraula / frase?
¿Qué significa esta palabra / frase?

What does this / that mean?
Què vol dir això?
¿Qué quiere decir esto?

What's the name of this fruit?
Com es diu aquesta fruita?
¿Cómo se llama esta fruta?

How do you say "Good morning" in Catalan?
Com es diu «Good morning» en català?
¿Cómo se dice «Good morning» en catalán?

What's this called in Spanish?
Com es diu això en castellà?
¿Cómo se llama esto en español?

How is this word pronounced?
Com es pronuncia aquesta paraula?
¿Cómo se pronuncia esta palabra?

Am I saying it right?
Ho dic bé?
¿Lo digo bien?

Translate this sentence into English for me.
Tradueixi'm a l'anglès aquesta frase.
Tradúzcame al inglés esta frase.

Spell it, please.
Lletra a lletra / Lletregi-la, sisplau.
Deletréela, por favor.

Write it for me.
Escrigui-me-la.
Escríbamela.

Where did you learn Catalan?
On va aprendre el català?
¿Dónde aprendió el catalán?

At university. On a course.
A la universitat. En un curs.
En la universidad. En un curso.

How long have you been studying Catalan?
Des de quan estudia català?
¿Desde cuándo estudia catalán?

I've been studying it for more than three years.
Ja porto més de tres anys estudiant-lo.
Llevo ya más de tres años estudiándolo.

5. **THE CLIMATE.** EL CLIMA. *EL CLIMA.*

What's the weather like?
Quin temps fa?
¿Qué tiempo hace?

The weather is bad.
Fa mal temps.
Hace mal tiempo.

I'm hot.
Tinc calor.
Tengo calor.

I'm cold.
Tinc fred.
Tengo frío.

It's (very) windy.
Fa (molt) vent.
Hace (mucho) viento.

It's raining.
Plou.
Llueve.

The weather is good.
Fa bon temps. Fa bo.
Hace buen tiempo.

It's (very) hot
Fa (molta) calor.
Hace (mucho) calor.

It's (very) cold.
Fa (molt) fred.
Hace (mucho) frío.

It's cool.
Fa fresca.
Hace fresco.

It's sunny.
Fa sol.
Hace sol.

It's very humid.
Hi ha molta humitat.
Hay mucha humedad.

It's going to rain / snow tomorrow.
Demà plourà / nevarà.
Mañana lloverá / nevará.

The weather is heavy.
Fa xafogor.
Hace bochorno.

It's threatening to rain
Amenaça tempesta.
Amenaza tormenta.

What's the temperature?
Quants graus hi ha?
¿A cuántos grados estamos?

It's four degrees above / below zero.
Tenim quatre graus sobre / sota cero. Hi ha quatre graus positius / negatius.
Tenemos cuatro grados sobre / bajo cero. Tenemos cuatro grados positivos / negativos.

It's icy.
Glaça.
Hiela.

The temperature is rising / falling.
Les temperatures pugen / baixen.
Las temperaturas suben / bajan.

6. **TRAVEL**. VIATGE. *VIAJE*

6.1 **At the border.** A la frontera. *En la frontera.*

When will we reach the border?
Quan arribarem a la frontera?
¿Cuándo llegaremos a la frontera?

We are at the Spanish border.
Som a la frontera espanyola.
Estamos en la frontera española.

Fill out / in this card.
Ompli aquesta fitxa.
Rellene esta ficha.

Passport control.
Control de passaports.
Control de pasaportes.

Your passport, please.
El seu passaport, sisplau.
Su pasaporte, por favor.

Do you have a visa?
Té visat?
¿Tiene visado?

We don't need a visa.
No ens cal visat.
No necesitamos visado.

May I telephone my embassy?
Puc telefonar a la meva ambaixada?
¿Puedo telefonear a mi embajada?

Customs.
Control de duana.
Control de aduana.

Do you have anything to declare?
Té res per a declarar?
¿Tiene algo que declarar?

I have nothing to declare.
No tinc res per a declarar.
No tengo nada que declarar.

Which is your luggage / baggage?
Quin és el seu equipatge?
¿Cuál es su equipaje?

Is this yours?
Això és de vostè?
¿Esto es de usted?

Let me see your purse / handbag.
Deixi'm veure la seva bossa de mà.
Déjeme ver su bolso de mano.

Open this suitcase / bag.
Obri aquesta maleta / bossa.
Abra esta maleta / bolsa.

All right. You may close it now.
Està bé. Ja pot tancar-la.
Está bien. Ya puede cerrarla.

6.2 Travelling by car. Asking for information and directions.
Viatge amb automòbil. Demanant informació i orientació.
Viaje en automóvil. Pidiendo información y orientación.

Am I going the right way to get to Lleida?
Vaig bé per anar a Lleida?
¿Voy bien para Lérida?

Where does this road lead / go to?
On porta aquesta carretera?
¿A dónde lleva esta carretera?

How do I get to Girona?
Com arribo a Girona?
¿Cómo llego a Gerona?

Where are we?
On som?
¿Dónde estamos?

Where do I have to turn?
On he de girar?
¿Dónde tengo que girar?

Can you point it out to me on the map?
Pot indicar-m'ho en el mapa?
¿Puede indicármelo en el mapa?

Where can I find a car repair shop / garage?
On trobo un (auto) taller?
¿Dónde puedo encontrar un taller de reparación de automóviles?

How far away is the nearest gas / petrol station?
A quina distància és la pròxima gasolinera?
¿A qué distancia está la próxima gasolinera?

Is the nearest service station far away?
És lluny la pròxima estació de servei?
¿Está lejos la próxima estación de servicio?

Where?
On?
¿Dónde?

straight ahead / on
tot recte
todo derecho

up (there)
amunt
arriba

right here
aquí mateix
aquí mismo

down
avall
abajo

that way
cap allí
hacia allí

(up) ahead
endavant
adelante

behind; back (there)
endarrere
atrás

to the east
a l'est
al este

far
lluny
lejos

to the south
al sud
al sur

to the north
al nord
al norte

two kilometers from here
a dos quilòmetres d'aquí
a dos kilómetros de aquí

near; close
prop
cerca

to the west
a l'oest
al oeste

on the other side
a l'altra banda
al otro lado

We are here.
Som aquí.
Estamos aquí.

Continue on / down this road for twenty kilometers.
Segueixi per aquesta carretera vint quilòmetres.
Continúe por esta carretera veinte kilómetros.

Turn right / left.
Tombi a la dreta / a l'esquerra.
Tuerza a la derecha / izquierda.

At the first fork / branch in the road.
A la primera bifurcació.
En la primera bifurcación.

At the first / second corner.
A la primera / segona cantonada.
En la primera / segunda esquina.

This road goes to Tarragona.
Aquesta carretera porta a Tarragona.
Esta carretera lleva a Tarragona.

The sea is ten kilometers from here.
El mar és a deu quilòmetres d'aquí.
El mar está a diez kilómetros de aquí.

I'll show it to you on the map.
Li ho indico en el mapa.
Se lo enseño en el mapa.

6.3 At the gas / petrol station
A la gasolinera
En la gasolinera

Fill it up, please.
Ple, sisplau.
Lleno, por favor.

Twenty liters of regular (3-star) gas / petrol, please.
Vint litres de gasolina normal, sisplau.
Veinte litros de gasolina normal, por favor.

Give me two thousand pesetas of super (4-star) petrol.
Posi'm súper per dues mil pessetes.
Póngame súper por dos mil pesetas.

I want thirty liters of gas / diesel oil.
Vull trenta litres de gas-oil.
Quiero treinta litros de gasóleo.

How many octanes is the super / regular.
De quants octans és la súper / normal?
¿De cuántos octanos es la súper / normal?

Do you have unleaded gas / petrol?
Tenen gasolina sense plom?
¿Tienen gasolina sin plomo?

Could you please check the oil level?
Faci el favor de comprovar el nivell de l'oli.
Por favor, compruebe el nivel del aceite.

I need an oil change.
Em cal canvi d'oli.
Me hace falta cambio de aceite.

Could you check the tires / tyres?
Vol revisar els pneumàtics?
¿Quiere revisar los neumáticos?

Can you repair it?
Pot reparar-lo?
¿Puede repararlo?

Where can I find a repair shop / garage?
On trobo un taller de reparacions?
¿Dónde puedo encontrar un taller de reparaciones?

Could you call the breakdown service?
Pot avisar el servei d'assistència?
¿Puede avisar el servicio de asistencia?

6.4 Automobile repair. Maintenance
Reparació d'automòbils. Manteniment
Reparación de automóviles. Mantenimiento.

Adjust / Tune up
Posi al punt
Ponga a punto

the ignition,
l'encesa,
el encendido,

the wheels,
les rodes,
las ruedas,

the lights.
l'enllumenament.
el alumbrado.

Change
Canviï
Cambie

the spark plugs,
les bugies,
las bujías,

the left front wheel.
la roda esquerra del davant.
la rueda delantera izquierda.

The right rear wheel is flat.
La roda dreta del derrere està rebentada.
La rueda trasera derecha está pinchada.

Check
Revisi
Revise

the pressure of the tires / tyres,
la pressió dels pneumàtics,
la presión de los neumáticos,

the oil level.
el nivell de l'oli.
el nivel del aceite.

My car has broken down.
El meu cotxe està avariat.
Mi coche está averiado.

The battery is dead.
La bateria està exhaurida.
La batería está agotada.

How long will you take to repair it?
Quant trigarà a reparar-lo?
¿Cuánto tardará en repararlo?

The engine
El motor
El motor

doesn't work properly,
falla,
falla,

pings / knocks,
pica,
pica / golpea,

stalls,
es cala,
se cala,

doesn't run,
no tira,
no tira,

doesn't start,
no s'engega,
no arranca,

jerks / shakes,
sotragueja; fa sotragades,
da sacudidas,

heats up too much,
s'escalfa massa,
se calienta demasiado,

makes too much noise.
fa massa soroll.
hace demasiado ruido.

It doesn't work.
No funciona.
No funciona.

I can't put it into second gear.
La segona (marxa) no entra.
La segunda (marcha) no entra.

6.5 Car rental
Lloguer de cotxes
Alquiler de coches

Do you rent cars?
Lloguen cotxes, vostès?
¿Alquilan ustedes coche?

I want to rent a four-seat, four-door car for one week.
Vull llogar per una setmana un cotxe de quatre portes i quatre places.
Quiero alquilar por una semana un coche de cuatro puertas y cuatro plazas.

How much is the rental per day?
Quant és el lloguer per dia?
¿Cuánto es el alquiler por día?

Must I also pay for mileage?
Cal pagar també el quilometratge?
¿Hay que pagar también el kilometraje?

Who takes care of the gas / petrol?
A càrrec de qui va la gasolina?
¿A cargo de quién va la gasolina?

Does the price also include insurance?
El preu inclou també l'assegurança?
¿El precio incluye también el seguro?

Where can I pick up the car?
On puc recollir el cotxe?
¿Dónde puedo recoger el coche?

Where do I leave off the car?
On he de tornar el cotxe?
¿Dónde tengo que entregar el coche?

6.6 Road accident
Accident de circulació
Accidente de tráfico

There has been an accident.
Hi ha hagut un accident.
Ha habido un accidente.

There are seriously injured persons.
Hi ha ferits greus.
Hay heridos graves.

There are only slightly injured persons.
Només hi ha ferits lleus.
Sólo hay heridos leves.

There are no personal injuries.
Només hi ha danys materials.
Sólo hay daños materiales.

Call
Avisi
Avise a

an ambulance,
l'ambulància,
la ambulancia,

the police,
la policia,
la policía,

the fire brigade,
els bombers,
los bomberos,

a tow-truck / wrecker.
la grua.
la grúa.

Call a doctor.
Cridi un metge.
Llame a un médico.

It wasn't anything (serious).
No ha passat res (de greu).
No ha pasado nada (grave).

Is your car insured?
Té assegurat el seu cotxe?
¿Tiene asegurado su coche?

6.7-6.9 **Travelling by train**
Viatge amb tren
Viaje en tren

6.7 **At the railroad / railway station**
A l'estació de ferrocarrils / RENFE
En la estación de ferrocarriles / RENFE

How do I get to the station?
Com puc arribar a l'estació?
¿Cómo puedo llegar a la estación?

Where is / are
On és / són
¿Dónde está(n)

the buffet? la cantina? *la cantina?*	**the restaurant?** el restaurant? *el restaurante?*
the information desk? la informació? *la información?*	**the ticket office?** la taquilla? *la taquilla?*
platform three? l'andana tres? *el andén tres?*	**track two?** la via dos? *la vía dos?*

the checkroom? / the left-luggage office?
la consigna?
la consigna?

the train to Valencia?
el tren per a València?
el tren para Valencia?

the waiting room?
la sala d'espera?
la sala de espera?

the toilet? / the restrooms?
els lavabos?
el lavabo? / los aseos?

When is there an express (train) to Lleida?
Quan hi ha tren ràpid per a Lleida?
¿Cuándo hay tren rápido para Lérida?

When does the last train leave for Barcelona?
Quan surt l'últim tren cap a Barcelona?
¿Cuándo sale el último tren para Barcelona?

When does the express arrive from Madrid?
Quan arriba el ràpid de Madrid?
¿Cuándo llega el rápido de Madrid?

Does the express from Paris have a sleeping car?
Porta vagó-llit l'exprés de París?
¿Lleva coche cama el expreso de París?

How much is a bunk / berth ticket?
Quant val el bitllet de llitera?
¿Cuánto cuesta el billete de litera?

Must I pay a supplement for the ten past eight train?
Cal pagar suplement per al tren de les vuit i deu?
¿Hay que pagar suplemento para el tren de las ocho y diez?

Does this train connect with another one to Madrid?
Té enllaç aquest tren per a Madrid?
¿Tiene enlace este tren para Madrid?

Where do I transfer / change over?
On cal fer transbord?
¿Dónde hay que hacer transbordo?

Does the train to Valencia depart from here?
Surt d'aquí el tren de València?
¿Sale de aquí el tren de Valencia?

Which track does the express from Girona arrive on?
A quina via arriba el ràpid de Girona?
¿A qué vía llega el rápido de Gerona?

Is the express from Paris delayed?
Porta retard l'exprés de París?
¿Trae retraso el expreso de París?

6.8 Signs. Information over the loudspeaker
Rètols. Informacions per altaveu
Rótulos. Informaciones por el altavoz

Arrivals.
Arribades.
Llegadas.

Departures.
Sortides.
Salidas.

Access to tracks.
Accés vies.
Acceso vías.

Express from Madrid going to Port Bou now arriving on track two.
Pròxima circulació per via dos ràpid procedent de Madrid que va a Port Bou.
Próxima circulación por vía dos rápido procedente de Madrid que va a Port Bou.

Suburban / local train to Mataró now arriving on track three.
Entrarà per via tres rodalies que va a Mataró.
Por vía tres va a efectuar su entrada cercanías con destino a Mataró.

Express from Valencia now stationed on track five.
Aturat en via cinc exprés procedent de València.
Estacionado en vía cinco expreso procedente de Valencia.

It will be departing shortly.
Aviat sortirà.
Saldrá en breve.

It is non-stop / direct to Sitges.
És directe a Sitges.
Es directo a Sitges.

It does not stop in Figueres.
No s'atura a Figueres.
No para en Figueres.

6.9 Buying tickets
Comprant bitllets
Comprando billetes

Give me a ticket to Tarragona, please.
Doni'm, sisplau, un bitllet per a Tarragona.
Déme, por favor, un billete para Tarragona.

ticket
bitllet
billete

group ticket
bitllet col.lectiu
billete colectivo

group ticket for eight persons
bitllet col.lectiu per a vuit persones
billete colectivo para ocho personas

first class ticket
bitllet de primera (classe)
billete de primera (clase)

half-price ticket
mig bitllet
medio billete

child's (fare) ticket
bitllet d'infant
billete de niño

seat reservation
reserva de seient
reserva de asiento

reduced rate ticket
bitllet de tarifa reduïda
billete de tarifa reducida

second class ticket
bitllet de segona (classe)
billete de segunda (clase)

round-trip / return ticket
bitllet d'anar i tornar
billete de ida y vuelta

supplement
suplement
suplemento

sleeping car ticket
bitllet de vagó-llit
billete de coche cama

reduction
reducció
reducción

bunk / berth ticket
bitllet de llitera
billete de litera

one-way / single ticket
bitllet d'anar
billete de ida

platform ticket
bitllet d'andana
billete de andén

6.10 **Travelling by plane**
Viatge amb avió
Viaje en avión

Where would you like to sit? By the window, by the aisle or in the middle?
On vol seure? Al costat de la finestreta, al costat del passadís o al centre?
¿Dónde quiere sentarse? ¿Al lado de la ventanilla, al lado del pasillo o en el centro?

Do not pass with pacemaker.
No passeu amb marcapàs.
No pasar con marcapasos.

T.W.A. flight ... to New York, now boarding at gate number four.
Vol TWA, número..., amb destinació a Nova York, porta d'embarcament quatre.
Vuelo T.W.A., número..., con destino a Nueva York, puerta de embarque cuatro.

No smoking, please.
No fumin, sisplau.
Absténganse de fumar.

Place the back of your seats in an upright position.
Mantinguin en posició vertical el respatller dels seients.
Mantengan en posición vertical el respaldo de sus asientos.

Fasten your safety belts.
Cordin-se els cinturons de seguretat.
Abróchense los cinturones de seguridad.

6.11 Travelling by ship
Viatge amb vaixell
Viaje en barco

Before arriving in Valencia, we'll be stopping in Ibiza.
Abans d'arribar a València, fem escala a Eivissa.
Antes de llegar a Valencia, hacemos escala en Ibiza.

I feel dizzy. Where can I get something for seasickness?
Em marejo. On puc aconseguir algun remei per al mareig?
Me mareo. ¿Dónde puedo conseguir algún remedio para el mareo?

Is there a doctor on board? Where can I find him/her?
Hi ha metge de bord? On el trobo?
¿Hay médico de a bordo? ¿Dónde lo encuentro?

6.12 At the travel agency
A l'agència de viatges
En la agencia de viajes

Could I get a brochure of the services you offer?
Puc rebre un prospecte / folletó sobre els seus serveis?
¿Puedo recibir un folleto sobre sus servicios?

Do you sell
Venen bitllets
¿Venden billetes de

bus / coach	**plane**	**train... tickets?**
d'autocar	d'avió	de tren?
autocar	*avión*	*tren?*

Do you take care of room reservations?
S'encarreguen de la reserva d'habitacions?
¿Se encargan de la reserva de habitaciones?

Do you organize trips?
Organitzen excursions?
¿Organizan excursiones?

Do you have a car rental service?
Tenen servei de lloguer de cotxes?
¿Tienen servicio de alquiler de coches?

Where can I sign up for a trip to Andorra?
On puc inscriure'm per a una excursió a Andorra?
¿Dónde puedo inscribirme para una excursión a Andorra?

Do you organize trips to Majorca?
Organitzen excursions a Mallorca?
¿Organizan excursiones a Mallorca?

What's the price of the tour of Andalusia?
Quin és el preu del circuit d'Andalusia?
¿Cuál es el precio del circuito de Andalucía?

Between what dates is the off-season rate valid?
En quines dates és vàlida la tarifa de temporada baixa?
¿En qué fechas es válida la tarifa de temporada baja?

When does the high season end?
Quan acaba la temporada alta?
¿Cuándo acaba la temporada alta?

Where does the bus / coach depart from?
D'on surt l'autocar?
¿De dónde sale el autocar?

When and where does the bus / coach arrive the last day?
Quan i on arriba l'autocar l'últim dia?
¿Cuándo y dónde llega el autocar el último día?

7. LODGING
ALLOTJAMENT
ALOJAMIENTO

7.1 Looking for accommodation.
Buscant allotjament.
Buscando alojamiento.

Is there a (two-star) hotel near here?
Hi ha prop d'aquí un hotel (de dues estrelles)?
¿Hay aquí cerca un hotel (de dos estrellas)?

Could you recommend me a good hostal that's not too expensive?
Podria recomanar-me un bon hostal que no sigui molt car?
¿Podría recomendarme un buen hostal que no sea muy caro?

I'd like to rent a room in a private home.
Voldria llogar una habitació en una casa particular.
Quisiera alquilar una habitación en una casa particular.

I'm looking for a hotel with a garage.
Busco un hotel que tingui garatge.
Busco un hotel que tenga garaje.

I would like to stay near the beach.
Voldria allotjar-me prop de la platja.
Quisiera alojarme cerca de la playa.

Could you point out a hotel near the (city) centre for me?
Tingui la bondat d'indicar-me un hotel cèntric.
¿Podría indicarme un hotel céntrico?

7.2-7.4 **The hotel.** L'hotel. *El hotel*

7.2 **Arrival**. Arribada. *Llegada*

I have a room reserved / booked here. My name is ...
Tinc aquí una habitació reservada. El meu nom és...
Tengo aquí una habitación reservada. Mi nombre es...

Do you have vacant rooms?
Tenen habitacions lliures?
¿Tienen habitaciones libres?

I need a double / single room
Vull una habitació individual / doble
Necesito una habitación sencilla / doble

with bathroom,
amb bany,
con baño,

without bathroom,
sense bany,
sin baño,

with hot and cold water,
amb aigua freda i calenta,
con agua fría y caliente,

with a washbasin,
amb lavabo,
con lavabo,

with an additional bed,
amb un llit supletori,
con una cama supletoria,

with a toilet,
amb wàter,
con water,

with a shower,
amb dutxa,
con ducha,

for one night,
per a una nit,
para una noche,

for two days,
per a dos dies,
para dos días,

for one week,
per a una setmana,
para una semana,

for two weeks.
per a dues setmanes.
para dos semanas.

I'd like a view of the sea / the mountains.
Voldria vista al mar / a les muntanyes.
Quisiera vista al mar / a las montañas.

I'd like full board.
Voldria pensió completa.
Quisiera pensión completa.

I'd like half board.
Voldria mitja pensió.
Quisiera media pensión.

I want only the room.
Desitjo l'habitació sola.
Deseo solo la habitación.

What's the price of a room for one night?
Quin és el preu de l'habitació per a una nit?
¿Cuál es el precio de la habitación para una noche?

Per person?
Per persona?
¿Por persona?

Is breakfast included?
Inclòs l'esmorzar? Inclòs el desdejuni?
¿Incluido el desayuno?

How much must I pay on account?
Quant cal pagar a compte?
¿Cuánto hay que pagar a cuenta?

May I see the room?
Podria veure l'habitació?
¿Podría ver la habitación?

I don't like it.
No m'agrada.
No me gusta.

I like it.
M'agrada.
Me gusta.

All right. It's fine.
Em convé.
Vale. Está bien.

Have my luggage sent up.
Faci pujar el meu equipatje.
Mande subir mi equipaje.

7.3 **After occupying the room**
Després d'ocupar l'habitació
Después de ocupar la habitación

In my room
A la meva habitació
En mi habitación

I need a chair,
falta una cadira,
falta una silla,

the telephone doesn't work,
no funciona el telèfon,
no funciona el teléfono,

there is no toilet paper,
no hi ha paper higiènic,
no hay papel higiénico,

there is no electricity.
no hi ha corrent (elèctric).
no hay corriente (eléctrica).

My room number is: ...
El número de la meva habitació és: ...
El número de mi habitación es: ...

Could you show me how the air conditioning works?
Podria ensenyar-me com funciona l'aire condicionat?
¿Podría enseñarme cómo funciona el aire acondicionado?

Could you please bring me
Faci el favor de portar
Haga el favor de traer

soap,
sabó,
jabón,

a glass?
un got.
un vaso.

In my room
A la meva habitació
En mi habitación

the lightbulb is burnt out,
la bombeta està fosa,
la bombilla está fundida,

the faucet / tap drips,
l'aixeta degota,
el grifo gotea,

the window doesn't open,
no es pot obrir la finestra,
no se puede abrir la ventana,

the closet / cupboard doesn't close.
no es pot tancar l'armari.
no se puede cerrar el armario.

My room hasn't been made up.
La meva habitació no està arreglada.
Mi habitación no está arreglada.

What's the current here?
Quin és el voltatge aquí?
¿Qué voltaje hay aquí?

I need a multiple socket / an adaptor.
Em fa falta un lladre / adaptador.
Necesito un ladrón / adaptador.

Where is
On és
¿Dónde está

the dining room,
el menjador,
el comedor,

the lounge,
el saló,
el salón,

the bar?
el bar?
el bar?

Would it be possible to have
Hi ha la possibilitat que em
Es posible que me

my clothes washed,
rentin la roba,
laven la ropa,

my shoes cleaned,
netegin les sabates,
limpien los zapatos,

my trousers pressed,
planxin els pantalons,
planchen los pantalones,

a button sewed?
cusin un botó?
cosan un botón?

Where can I
On es pot
¿Dónde se puede

buy stamps,
comprar segells,
comprar sellos,

sign up for trips / activities,
apuntar-se a excursions / activitats,
apuntarse a excursiones / programas,

exchange money?
canviar diners?
cambiar dinero?

Call me at seven tomorrow.
Demà cridi'm a les set.
Mañana llámeme a las siete.

I've lost my room key.
He perdut la clau de la meva habitació.
He perdido la llave de mi habitación.

I've left the key in my room.
He deixat la clau dintre de la meva habitació.
He dejado la llave en mi habitación.

If anyone asks for me, I'll be back around five.
Si em busquessin, torno cap a les cinc.
Si me buscaran, vuelvo a eso de las cinco.

7.4 The **departure**. La sortida. *La partida*

I'm leaving tomorrow
Marxo demà
Me voy mañana

morning,
al matí,
por la mañana,

at noon.
al migdia.
al mediodía.

What time must I check out?
A quina hora he de deixar lliure l'habitació?
¿A qué hora tengo que dejar libre la habitación?

Have my bill prepared.
Tingui el compte preparat.
Tenga mi cuenta preparada.

The bill, please.
El compte, sisplau.
La cuenta, por favor.

Aren't you mistaken? I've only been here for two nights.
No s'equivoca? Només hi he estat dues nits.
¿No se equivoca? Sólo he estado dos noches.

Call me a taxi.
Cridi'm un taxi.
Llámeme un taxi.

Send for my luggage to be brought down.
Mani baixar el meu equipatje.
Mande bajar mi equipaje.

7.5 **Camping**. Càmping. *Cámping*

Is there a camping site near here?
Hi ha per aquí un càmping?
¿Hay por aquí un cámping?

Is it permitted to camp here?
És permès acampar aquí?
¿Se permite acampar aquí?

Is there room
Hi ha lloc
¿Hay sitio

for a tent?
per a una tenda?
para una tienda?

for a trailer / caravan?
per a una caravana?
para una caravana?

for a trailer-home?
per a una autocaravana?
para una autocaravana?

How much does one night cost?
Quant cal pagar per una nit?
¿Cuánto hay que pagar por una noche?

Do you rent tents?
Lloguen tendes?
¿Alquilan tiendas?

Where can I change (fill) the gas cylinder / tank?
On puc canviar (fer omplir) la bombona de gas?
¿Dónde puedo cambiar (hacer llenar) la bombona de gas?

Where can one **cook?**
On es pot cuinar?
¿Dónde se puede cocinar?

wash the dishes?
rentar els plats?
fregar los platos?

wash clothes?
rentar roba?
lavar ropa?

Can we make a fire?
Podem encendre una foguera?
¿Podemos encender una hoguera?

How far away is the nearest grocery?
A quina distància es troba la botiga de queviures més propera?
¿A qué distancia está la tienda de comestibles más cercana?

8. **THE CITY**. LA CIUTAT. *LA CIUDAD*

8.1 **Visiting the city**
Visita de la ciutat
Visita de la ciudad

Can you provide me with a map of the city?
Pot facilitar-me un plànol de la ciutat?
¿Puede facilitarme un plano de la ciudad?

What are the city's most important monuments?
Quins són els monuments més importants de la ciutat?
¿Cuáles son los monumentos más importantes de la ciudad?

Can you recommend me an itinerary for visiting the city in
Pot recomenar-me un itinerari per a una visita de la ciutat en
¿Puede recomendarme un itinerario para una visita de la ciudad en

a day, **two days?**
un dia, dos dies?
un día, dos días?

Do you organize guided tours of the city?
Organitzen visites comentades de la ciutat?
¿Organizan visitas comentadas de la ciudad?

What language does the guide speak (in)?
En quina llengua parla el guia?
¿En que lengua habla el guía?

How much does it cost?
Quant costa la participació?
¿Cuánto cuesta la participación?

Where does the bus / coach leave from?
D'on surt l'autocar?
¿De dónde sale el autocar?

8.2 Asking for information in the city
Demanant informació a ciutat
Pidiendo información en la ciudad

How far (away) is it?
A quina distància es troba?
¿A qué distancia está?

Is the city center far from here?
És lluny el centre de la ciutat?
¿Está lejos el centro de la ciudad?

How can I get to the city center?
Com puc arribar al centre de la ciutat?
¿Cómo puedo llegar al centro de la ciudad?

Where is the city hall?
On és l'ajuntament?
¿Dónde se encuentra el ayuntamiento?

Is there a mailbox / letter box near here?
Hi ha una bústia aquí a prop?
¿Hay aquí cerca un buzón?

Is it worth going by car?
Val la pena d'anar-hi amb cotxe?
¿Vale la pena ir en coche?

It's very close / nearby.
És molt a prop.
Está muy cerca.

You can walk there.
Pot anar-hi a peu.
Puede ir a pie.

Turn right at the third corner.
A la tercera cantonada tombi a la dreta.
En la tercera esquina doble a la derecha.

It's a bit far.
És una mica lluny.
Está un poco lejos.

Which bus / coach, subway / underground should I take?
Quin autobús, metro he d'agafar?
¿Qué autobús, metro tengo que tomar?

Where is the bus / coach stop? the subway / tube station?
On és la parada de l'autobús? / l'estació de metro?
¿Dónde está la parada de autobuses? / la estación de metro?

One hundred and fifty meters from here.
A cent cinquanta metres d'aquí.
A ciento cincuenta metros de aquí.

On the corner.
A la cantonada.
En la esquina.

The second street on the left, on the right.
Al segon carrer a l'esquerra, a la dreta.
En la segunda calle a la izquierda, a la derecha.

Where do I get off?
On he de baixar?
¿Dónde tengo que bajar?

How many stops away is it?
Quantes parades he de fer?
¿Cuántas paradas tengo que seguir?

Do I have to transfer / change over?
He de fer transbord?
¿Tengo que transbordar?

How much is the ticket?
Quant val el bitllet?
¿Cuánto vale el billete?

Here.
Aquí.
Aquí.

Straight ahead / on.
Tot recte.
Todo derecho.

On / To the right.
A la dreta.
A la derecha.

On / To the left.
A l'esquerra.
A la izquierda.

8.3 Urban transport. Signs. Information over the loudspeaker
Transport urbà. Rètols. Informacions per altaveu
Transporte urbano. Rótulos. Informaciones por el altavoz

Line 5 (five).
Línia 5 (cinc).
Línea 5 (cinco).

Direction Horta.
Direcció Horta.
Dirección Horta.

Exit to Bailen.
Sortida Bailèn.
Salida Bailén.

Next station: Diagonal.
Pròxima estació: Diagonal.
Próxima estación: Diagonal.

Connection with line three.
Correspondència amb línia tres.
Correspondencia con línea tres.

Attention! To open, push handle up (on metro).
Atenció. Per obrir, accioneu la palanca.
Atención. Para abrir, accionar la palanca.

Request your stop.
Demaneu / sol.liciteu parada.
Solicite parada.

8.4 The taxi. El taxi. *El taxi*

Please call me a taxi.
Cridi'm un taxi, sisplau.
Por favor, llámeme un taxi.

Where can I find a taxi?
On puc trobar un taxi?
¿Dónde puedo encontrar un taxi?

Is there a taxi rank near here?
Hi ha prop d'aquí una parada de taxis?
¿Hay por aquí una parada de taxis?

Send me a taxi tomorrow morning at seven.
Enviï'm un taxi demà a les set del matí.
Mándeme un taxi mañana a las siete de la mañana.

My address is number twelve, Main Street.
La meva adreça és Carrer Major, número dotze.
Mi dirección es Calle Mayor, número doce.

Take me to Lesseps Square.
Porti'm a la Plaça Lesseps.
Lléveme a la Plaza Lesseps.

How much would it cost me to go to the airport?
Quant em costaria anar a l'aeroport?
¿Cuánto me costaría ir al aeropuerto?

How long does it take to get to the station?
Quant triga a arribar a l'estació?
¿Cuánto tarda en llegar a la estación?

I'm in a hurry.
Tinc pressa.
Tengo prisa.

Wait for me here a moment.
Esperi'm aquí un moment.
Espéreme aquí un momento.

We have arrived.
Hem arribat.
Hemos llegado.

Stop here.
Pari aquí.
Pare aquí.

How much do I owe you?
Què li dec?
¿Qué le debo?

How much does the taximeter mark?
Quant marca el taxímetre?
¿Cuánto marca el taxímetro?

Here. Keep the change.
Tingui. Quedi's el canvi.
Tenga. Quédese con la vuelta.

8.5 **Parking**. Pàrking. *Aparcamiento*

May I leave my car here?
Puc deixar aquí el meu cotxe?
¿Puedo dejar aquí mi coche?

You'll find an underground parking lot / car park two hundred meters from here.
A dos-cents metres trobarà un pàrking subterrani.
A doscientos metros encontrará un aparcamiento subterráneo.

Take a ticket upon entering.
En entrar, prengui el tiquet.
Al entrar, recoja el ticket.

It is forbidden to park here.
És prohibit estacionar aquí.
Está prohibido estacionar aquí.

Do not park here because the police
No aparqui aquí, perquè la policia
No aparque aquí, porque la policía

will fine you,
el multarà,
le va a multar,

will tow away your car.
s'emportarà el seu cotxe.
se llevarà su coche.

You can only park here if you put coins in the parking meter.
Només pot aparcar aquí si tira monedes al parkímetre.
Sólo puede aparcar aquí si echa monedas en el parquímetro.

You can park for an hour and a half at the most.
Pot aparcar una hora i mitja com a màxim.
Puede aparcar una hora y media como máximo.

8.6 **Police**. Policia. *Policía*

Police!
Policia!
¡Policía!

Thief! Stop thief!
Lladres! Al lladre!
¡Ladrón! ¡Al ladrón!

Please call the police.
Cridi la policia, sisplau.
Llame a la policía, por favor.

Where is the police station?
On és la comissaria de policia?
¿Dónde encuentro la comisaría de policía?

I've lost my papers.
He perdut els meus documents.
He perdido mis documentos.

I'm lost.
M'he perdut.
Me he perdido.

I've been robbed.
M'han robat.
Me han robado.

It was this man.
Ha estat aquest home.
Ha sido este hombre.

It was this woman.
Ha estat aquesta dona.
Ha sido esta mujer.

It was them.
Han estat aquests.
Han sido éstos.

I have witnesses.
Tinc testimonis.
Tengo testigos.

Are you willing to serve as a witness?
Està vostè disposat / disposada a fer de testimoni?
¿Está usted dispuesto / dispuesta a servir de testigo?

They've stolen
M'han robat
Me han robado

my camera,
la cambra fotogràfica,
la cámara fotográfica,

my car,
el cotxe,
el coche,

my money,
els diners,
el dinero,

my wallet,
la cartera,
la cartera,

my handbag / purse.
la bossa de mà.
el bolso.

I've been held up and they've stolen
M'han atracat i m'han pres
Me han atracado y me han quitado

my ring,
l'anell,
el anillo,

my bracelet,
la polsera,
la pulsera,

my necklace,
el collaret,
el collar,

my watch.
el rellotge.
el reloj.

I want to report
Voldria denunciar
Quisiera denunciar

an accident,
un accident,
un accidente,

a rape,
una violació,
una violación,

a holdup,
un atracament,
un atraco,

a robbery.
un robatori.
un robo.

Please take note.
Tinguin la bondat de prendre acta.
Tengan la bondad de levantar acta.

Can you give a description of the robber?
Pot fer una descripció de l'atracador?
Puede dar una descripción del atracador?

Would you recognize the thief?
Podria reconèixer el lladre?
¿Podría reconocer al ladrón?

I'm an American / British citizen.
Sóc ciutadà americà / anglès. Sóc ciutadana americana / anglesa.
Soy ciudadano americano / inglés. Soy ciudadana americana / inglesa.

I would like an interpreter / a lawyer.
Voldria un intèrpret / advocat.
Quisiera un intérprete / abogado.

I haven't done anything.
No he fet res.
No he hecho nada.

I want to speak with the American / British consul.
Vull parlar amb el cònsol d'Amèrica / d'Anglaterra.
Quiero hablar con el cónsul de America / Inglaterra.

You have commited an infraction.
Vostè ha comès una infracció.
Usted ha cometido una infracción.

You are parked in a no-parking area.
Vostè ha aparcat en zona prohibida.
Usted ha aparcado en zona prohibida.

I have to fine you.
He de multar-lo / multar-la.
Tengo que multarle.

9. **FREE TIME**
TEMPS LLIURE
TIEMPO LIBRE

9.1 **Pastimes.** Lleure. *Ocio*

What's your favorite pastime?
Quina és la seva diversió favorita?
¿Cuál es su entretenimiento favorito?

I like / I would like
M'agrada / m'agradaria
Me gusta / gustaría

to play pool/billiards,
jugar al billar,
jugar al billar,

to play cards,
jugar a cartes,
jugar a las cartas,

to go on trips,
fer excursions,
hacer excursiones,

to read,
llegir,
leer,

to go horseback riding,
muntar a cavall,
montar a caballo,

to visit museums and exhibitions,
visitar museus i exposicions,
visitar museos y exposiciones,

to listen to the radio,
escoltar la ràdio,
escuchar la radio,

to play chess,
jugar als escacs,
jugar al ajedrez,

to surf,
practicar surfing,
practicar el surfing,

to dance,
ballar,
bailar,

to play tennis,
jugar al tennis,
jugar al tenis,

to watch television,
veure la tele(visió),
ver la tele(visión),

to swim.
nedar.
nadar

My wife is a cinema / theater lover.
La meva dona és aficionada al cine / teatre.
Mi mujer es aficionada al cine / teatro.

Do you collect anything?
Vostè és col.leccionista d'alguna cosa?
¿Usted es coleccionista de algo?

I collect stamps.
Col·lecciono segells
Colecciono sellos

I devote all of my free time to
Dedico tot el meu temps lliure a
Dedico todo mi tiempo libre a

angle fishing,
la pesca amb canya,
la pesca con caña,

beekeeping,
l'apicultura,
la apicultura,

hunting.
la caça.
la caza.

I'm extremely fond of gathering mushrooms.
Sóc un boletaire apassionat.
Soy un buscador apasionado de setas.

Do you feel like playing
Té ganes de jugar
¿Tiene ganas de jugar

dominoes,
al dòmino,
al dominó,

cards,
a cartes,
a las cartas,

darts?
als daus?
a los dados?

Can you show me what the Spanish deck of cards looks like?
Pot ensenyar-me com és la baralla espanyola?
¿Puede enseñarme cómo es la baraja española?

We could go dancing tonight.
Aquesta nit podríem sortir a ballar.
Esta noche podríamos salir a bailar.

Do you know of a good dance hall near here?
Coneix aquí prop una bona sala de festes?
¿Conoce aquí cerca una buena sala de fiestas?

May I turn on the T.V.?
Puc encendre / engegar la tele?
¿Puedo encender la tele?

Turn down the radio, please.
Baixi el volum de la ràdio, sisplau.
Baje el volumen de la radio, por favor.

Could you tell me the opening hours of the Museum of Art of Catalonia?
Pot dir-me l'horari del Museu d'Art de Catalunya?
¿Puede decirme el horario del Museo de Arte de Cataluña?

What are the Picasso Museum's opening hours?
Quan es pot visitar el Museu Picasso?
¿Cuándo se puede visitar el Museo Picasso?

Where is Picasso's "Guernica" exhibited?
On és exposat el «Guernica» de Picasso?
¿Dónde está expuesto el «Guernica» de Picasso?

Are there bullfights at this time of year?
Se celebren «*corridas*» en aquesta temporada?
¿Se celebran corridas en esta temporada?

9.2 **At the theater**. Al teatre. *En el teatro*

I would like to go to the theater tonight. Could you recommend me an entertaining play?
Aquesta nit voldria anar al teatre. Podria recomanar-me una peça entretinguda?
Esta noche quisiera ir al teatro. ¿Podría recomendarme una obra entretenida?

If you don't speak / understand the language, I would recommend a musical show.
Si no saben bé la llengua, els recomanaria un espectacle musical.
Si no hablan / entienden la lengua, les recomendaría un espectáculo musical.

What show is playing tomorrow?
Quina obra fan demà?
¿Qué obra darán mañana?

Could you please reserve me two seats for tomorrow's performance?
Seria tan amable de reservar-me dues localitats per a la funció de demà?
¿Haría el favor de reservarme dos localidades para la función de mañana?

Two seats in the second row on the first floor, please.
Sisplau, dues entrades de la segona fila del primer pis.
Por favor, dos entradas de la segunda fila del primer piso.

What time does the show start?
A quina hora comença la funció?
¿A qué hora comienza la función?

Once the show has begun, you will not be allowed to enter the theater.
Un cop començada la representació, no podran entrar a la sala.
Una vez iniciada la representación, no podrán entrar en la sala.

9.3 **At the cinema**. Al cine. *En el cine*

Do you have a theater and cinema guide?
Té una cartellera de teatres i cines?
¿Tiene usted una cartelera de espectáculos?

I would like to go see a / an
M'agradaria anar a veure una pel.lícula
Me gustaría ir a ver una película

detective film,
policíaca; de lladres i serenos,
policíaca,

comedy,
còmica,
cómica; de risa,

adventure film,
d'aventures,
de aventuras,

love film,	**sex film,**
d'amor,	de sexe,
de amor,	*de sexo,*
science fiction film,	**western.**
de ciència-ficció,	de l'oest.
de ciencia-ficción,	*del oeste.*

Could you tell me where they're showing an / a
Podria dir-me en quin cine fan aquest vespre una pel.lícula
¿Podría decirme dónde ponen esta noche una película

English,	**French,**
anglesa,	francesa,
inglesa,	*francesa,*
Italian,	
italiana,	
italiana,	

original version film tonight?
en versió original?
en versión original?

What time are the showings?
A quina hora comencen les sessions?
¿A qué hora comienzan las sesiones?

Two tickets for the afternoon showing, please. If it's possible, in the center of row eight in the orchestra / stalls.
Sisplau, dues entrades per a la sessió de la tarda. Si pot ser centrals, en la fila vuit de la platea.
Por favor, dos entradas para la sesión de la tarde. Si puede ser, centrales, en la fila ocho de la platea.

I'm sorry, but it's a continuous showing and the tickets aren't numbered.
Ho sento, però la sessió és contínua i les entrades no són numerades.
Lo siento, pero la sesión es continua y las entradas no son numeradas.

9.4 Signs, anouncements in the theater and cinema.
Rètols, avisos al teatre i al cine
Rótulos, avisos en el teatro y en el cine

Monday, day off.
Dilluns, descans semanal.
Lunes, descanso semanal.

Not recommended for persons under 18 (eighteen).
No recomenada a més joves de 18 (divuit) anys.
No recomendada para menores de 18 (dieciocho) años.

Tickets on sale fifteen days in advance.
Venda anticipada de localitats amb quinze dies d'antelació.
Venta anticipada de localidades con quince días de antelación.

Reservations by telephone.
Reserves per telèfon.
Reservas por teléfono.

Special group rates.
Preus especials per a grups.
Precios especiales para grupos.

Original version, subtitles in Spanish.
VOSE; Versió original subtitulada en espanyol.
V.O.S.E.; Versión original subtitulada en español.

Original version in French.
Versió original en francès: VOFr.
Versión original en francés: V.O.Fr.

All tickets are sold out.
Totes les localitats estan exhaurides. Exhaurides les localitats.
Todas las localidades están agotadas. Agotadas las localidades.

9.5 At the beach
A la platja
En la playa

What beach would you recommend us?
Quina platja podria recomanar-nos?
¿Qué playa podría recomendarnos?

What's the temperature of the water today?
Quants graus té avui l'aigua?
¿A cuántos grados está hoy el agua?

Where can we get undressed?
On podem despullar-nos?
¿Dónde podemos desvestirnos?

Is it dangerous for children?
No hi ha perill per als nens?
¿No hay peligro para los niños?

How much does it cost per hour (for two hours) to rent
Quant costa el lloguer per una hora (per dues hores)
¿Cuánto cuesta el alquiler por un hora (por dos horas)

a deck / lawn chair,
d'una gandula,
de una hamaca,

an air bed,
d'un matalàs inflable,
de un colchón neumático,

a paddle boat,
d'un patí,
de un patín,

a boat?
d'un bot?
de un bote?

Be careful not to step on sea urchins!
Compte a no trepitjar eriçons de mar!
¡Cuidado de no pisar erizos de mar!

Can one swim / fish here?
Es pot banyar / pescar aquí?
¿Se puede bañar / pescar aquí?

10. **MEALS. RESTAURANT**
ÀPATS. RESTAURANT
COMIDAS. RESTAURANTE

10.1 **Meals. Generalities**
Àpats. Generalitats
Comidas. Generalidades

We would like to have lunch / supper.
Voldríem dinar / sopar.
Quisiéramos comer (almorzar) / cenar.

Could you recommend us a typical Catalan / Spanish restaurant?
Pot recomanar-nos un restaurant típic català / espanyol?
¿Puede recomendarnos un restaurante típico catalán / español?

Is there a beer house / wine cellar near here?
Hi ha aquí a la vora una cerveseria / un celler?
¿Hay aquí cerca una cervecería / bodega?

Please reserve a table for four at eight thirty tonight.
Reservi'ns sisplau una taula per a quatre persones, per a dos quarts de nou d'aquesta nit.
Resérvenos, por favor, una mesa para cuatro personas para las ocho y media de esta noche.

Aren't you hungry / thirsty?
No tens gana / set?
¿No tienes hambre / sed?

I'm very hungry.
Tinc molta gana.
Tengo mucha hambre.

I'm thirsty.
Tinc set.
Tengo sed.

Let's go eat / drink something!
Anem a menjar / prendre alguna cosa!
¡Vamos a comer / tomar algo!

Let's have breakfast.
Anem a esmorzar.
Vamos a desayunar.

I'll invite you to
L'invito a
Le / La invito a

lunch
dinar
comer (almorzar)

a snack
berenar
merendar

dinner / supper.
sopar.
cenar.

I'll invite you to a drink.
L'invito a prendre una copa.
Le / La invito a tomar una copa.

Let's have dinner / supper together!
Sopem plegats!
¡Cenemos juntos!

You must try the Catalan / Spanish specialties.
Ha de tastar les especialitats catalanes / espanyoles.
Tiene que probar las especialidades catalanas / españolas.

Let's go into this restaurant!
Entrem en aquest restaurant!
¡Vamos a entrar en este restaurante!

10.2 **Breakfast - at the hotel**
Esmorzar - a l'hotel
Desayuno - en el hotel

Is breakfast included in the room price?
L'esmorzar està inclòs en el preu de l'habitació?
¿El desayuno está incluido en el precio de la habitación?

We would like to have breakfast.
Voldríem esmorzar.
Quisiéramos desayunar.

Could you please tell me what time they serve breakfast?
Digui'm, sisplau, a quines hores serveixen l'esmorzar?
Dígame, por favor, ¿entre qué horas sirven el desayuno?

Have my breakfast sent up to my room.
Faci'm pujar l'esmorzar a la habitació.
Hágame subir el desyuno a la habitación.

Where is the dining room?
On és el menjador?
¿Dónde esté el comedor?

Where can we sit?
On podem seure?
¿Dónde podemos sentarnos?

What would you like,
Què desitgen prendre,
¿Qué desean tomar,

white coffee,	**tea,**	**cocoa?**
cafè amb llet,	te,	cacau?
café con leche,	*té,*	*cacao?*

Bring me a fruit juice.
Porti'm un suc de fruita.
Tráigame un zumo de fruta.

With or without sugar?
Amb sucre o sense?
¿Con o sin azúcar?

Waiter, bring me another coffee.
Cambrer, porti'm un altre cafè.
Camarero, tráigame otro café.

Bring us a few / some
Porti'ns una mica / unes
Tráiganos un poco / unas

slices of bread,
llesques de pa,
rebanadas de pan,

(bread) rolls.
uns panets.
unos panecillos

10.3 **Drinks; beverages**
Begudes
Bebidas

Can I invite you to a drink?
Puc invitar-lo / invitar-la a prendre una copa?
¿Puedo invitarle / invitarla a tomar una copa?

Thank you. I accept your invitation.
Gràcies. Accepto la seva invitació.
Gracias. Acepto su invitación.

What shall we have?
Què prendrem?
¿Qué vamos a tomar?

What would you gentlemen like to drink?
Què volen prendre els senyors?
¿Qué desean tomar, los señores?

Bring a bottle of ice cold beer / ale.
Porti una ampolla de cervesa gelada.
Traiga una botella de cerveza helada.

A bottle / A liter of wine.
Una ampolla / Un litre de vi.
Una botella / Un litro de vino.

Which wine do you recommend?
Quin vi recomana?
¿Qué vino recomienda?

Bring some more ice (cubes), please.
Porti més glaçons, sisplau.
Traiga más (cubitos de) hielo, por favor.

Cheers! To your health! (polite)
Salut! A la seva salut!
¡Salud! ¡A su salud!

Cheers! To your health!
Salut! A la teva salut!
¡Salud! ¡A tu salud!

10.4 Lunch and dinner - at a restaurant
Dinar i sopar - en un restaurant
Almuerzo y cena - en un restaurante

Where shall we sit, here or in the corner?
On seiem, aquí o al racó?
¿Dónde vamos a sentarnos, aquí o en el rincón?

The waiter will be with you in a moment.
El cambrer vindrà de seguida.
El camarero viene en seguida.

Is this table free?
És lliure aquesta taula?
¿Está libre esta mesa?

We'll sit here.
Seguem aquí.
Vamos a sentarnos aquí.

Waiter, bring us another chair, please.
Cambrer, porti'ns una cadira més, sisplau.
Camarero, tráiganos otra silla más, por favor.

Excuse me, is this chair free?
Perdoni, és lliure aquesta cadira?
Perdone, ¿está libre esta silla?

We would like to eat / drink something.
Voldríem menjar / beure alguna cosa.
Quisiéramos comer / beber algo.

Waiter, the menu, please.
Cambrer, la carta, sisplau.
Camarero, la carta, por favor.

Bring another knife / fork.
Porti un altre ganivet / una altra forquilla.
Traiga otro cuchillo / tenedor.

I / We need a spoon
Falta una cullera
Falta una cuchara

a place setting
un cobert
un cubierto

the salt (shaker).
un saler.
el salero.

What's on the menu?
Què és el menú?
¿Qué es el menú?

I'll have today's set menu
Serveixi'm el menú (del dia).
Sírvame el menú (del día)

10.5 **Ordering**. Comanda. *Pedido*

What apéritif shall we order?
Quin aperitiu demanem?
¿Qué aperitivo vamos a pedir?

What shall we have for starters?
Què mengem per començar?
¿Qué comeremos para empezar?

Salad?
Amanida?
¿Ensalada?

Do you like olives?
Lo agraden les olives?
¿Le gustan las aceitunas?

What would you like for your first course, soup or something else?
Què desitja com a primer plat, sopa o alguna altra cosa?
¿Qué desea como primer plato, sopa o alguna otra cosa?

Pasta or rice?
Pasta o arròs?
¿Pasta o arroz?

What would you prefer: meat, fish or a vegetable dish?
Què puc recomanar-li: carn, peix o algun plat de verdura?
¿Qué le puedo recomendar: carne, pescado o algún plato de verdura?

Do you prefer fowl?
Prefereix aviram?
¿Prefiere aves?

Do you like game (meat)?
Li agrada la (carn d'animals de) caça?
Le gusta la (carne de animales de) caza?

They cook it very well here.
Aquí la preparen molt bé.
Aquí la preparan muy bien.

How do you like your meat, well-done, medium or rare?
Com li agrada la carn, molt feta, al punt o poc feta?
¿Cómo le gusta la carne, bien hecha, al punto o poco hecha?

You must try one of the specialties from here.
Ha de tastar alguna especialitat d'aquí.
Tiene que probar alguna especialidad de aquí.

Waiter!
Cambrer!
¡Camarero!

What shall I bring you?
Què els porto?
¿Qué les traigo?

For starters, bring us prawn cocktail.
Per començar portin'ns còctel de gambes.
Para comenzar tráiganos cóctel de gambas.

Which soup do you recommend?
Quina sopa recomana?
¿Qué sopa recomienda?

Which is the "vichissoise" soup?
Quina sopa és la vichissoise?
¿Qué sopa es la vichissoise?

As our main course, we would like to have fish or game.
Com a plat principal, voldríem menjar peix o caça.
Como plato principal, quisiéramos comer pescado o caza.

What would you recommend?
Què pot recomanar-nos?
¿Qué nos puede recomendar?

We'll order dessert later on.
Demanarem les postres més tard.
Pediremos los postres más tarde.

Enjoy your meal!
Bon profit!
¡Buen provecho! ¡Que aproveche!

You too.
Igualment.
Igualmente.

Do you like it?
Li agrada?
¿Le gusta?

This dish is excellent / delicious.
Aquest plat és excel·lent / deliciós.
Este plato es excelente / delicioso.

Wouldn't you like to dress the salad?
No vol amanir l'amanida?
¿No quiere aliñar / aderezar la ensalada?

What would you like to go with it?
Quin acompanyament desitja?
¿Qué guarnición desea?

What sauce would you like with your meat?
Quina salsa vol amb la carn?
Qué salsa quiere con la carne?

Would you like bread?
Vol pa?
¿Quiere pan?

What shall we drink?
Què prendrem?
¿Qué vamos a tomar?

Waiter, which wine do you recommend with this meat?
Cambrer, quin vi recomana amb aquesta carn?
Camarero, ¿qué vino recomienda con esta carne?

Do you want red or white wine?
Vol vi negre o blanc?
¿Quiere vino tinto o blanco?

Waiter, do you have a house wine?
Cambrer, tenen vi de la casa?
Camarero, ¿tienen vino de la casa?

Bring a bottle of "cava" (sparkling wine).
Porti una ampolla de cava.
Traiga una botella de cava.

To your health.
A la seva salut.
A su salud.

What shall we have for dessert?
Què menjarem de postres?
¿Qué vamos a comer de postre?

Would you like fruit, cheese or sweets?
Vol fruita, formatge o dolços?
¿Quiere fruta, queso o dulces?

Would you like coffee?
Prendrà cafè?
¿Tomará café?

Would you like a brandy? It aids digestion.
Vol un conyac? Ajuda a fer la digestió.
¿Quiere un coñac? Ayuda la digestión.

A toast to our friends.
Brindem pels nostres amics.
Brindemos por nuestros amigos.

10.6 **The bill.** El compte. *La cuenta*

Let's pay.
Paguem.
Vamos a pagar.

Waiter, the bill, please.
Cambrer, el compte, sisplau.
Camarero, la cuenta, por favor.

Please don't. I'll pay.
Deixi-ho, l'invito jo.
Déjelo, le invito yo.

I'm paying this time.
Aquesta vegada pago jo.
Esta vez pago yo.

Let's split the bill.
Compartim el compte.
Vamos a compartir la cuenta.

How large a tip does one leave?
Quanta propina es deixa?
¿Cuánta propina se deja?

Excuse me, but this bill is wrong.
Perdoni, però aquest compte és errat / equivocat.
Perdone, pero esta cuenta está equivocada.

Waiter, it's / that's for you.
Cambrer, és per a vostè.
Camarero, es para usted.

I appreciate your invitation.
Li agraeixo molt la invitació.
Le agradezco mucho la invitación.

10.7 Restaurant signs
Rètols al restaurant
Letreros en el restaurante

parking (lot)
aparcament; pàrking
aparcamiento; parking

typical Catalan / Spanish cuisine
cuina típica catalana / espanyola
cocina típica catalana / española

pavement; tables / terrace
terrassa
terraza

dining room
menjador
comedor

kitchen
cuina
cocina

checkroom; cloakroom
guarda-roba m
guardarropa

washroom(s)
lavabo(s)
lavabo(s)

toilet(s); restroom(s)
lavabo(s)
aseo(s); servicio(s)

men
homes
caballeros

women
dones
señoras

public telephone
telèfon públic
teléfono público

menu; list of dishes
carta (de plats)
carta (de platos)

price list
llista de preus
lista de precios

menu; bill of fare
menú
menú

the chef suggests / recommends
el xef us suggereix / recomana
El chef le sugiere / recomienda

service charge included
servei inclòs
servicio incluido

V.A.T. included
IVA inclòs
I.V.A. incluido

checks and credit cards are not accepted
no s'admeten talons i targetes de crèdit
no se admiten cheques / talones y tarjetas de crédito

10.8-10.22 **The menu**. La carta. *La carta*

10.8 **Hors d'oeuvres**
Entremesos
Entremeses

assorted cold cuts / meats
assortiment de carn freda
surtido de fiambres

caviar
caviar
caviar

(green, black) olives
olives (verdes, negres)
aceitunas (verdes, negras)

patés
patés
patés

prawn cocktail
còctel de gambes
cóctel de gambas

foie gras
foie gras
foie gras

ham (cured)
pernil
jamón

potato / Russian salad
ensalada russa
ensalada rusa

seafood salad / cocktail
amanida / còctel de marisc
ensalada / cóctel de mariscos

10.9 **Salads**. Amanides. *Ensaladas*

asparagus with mayonnaise
espàrrecs amb maionesa
espárragos con mayonesa

lettuce
enciam
lechuga

cucumbers
cogombres
pepinos

mixed salad
amanida mixta
ensalada mixta

raw vegetable salad
crudités
crudités

tomato salad
amanida de tomàquet
ensalada de tomate

10.10 **Pastas and rices.** Pastes i arrossos. *Pastas y arroces*

canneloni
canelons
canelones

macaroni
macarrons
macarrones

noodles
tallarines f pl
tallarines m pl

"paella" (rice dish)
paella; arròs a la cassola
paella

pilaf rice
pilaf; arròs pilaf
pilaf; arroz pilaf

pizza
pizza
pizza

ravioli
raviolis
raviolis

spaghetti
espaguetis
espaguetis

10.11 **Accompaniments and sauces**
Acompanyaments i salses
Guarniciones y salsas

croquettes
croquetes
croquetas

garlic mayonnaise
allioli
alioli

ketchup
catsup
catsup

mashed potatoes
puré de patates
puré de patatas

mayonnaise
maionesa; salsa maionesa
mayonesa; salsa mayonesa

potatoes
patates
patatas

potato chips / crisps
patates fregides
patatas fritas

rice
arròs
arroz

tomato sauce
salsa de tomàquet
salsa de tomate

10.12 **Soups**. Sopes. *Sopas*

broth; stock
brou
caldo

consommé
consomé
consomé

cream of vegetable soup
crema de llegums / verdures
crema de legumbres / verduras

"escudella" stew
escudella
«escudella»

"gazpacho" (cold tomato and garlic soup)
gaspatxo
gazpacho

fish soup
sopa de peix
sopa de pescado

meatball soup
sopa de mandonguilles
sopa de albóndigas

seafood soup
sopa de marisc
sopa de marisco

tomato soup
sopa de tomàquet
sopa de tomate

vegetable soup
sopa de verdures
sopa de verduras

10.13 **Vegetable dishes**
Plats de verdura
Platos de verdura

"fabada" (Asturian dish made of beans, sausage and bacon).
mongetes estofades; cassola de faves
fabada; cazuela de habas

lentil stew
cassola de llenties
cazuela de lentejas

mixed vegetables
minestra de verdures
menestra de verduras

pea soup
puré de pèsols
puré de guisantes

10.14 Methods of preparation
Maneres de preparació
Maneras de preparación

(a)live
viu, viva
vivo, -a

baked
al forn
al horno

barbecued
a la graella
a la parrilla

boiled
bullit, -ida
hervido, -ida

braised
a la brasa
a la brasa; braseado, -a

browned
ofegat, -ada
rehogado, -ada

candied
confitat, -ada
confitado, -ada

cooked; boiled
cuit, -a
cocido, -a

covered / fried in batter
arrebossat, -ada
rebozado, -ada

dry
sec, -a
seco, -a

flambé
flamejat, -ada
flameado, -ada

fried
fregit, -ida
frito, -a

gratin
gratinat, -ada
gratinado, -ada

grilled
a la planxa
a la plancha

ground; minced
picat, -ada
picado, -ada

natural
al natural
al natural

pickled
en escabetx
en escabeche

roasted
rostit, -da
asado, -a

salted
salat, -ada
salado, -a

sautéed
saltat, -ada
salteado, -a

smoked
fumat, -ada
ahumado, -a

stuffed
farcit, -ida
relleno, -a

with cream
amb crema
a la crema

with vinaigrette
a la vinagreta
a la vinagreta

10.15 **Meats**. Carns. *Carnes*

assorted barbecued meats
graellada de carn
parrillada de carne

fillet; sirloin
filet
filete

Hungarian goulash
goulash a l'hongaresa
goulash a la húngara

meat fried in breadcrumbs
carn arrebossada
carne rebozada

meatballs
mandonguilles
albóndigas

meat rolls
rotllos de carn
rollos de carne

pork loin
llom de porc
lomo de cerdo

pork rib / chop
costella de porc
chuleta de cerdo

ragout
ragout
ragout

roastbeef
rosbif
rosbif

roasted / barbecued meat
rostit
asado

steak
bistec
bistec; bisté

steak tartare
bistec tàrtar
bistec tártar

stuffed pepper
pebrot farcit
pimiento relleno

veal cutlet; escalope
escalopa
escalope

veal rolls
rotllos de vedella
revueltos de ternera

stew
estofat
estofado

tripe
tripes
tripas; callos

veal pats
medallons de vedella
medallones de ternera

Viennese-style escalope
escalopa a la vienesa
escalope a la vienesa

10.16 Domestic animals and their meats
Animals domèstics i la seva carn
Animales domésticos y su carne

beef
carn de bou
carne de res

kid
cabrit
cabrito

mutton
moltó; xai
carnero

rabbit
conill
conejo

suckling pig
porcell; garrí
lechón; cochinillo

calf; veal
vedella; carn de vedella
ternera; carne de ternera

lamb
anyell; bé
cordero

ox
bou
buey

sheep
ovella; xai
oveja

10.17 **Game and fowl**
Caça i aviram
Caza y aves

chicken
pollastre
pollo

deer; venison
cérvol
ciervo; venado

duck
ànec
pato

goose
oca
ganso; oca

hare
llebre; conill de bosc
liebre

hen
gallina
gallina

quail
guatlla
codorniz

turkey
gall dindi
pavo

wild boar
senglar; porc senglar
jabalí

wild goose
oca salvatge
ganso salvaje

10.18 **Fish. Seafood**
Peix. Marisc
Pescado. Mariscos

assorted grilled fish
graellada de peix
parrillada de pescado

fish and seafood stew.
sarsuela de peix i marisc
zarzuela de pescado y marisco

(live) oysters
ostres (vives)
ostras (vivas)

octopus in its own ink
pops amb la tinta
pulpos en su tinta

10.19 Fresh and salt water fish
Peixos d'aigua dolça i de mar
Peces de agua dulce y de mar

anchovy
anxova
anchoa

carp
carpa
carpa

cod(fish)
bacallà
bacalao

eel
anguila
anguil(l)a

hake
lluç
merluza

herring
areng
arenque

salmon
salmó
salmón

sardine
sardina
sardina

sole
llenguado
lenguado

tuna(fish)
tonyina
atún

trout
truita
trucha

10.20 Seafood. Snails
Marisc. Cargols
Mariscos. Caracoles

clam; mussel
musclo; cloïssa; copinya
almeja; mejillón

crab
cranc
cangrejo

cuttlefish
sípia; sèpia
sepia; jibia

lobster
llagosta
langosta

oyster
ostra
ostra

octopus
pop
pulpo

prawn
gamba
gamba

seafood
marisc
marisco

shrimp
gambeta
camarón

snail
cargol; bover
caracol; caracol comestible

squid
calamar(s)
calamar

10.21 Desserts and sweets. Pastries and cakes
Postres i plats dolços. Pastes i pastissos
Postres y platos dulces. Pastas y pasteles

assorted cheeses
safata de formatges
surtido de quesos

assorted pastries
rebosteria
repostería

a piece of cake
un tall de pastís
un corte de pastel

chocolate cake
pastís de xocolata
pastel de chocolate

chocolate mousse
mousse de xocolata
mousse de chocolate

cream caramel; flam
flam
flan

crêpes
creps
creps

crullers
xurros
churros

custard
crema
crema

doughnuts
bunyols
buñuelos

fresh fruit
fruita del temps
fruta del tiempo

fruit cocktail
macedònia de fruites
macedonia de frutas

marmalade; preserves
melmelada
mermelada

Pastries and cakes
Pastes i pastissos
Pastas y pasteles

pudding
púding
puding / pudín / budín

rice pudding
arròs amb llet
arroz con leche

tea pastries
pastes seques
pastes de té; pastas secas

yogurt with fruits
iogurt de fruites
yogur de frutas

10.22 **Ice cream and sweets**
Gelats i dolços
Helados y dulces

a bar of chocolate
una rajola de xocolata
una tableta de chocolate

candies; toffees; sweets
caramels; confits
caramelos; confites

chewing-gum
xiclet
chicle; goma de mascar

chocolate ice cream
gelat de xocolata
helado de chocolate

chocolates
bombons
bombones

cup of ice cream
copa de gelat
copa de helado

chocolate with almonds / hazel nuts
xocolata amb ametlles / avellanes
chocolate con almendras / avellanas

marzipan
massapà
mazapán

nougat
torró
turrón

sweets
dolços
dulces

three-scoop cup
copa de tres boles
copa de tres bolas

vanilla ice cream
gelat de vainilla
helado de vainilla

11. **PURCHASES. SERVICES**
COMPRES. SERVEIS
COMPRAS. SERVICIOS

11.1 **Portions; units**
Porcions; unitats
Porciones; unidades

Please give me
Doni'm, sisplau
Déme, por favor

two hundred grams of ham,
dos-cents grams de pernil,
doscientos gramos de jamón,

two hundred and fifty grams of cheese,
dos-cents cinquanta grams de formatge,
doscientos cincuenta gramos de queso,

half a kilo of grapes,
mig quilo de raïm,
medio kilo de uvas,

a kilo of bread,
un quilo de pa,
un kilo de pan,

a liter of milk,
un litre de llet,
un litro de leche,

forty centimeters,
quaranta centímetres,
cuarenta centímetros,

one meter.
un metro.
un metre.

Give me all of it.
Doni'm / Posi'm tot / sencer.
Déme / Póngame todo / entero.

Give me half (of it).
Doni-me'n la meitat.
Déme la mitad.

Slice it for me.
Doni-me'l a talls / a llesques.
Démelo en lonchas / en tajadas.

Give me
Doni-me'n
Déme

a few,
uns quants,
unos cuantos,

more,
més,
más,

less.
menys.
menos.

Give me
Doni'm
Déme

a (whole) chicken,
un pollastre (sencer),
un pollo (entero),

half a chicken,
mig pollastre,
medio pollo,

a quarter of a chicken.
un quart de pollastre.
un cuarto de pollo.

Give me
Doni'm
Déme

a packet of bread crumbs,
un paquet de pa ratllat,
un paquete de pan rallado,

a packet of cigarettes,
un paquet de cigarretes,
un paquete de cigarrillos,

a piece of cheese,
un tros de formatge,
un pedazo / trozo de queso,

a packet of butter,
un tros de mantega; una pastilla / un paquet de mantega,
un pedazo de mantequilla; una pastilla / un paquete de mantequilla.

a bar of soap,
una pastilla de sabó,
una pastilla de jabón,

a box of matches,
una capsa de mistos / llumins,
una caja de cerillas,

a box of cigars,
una capsa de cigars,
una caja de puros,

a packet / a box of chicken / beef cubes,
un paquet / una capsa de pastilles maggi,
un paquete / una caja de pastillas maggi,

a can of beer,
una llauna de cervesa,
una lata de cerveza,

a can,
una llauna,
una lata,

a can of tomato sauce,
una llauna de tomàquet,
una lata de tomate,

a pair of socks,
un parell de mitjons,
un par de calcetines,

a yogurt,
un iogurt,
un yogur,

a glass of wine,
un got / vas de vi,
un vaso de vino,

a loaf of bread,
una barra de pa,
una barra de pan,

a slice of melon
una tallada de meló,
una tajada de melón,

a slice of ham,
un tall de pernil,
una loncha / tajada de jamón,

a slice of hake,
una rodanxa de lluç,
una rodaja de merluza,

a slice of bread,
una llesca de pa,
una rebanada de pan,

a bar of chocolate
una rajola de xocolata,
una tableta de chocolate,

a roll of toilet paper,
un rotlle / rotllo de paper higiènic,
un rollo de papel higiénico,

a dozen eggs,
una dotzena d'ous,
una docena de huevos,

a bottle of wine / beer,
una ampolla de vi / cervesa,
una botella de vino / cerveza,

a jar of honey,
un pot de mel,
un tarro de miel,

a packet of instant soup,
un sobre de sopa maggi,
un sobre de sopa maggi,

a bag of chick-peas
una bossa de cigrons,
una bolsa de garbanzos,

11.2 **Measures**. Mesures. *Medidas*

Weights. Weight measures
Pesos. Mesures de pesos
Pesos. Medidas de pesos

gram
gram
gramo

decagram (10 grams)
decagram (10 grams)
decagramo (10 gramos)

kilogram; kilo
quilogram; quilo
kilogramo; kilo

quintal
quintar
quintal (métrico)

ton
tonelada
tonelada

Capacity and volume measures
Mesures de capacitat i de volum
Medidas de capacidad y de volumen

deciliter
decilitre
decilitro

liter
litre
litro

hectoliter
hectolitre
hectolitro

cubic centimeter
centímetre cúbic
centímetro cúbico

cubic meter
metre cúbic
metro cúbico

Lineal measures
Mesures de longitud
Medidas de longitud

milimeter
milímetre
milímetro

centimeter
centímetre
centímetre

decimeter
decímetre
decímetro

kilometer
quilòmetre
kilómetro

square meter
metre quadrat
metro cuadrado

Other measures
Altres mesures
Otra medidas

mile
milla
milla

pound
lliura
libra

meter
metre
metro

Surface measures
Mesures de superfície
Medidas de superficie

square kilometer
quilòmetre quadrat
kilómetro cuadrado

league
llegua
legua

hectare
hectàrea
hectárea

11.3 **Purchases. Generalities**
Compres. Generalitats
Compras. Generalidades

What stores / shops are there around here?
Quines botiques hi ha per aquí?
¿Qué tiendas hay por aquí?

Where can I buy envelopes?
On puc comprar sobres?
¿Dónde puedo conseguir sobres?

Where is the nearest tobacconist's / cigar shop / stationer's?
On es troba l'estanc més proper / la papereria més propera?
¿Dónde queda el estanco más próximo / la papelería más próxima?

What time do they open / close the stores?
A quina hora obren / tanquen les botigues?
¿A qué hora abren / cierran las tiendas?

Is it open / closed?
Està obert / tancat?
¿Está abierto / cerrado?

What would you like?
Què desitja / desitjen?
¿Qué desea / desean?

What can I do for you?
En què puc servir-li?
¿En qué puedo servirle?

Are you being served?
Ja l'atenen? Ja el / la serveixen?
¿Le / La atienden ya?

Who's next?
Qui toca?
¿Quién es el / la siguiente?

There is a little bit more, do you mind?
És una mica més, no li fa res?
Es un poco más, ¿no le importa?

Here you go.
Aquí ho té.
Aquí lo tiene.

Anything else?
Una altra cosa?
¿Algo más?

Is that all?
Això és tot?
¿Eso es todo?

That comes to two hundred pesetas all together.
Són dues-centes pessetes en total.
Son doscientas pesetas en total.

I also need some envelopes.
Necessito també uns sobres.
Necesito también unos sobres.

Do you also have stamps?
Té segells també?
¿Tiene sellos también?

Show me some postcards.
Ensenyi'm unes postals.
Enséñeme unas postales.

How much is this (one)?
Aquest / Aquesta quin preu té?
¿Este / Esta qué precio tiene?

How much is it?
Quant és?
¿Cuánto cuesta / vale?

How much do I owe you?
Què li dec?
¿Cuánto le debo?

It costs one hundred pesetas.
Val cent pessetes.
Vale cien pesetas.

Don't you have anything cheaper?
No en té de més barats?
¿No tiene nada más barato?

It's too expensive.
És massa car.
Es demasiado caro.

You only have this one?
Només té aquest / aquesta?
Solo tiene este / esta?

Don't you have another one?
No en té un altre / una altra?
¿No tiene otro / otra?

There aren't / isn't any?
No n'hi ha?
¿No hay?

Do you usually have it?
Acostumen tenir-ho?
¿Suelen tenerlo / tenerla?

When will you have more?
Quan en tindrà?
¿Cuándo tendrá?

Give me another (one).
Doni-me'n un altre.
Déme otro.

Could you exchange it for me?
Pot canviar-me'l?
¿Puede cambiármelo?

Who should I pay?
A qui he de pagar?
¿A quién tengo que pagar?

You can pay me.
Ja li cobro jo.
Ya le cobro yo.

Here's the bill.
Aquí té la factura.
Aquí tiene la factura.

Go ahead to the cashier's desk.
Passi per la caixa.
Pase por la caja.

Shall I wrap it?
S'ho embolico?
¿Se lo envuelvo?

Wrap it for me.
Emboliqui-me'l.
Envuélvamelo.

11.4 **At the marke**t. Al mercat. *En el mercado*

Buying vegetables and fruits
Comprant verdures i fruites
Comprando verduras y frutas

Give me a kilo of oranges.
Doni'm un quilo de taronges.
Déme un kilo de naranjas.

Give me half a kilo of ripe tomatoes.
Doni'm mig quilo de tomàquets madurs.
Déme medio kilo de tomates maduros.

They're not ripe enough.
No són prou madurs.
No están bastante maduros.

Riper, please.
Més madurs, sisplau.
Más maduros, por favor.

Greener; less ripe.
Més durs / verds.
Más duros.

Larger / smaller.
Més grans / petits.
Más grandes / pequeños.

Weigh this melon (for me).
Pesi ('m) aquest meló.
Pése (me) este melón.

How much does it weigh?
Quant pesa?
¿Cuánto pesa?

Are the vegetables fresh?
És fresca la verdura?
¿Es fresca la verdura?

Could you give me a bag?
Pot donar-me una bossa?
¿Puede darme una bolsa?

What's this fruit called in Catalan / Spanish?
Com es diu en català / castellà aquesta fruita?
¿Cómo se llama en catalán / español esta fruta?

11.5 **Butcher's shop**. Carnisseria. *Carnicería*

Give me
Doni'm
Déme

half a kilo of veal,
mig quilo de carn de vedella,
medio kilo de carne de ternera,

three hundred grams of pig's liver,
tres-cents grams de fetge de porc,
trescientos gramos de hígado de cerdo,

half a kilo of lard.
mig quilo de llard.
medio kilo de manteca.

Give me
Doni'm també
Déme también

two hundred and fifty grams of ham also.
dos-cents cinquanta grams de pernil.
doscientos cincuenta gramos de jamón.

Thinly sliced, please.
En talls fins, sisplau.
En lonchas / tajadas finas, por favor.

Thicker.
Més gruixudes.
Más gruesas.

This is too fatty.
Aquest és massa gras.
Este es demasiado graso.

Leaner, please.
Més magre, sisplau.
Más magro, por favor.

11.6 **Poultry shop.** Polleria. *Pollería*

Give me
Doni'm
Déme

a chicken,
un pollastre,
un pollo,

a turkey.
un gall dindi.
un pavo.

a duck, but not too large,
una oca no gaire grossa,
un pato no muy grande,

Give me half a kilo of chicken breasts.
Doni'm mig quilo de pit de pollastre.
Déme medio kilo de pechuga de pollo.

Do you have foie gras?
Té foie gras?
¿Tiene foie gras?

Do you have roasted chicken?
Té pollastre rostit?
¿Tiene pollo asado?

Give me a whole chicken,
Doni'm un pollastre sencer
Déme un pollo entero

half a chicken,
mig pollastre
medio pollo

a quarter of a chicken.
un quart de pollastre.
un cuarto de pollo.

Give me a dozen eggs.
Doni'm una dotzena d'ous.
Déme una docena de huevos.

Half a dozen.
Mitja dotzena.
Media docena.

11.7 **Fish shop**. Peixateria. *Pescadería*

Do you have fresh fish?
Tenen peix fresc?
¿Tienen pescado fresco?

What kind of fish do you have?
Quina mena de peixos tenen?
¿Qué tipo de pescado tienen?

Do you have fresh water fish or only salt water fish?
Tenen peix d'aigua o només peixos de mar?
¿Tienen pescado de agua dulce o solo pescado de mar?

I would like to buy kippered herring.
Voldria comprar arengs fumats.
Quisiera comprar arenques ahumados.

Do you have frozen tunafish?
Hi ha tonyina congelada?
¿Hay atún congelado?

Does this fish have many bones?
Té moltes espines aquest peix?
¿Tiene muchas espinas este pescado?

Give me four slices of this.
Doni'm quatre rodanxes d'aquest.
Déme cuatro rodajas de este.

I don't want the head / tail.
No vull el cap / la cua.
No quiero la cabeza / cola.

Could you scale it?
Pot treure les escates?
¿Puede quitar las escamas?

11.8 **Department store**. Magatzem. *Almacén*

Where is the entrance,
On és l'entrada?
¿Dónde está la entrada?

the information desk,
la informació?
la información?

the checkroom?
la consigna?
la consigna?

Where are
On són
¿Dónde están

the elevators; the lifts
els ascensors,
los ascensores,

the fitting rooms?
els emprovadors?
los probadores?

the escalators,
les escales mecàniques,
las escaleras mecánicas,

What floor is the shoe section on?
En quina planta és la sabateria?
¿En qué planta está la zapatería?

Where can I find
On és / són
¿Dónde puedo encontrar

sporting goods,
els articles d'esport,
los artículos de deporte,

dog food?
el menjar per a gossos?
la comida para perros?

It is / They are
És / Són
Está / Están

in the basement,
al soterrani,
en el sótano,

on the ground floor,
a la planta baixa,
en la planta baja,

on the first floor.
a la primera planta.
en la primera planta.

11.9 Articles of clothing; fashion
Peces de vestir; articles de moda
Prendas de vestir; artículos de moda

What size would you like it in?
De quina talla la desitja?
¿De qué talla la desea?

In thirty-eight.
De la trenta-vuit.
De la treinta y ocho.

What color?
De quin color?
¿De qué color?

A light / dark color.
D'un color clar / fosc.
De un color claro / oscuro.

Show me a long-sleeved striped / checked shirt.
Mostri'm una camisa de màniga llarga amb ratlles / quadres.
Muéstreme una camisa de manga larga a rayas / de cuadros.

It's in fashion. This is the latest fashion.
Està de moda. Això es la darrera moda.
Está de moda. Esto es la última moda.

May I try it on?
Puc emprovar-me-la?
¿Puedo probármela?

Try it on.
Emprovi-se-la.
Pruébesela.

The fitting rooms are at the back of the room.
Els emprovadors són al fons de la sala.
Los probadores están al fondo de la sala.

What do you think? Do you like how it fits?
Com és? Li queda bé?
¿Qué tal es? ¿Le queda bien?

No, the sleeves are too short / long.
No, les mànigues són massa curtes / llargues.
No, las mangas son demasiado cortas / largas.

This one is too wide / tight.
Aquesta és massa ampla / estreta.
Esta es demasiado ancha / estrecha.

It's too small / large.
És massa petita / gran.
Es demasiado pequeña / grande.

Give me a smaller / larger size.
Doni'm un número més petit / gran.
Déme un número menor / mayor.

Show me a smaller / larger size.
Ensenyi'm una talla més petita / gran.
Enséñeme una talla menor / mayor.

I don't like the color / the material / the sample.
No m'agrada el color / la tela / la mostra.
No me gusta el color / la tela / la muestra.

What material is it made of?
De quina tela està feta?
¿De qué tela está hecha?

Does it shrink when washed?
No s'encongeix en rentar?
¿No se encoge al lavar?

Can it be machine-washed?
Es pot rentar amb màquina?
¿Se puede lavar en máquina?

Will the colors fade?
No perd color?
¿No pierde color?

Does it wrinkle?
No s'arruga?
¿No se arruga?

It can only be dry-cleaned.
Només es pot rentar en sec.
Solo se puede lavar en seco.

It's a wrinkle-resistant cloth, it doesn't need ironing.
És una tela que no s'arruga, no cal planxar-la.
Es una tela inarrugable, no hay que plancharla.

11.10 **Shoe store; shoes. Footwear**
Sabateria; sabates. Calçat
Zapatería; zapatos. Calzado

I'd like to buy a pair of leather shoes.
Voldria comprar un parell de sabates de cuiro.
Quisiera comprar un par de zapatos de cuero.

What size do you take?
Quin número calça?
¿Qué número calza?

Forty-three.
El quaranta-tres.
El cuarenta y tres.

What color would you like them in?
De quin color les desitja?
¿De qué color los desea?

Black or grey.
Negre o gris.
Negro o gris.

Try these on.
Emprovi's aquestes.
Pruébese estos.

They are very fashionable.
Estan molt de moda.
Están muy de moda.

Here is the shoehorn.
Aquí té el calçador.
Aquí tiene el calzador.

Do they fit well?
Li queden bé?
¿Le quedan bien?

They're too tight.
M'estrenyen.
Me aprietan.

They're too large / small.
Em van massa grans / petites.
Me son demasiado grandes / pequeños.

These are a size smaller / larger.
Aquestes són un número més petit / gran.
Estos son de un número menor / mayor.

These are fine.
Aquestes ja em van bé.
Estos ya me van bien

I'll take them
Me les quedo.
Me los quedo.

11.11 Services; repairs
Serveis; reparacions
Servicios; reparaciones

Where can I find someone who fixes shoes / watches / electrical appliances?
On puc trobar una persona que repari sabates / rellotges / electrodomèstics?
¿Dónde puedo encontrar una persona que arregle zapatos / relojes / electrodomésticos?

My watch
S'ha espatllat el meu rellotge
Se ha estropeado mi reloj

our coffee pot,
la nostra cafetera
nuestra cafetera

the heading is broken.
la calefacció.
la calefacción.

It doesn't work
No funciona.
No funciona.

Can you repair it?
Pot reparar-lo / reparar-la?
¿Puede arreglarlo / arreglarla?

Do you do water, gas and electrical instalations and repairs?
Fa instal.lacions i reparacions d'aigua, gas i electricitat?
¿Hace instalaciones y reparaciones de agua, gas y electricidad?

When can you come?
Quan pot venir?
¿Cuándo puede venir?

Couldn't you come sooner?
No podria venir abans?
¿No podría venir antes?

Give me your telephone number.
Doni'm el seu número de telèfon.
Déme su número de teléfono.

Here's my card.
Aquí té la meva targeta.
Aquí tiene mi tarjeta.

11.12 Florist's. Flowers
Floristeria. Flors
Floristería. Flores

What's the name of this flower?
Com es diu aquesta flor?
¿Cómo se llama esta flor?

Give me a bunch / bouquet.
Doni'm un ram / pom.
Déme un ramo / ramillete.

How much is a bunch / bouquet of carnations / roses?
Quant val un ram de clavells / roses?
¿Cuánto cuesta un ramo de claveles / rosas?

Please prepare me
Prepari, sisplau,
Prepare, por favor,

a bridal bouquet
un ram de núvia
un ramo de novia

a wreath of flowers.
una corona de flors.
una corona de flores.

Be kind enough to send the flowers to this address.
Tingui la bondat d'enviar les flors a aquesta adreça.
Tenga la bondad de enviar las flores a esta dirección.

Attach this card.
Posi-hi aquesta targeta.
Ponga esta tarjeta.

Do you have
Teniu
¿Tienen

soil for flowers
terra per a flors
tierra para flores

fertilizer
adob
abono

flower pots
testos
macetas

flower seeds?
llavors de flors?
semillas de flores?

11.13 Jewelry shop. Jewels, costume jewelry
Joieria. Joies, bijuteria
Joyería. Joyas, bisutería

I would like to buy a jewel / gem.
Voldria comprar alguna joia.
Quisiera comprar alguna joya.

Show me a gold watch
Ensenyi'm un rellotge d'or
Enséñeme un reloj de oro

a gold chain
una cadena d'or
una cadena de oro

a gold ring.
un anell d'or.
un anillo de oro.

I would like something simpler.
Voldria una cosa més senzilla.
Quisiera algo más sencillo.

This (one) is too expensive.
Aquesta és massa cara.
Ésta es demasiado cara.

It's (made of) fine gold.
És d'or de llei.
Es de oro de ley.

It's (made of) silver.
És d'argent.
Es de plata.

It's gilt / silver plated.
És daurat / argentat.
Es dorado / plateado.

How many carats is it?
De quants quirats és?
¿De cuántos quilates es?

We would like to buy wedding rings.
Voldríem comprar aliances.
Quisiéramos comprar alianzas.

I'm looking for a ring with a precious stone.
Busco un anell amb alguna pedra preciosa.
Busco un anillo con alguna piedra preciosa.

11.14 **Souvenirs.** Records. *Recuerdos*

I'm looking for souvenirs of Catalonia / Spain.
Busco records de Catalunya / d'Espanya.
Busco recuerdos de Cataluña / de España.

Show me
Ensenyi'm articles
Enséñeme artículos

ceramics,
de ceràmica,
de cerámica,

goldware,
d'orfebreria,
orfebrería,

leather goods,
de marroquineria,
marroquinería,

costume jewelry,
de bijuteria,
bisutería,

silverware.
d'argenteria.
platería.

Do you have antique coins?
Té monedes antigues?
¿Tiene monedas antiguas?

I'd like to buy some craftwork:
Voldria comprar uns objectes d'artesania popular:
Quisiera comprar unos objetos de artesanía popular:

embroidered items,
brodats,
bordados,

lace articles,
puntes al coixí,
encajes,

castanets,
castanyoles,
castañuelas,

a lace shawl,
mantellina de puntes,
mantilla de encaje,

wooden figures,
figuretes de fusta,
figuritas de madera,

statues,
estàtues,
estatuas,

a painting.
un quadre.
un cuadro.

Do you have records of popular Catalan / Spanish music?
Té discos de música popular catalana / española?
¿Tiene discos de música popular catalana / española?

Is there an antique shop around here?
Hi ha per aquí una botiga d'antiguitats?
¿Hay por aquí una tienda de antigüedades?

11.15 Gifts. Toys
Regals. Joguines
Regalos. Juguetes

I'd like to buy a gift for my wife / my husband / my children.
Voldria comprar algun regal per a la meva dona / per al meu marit / per als meus fills.
Quisiera comprar algún regalo para mi mujer / mi marido / mis hijos.

Look over the articles on the counter.
Miri els articles que hi ha sobre el taulell.
Mire los artículos que hay sobre el mostrador.

You'll surely find something you like.
Segurament trobarà alguna cosa que li agradi.
Seguramente encontrará algo que le guste.

I'd like to buy some toys for a three year old girl and a five year old boy.
Voldria comprar algunes joguines per a una nena de tres anys i per a un nen de cinc (anys).
Quisiera comprar algunos juguetes para una niña de tres años y para un niño de cinco (años).

Do you have boxed games?
Tenen jocs de societat?
¿Tienen juegos de sociedad?

Show me a doll and a carriage / toy car.
Mostri'm una nina i un cotxet.
Muéstreme una muñeca y un cochecito.

Does it run on batteries?
Funciona amb piles?
¿Funciona con pilas?

Let me have a ball and some roller skates.
Doni'm una pilota i un patí de rodes.
Déme una pelota / un balón y un patín de ruedas.

Do you sell sporting goods?
Té articles d'esport?
¿Tiene artículos de deporte?

Do you have tennis rackets?
Té raquetes de tennis?
¿Tiene raquetas de tenis?

11.16 Newsstand. Book shop
Quiosc. Llibreria
Quiosco. Librería

Have the
Han sortit ja els diaris
Han salido ya los periódicos

morning,
del matí,
de la mañana,

afternoon newspapers come out yet?
de la tarda?
de la tarde?

Please show me an English or German newspaper.
Ensenyi'm, sisplau, un diari anglès o alemany.
Enséñeme, por favor, un periódico inglés o alemán.

Give me a newspaper in Catalan.
Doni'm un diari en català.
Déme un periódico en catalán.

Are / Is there **crossword puzzles,**
Hi ha en aquest diari mots encreuats,
¿Hay en este periódico crucigramas,

a theater and film guide in this newspaper?
cartellera de teatre i de cine?
cartelera de teatro y de cine?

Where is there a book shop near here?
On hi ha per aquí una llibreria?
¿Dónde hay por aquí una librería?

I'd like to buy a book in Catalan / Spanish.
Voldria comprar un llibre en català / espanyol.
Quisiera comprar un libro en catalán / español.

Do you have Catalan novels translated into English / French?
Teniu novel.les catalanes en traducció anglesa / francesa?
¿Tienen novelas catalanas en traducción inglesa / francesa?

What subject are you interested in?
Quin tema l'interessa?
¿Qué tema le interesa?

Show me books on
Ensenyi'm llibres sobre
Enséñeme libros sobre

architecture **painting,**
arquitectura, pintura,
arquitectura, pintura,

monuments,
monuments,
monumentos,

folklore,
folklore,
folklore,

sculpture,
escultura,
escultura,

the Olympics,
l'olimpíada,
la olimpíada,

Miró and Dalí.
Miró i Dalí.
Miró y Dalí.

I want
Vull
Quiero

a history of Catalan art,
una història de l'art català,
una historia del arte catalán,

a book on the history of Catalonia,
un llibre sobre la història de Catalunya,
un libro sobre la historia de Cataluña,

an anthology of Spanish literature,
una antologia de la literatura espanyola,
una antología de la literatura española,

a Spanish - Catalan dictionary.
un diccionari castellà - català.
un diccionario español - catalán.

Where can I find
On trobo
¿Dónde encuentro

children's stories,
rondalles per a nens,
cuentos infantiles,

guide books?
guies?
guías?

Could you show me another issue,
Podria ensenyar-me un altre exemplar,
¿Podría enseñarme otro ejemplar,

a more recent edition?
una edició més recent?
una edición más reciente?

Do you sell
Veneu
¿Venden

records,
discos,
discos,

cassettes,
cassettes,
casetes,

musical scores,
partitures,
partituras,

used books,
llibres de vell,
libros usados,

text books?
llibres de text?
libros de texto?

11.17 **Cigar store; Tobacconist's**. Estanc. *Estanco*

Let me have a pack of cigarettes.
Doni'm un paquet de cigarretes.
Déme un paquete de cigarrillos.

Give me a box of matches.
Doni'm una capsa de mistos / llumins.
Déme una caja de cerillas.

Do you have lighter fluid?
Té gasolina per a l'encenedor?
¿Tiene gasolina para el encendedor / mechero?

Do you have lighter flints?
Té pedres per l'encenedor?
Tiene piedras para el mechero?

Could you fill this lighter for me?
Pot carregar-me aquest encenedor de gas?
¿Puede cargarme este mechero de gas?

Let me see some pipes.
Ensenyi'm unes pipes.
Enséñeme unas pipas.

Let me have some postcards and stamps.
Doni'm postals i segells.
Déme postales y sellos.

Let me have twenty-five envelopes.
Doni'm vint-i-cinc sobres.
Déme veinticinco sobres.

Do you smoke?
Vostè fuma?
¿Fuma usted?

I don't smoke.
No fumo.
No fumo.

I smoke a lot.
Fumo molt.
Fumo mucho.

Do you mind if I smoke?
No li molesta si fumo?
¿No le molesta si fumo?

Does the smoke bother you?
No li molesta el fum?
¿No le molesta el humo?

Do you have a light?
Té foc?
¿Tiene fuego?

Thank you (for the light).
Gràcies (pel foc).
Gracias (por el fuego).

11.18 **Watchmaker's.** Rellotgeria. *Relojería*

My watch has stopped.
El meu rellotge s'ha aturat.
Se me ha parado el reloj.

I think it's broken.
Crec que s'ha espatllat.
Creo que se ha estropeado.

My watch gains / loses three minutes per day.
El meu rellotge va avançat / endarrerit tres minuts per dia.
Mi reloj va adelantado / atrasado tres minutos por día.

Look and see what's wrong with it.
Miri'm què té.
Mírelo qué tiene.

Can you repair it?
Pot reparar-lo?
¿Puede arreglarlo?

How much will it cost to repair it?
Quant costarà la reparació?
¿Cuánto costará la reparación?

When can I come to pick it up?
Quan puc venir a recollir-lo?
¿Cuándo puedo venir a recogerlo?

It's ready.
Ja està.
Ya está.

Please set the hour.
Posi'l a l'hora, sisplau.
Ponga, por favor, la hora. Póngalo en hora.

Give me a (leather / metal) watchband.
Doni'm una corretja (de pell; de metall).
Déme una correa (de cuero; de metal).

Change the battery.
Canviï-li la pila.
Cámbiele la pila.

11.19 **Optician's. Photography. Optician's; optical**
Foto - Òptica. Òptica; òptic.
Foto - Óptica. Óptica; óptico.

I've broken my glasses.
Se m'han trencat les ulleres.
Se me han roto las gafas.

The frames are broken.
Se m'ha trencat la muntura.
Se me ha roto la montura.

Can you fix them?
Pot arreglar-les?
¿Puede arreglarlas?

Can you fix it?
Pot arreglar-la?
¿Puede arreglarla?

I need new frames.
Necessito una muntura nova.
Necesito una montura nueva.

Let me have a glasses case.
Doni'm un estoig d'ulleres.
Déme un estuche de gafas.

Do you have sunglasses?
Té ulleres de sol?
¿Tiene gafas de sol?

I need bifocal lenses.
Necessito vidres bifocals.
Necesito cristales bifocales.

Do you have soft / hard contact lenses?
Té lents toves / dures?
¿Tiene lentillas blandas / duras?

I need five diopter lenses.
Necessito vidres de cinc diòptries.
Necesito cristales de cinco dioptrias.

Show me
Ensenyi'm
Enséñeme

a barometer,
un baròmetre,
un barómetro,

a compass,
una brúixola / búixola,
una brújula,

some binoculars,
uns prismàtics / binocles,
unos prismáticos,

a microscope,
un microscopi,
un microscopio,

a magnifying glass,
unes lents d'augment,
unos lentes de aumento,

a telescope.
un telescopi.
un telescopio.

Photographer. Photo.
Fotògraf. Foto.
Fotógrafo. Foto.

Do you have a photographic laboratory?
Tenen laboratori fotògrafic?
¿Tienen laboratorio fotográfico?

Do you have a video laboratory?
Tenen laboratori de vídeo?
¿Tienen laboratorio de vídeo?

Do you make studio photographs?
Fan fotografies d'estudi?
¿Hacen fotografías de estudio?

Do you repair cameras?
Reparen màquines fotogràfiques?
¿Arreglan máquinas fotográficas?

Do you develop color photographs?
Revelen fotografies en color?
¿Revelan fotografías en color?

Do you make enlargements?
Fan ampliacions?
¿Hacen ampliaciones?

I urgently need identity card photos.
Necessito urgentment fotos de carnet.
Necesito urgentemente fotos de carnet.

Where is there an automatic photo booth near here?
On hi ha per aquí un fotomaton?
¿Dónde hay por aquí un fotomatón?

Develop this roll, please.
Reveli, sisplau, aquest rodet.
Revele, por favor, este rollo.

Make two copies of each photo / negative.
Faci dues còpies de cada foto / negatiu.
Haga dos copias de cada foto / negativo.

When will it be ready?
Quan el tindrà?
¿Para cuándo lo tendrá?

Give me three rolls of
Doni'm tres rodets de
Déme tres rollos de

color film,
pel.lícula en color,
película en color,

black and white film,
pel.lícula en blanc i negre,
película en blanco y negro,

color slide film.
pel.lícula en color per a diapositives.
película en color para diapositivas.

11.20 **Perfumery; drugstore / drysaltery**
Perfumeria; drogueria
Perfumería; droguería

Show me a good perfume.
Ensenyi'm un bon perfum.
Enséñeme, por favor, un buen perfume.

This one is too strong.
Aquest és massa fort.
Este es demasiado fuerte.

I'd like a more discreet perfume.
Volia un perfum més discret.
Quería un perfume más discreto.

It's for an older woman.
És per a una senyora gran.
Es para una señora mayor.

What colognes do you have?
Quina colònia té?
¿Qué colonia tiene?

Is this a brand from here?
Aquesta és una marca d'aquí?
¿Esta es una marca de aquí?

Give me a night cream for dry / greasy / delicate skin.
Doni'm una crema de nit per a cutis sec / gras / fi.
Déme una crema de noche para cutis seco / graso / fino.

Give me a make-up kit.
Doni'm un maquillatge compacte.
Déme un maquillaje compacto.

11.21 **Hairdresser's; Barber's. Generalities.**
Perruqueria. Generalitats.
Peluquería. Generalidades.

Where is there a good men's / women's / children's / unisex hairdresser's near here?
On hi ha aquí una bona perruqueria de senyors / senyores / nens / perruqueria unísex?
¿Dónde hay aquí una buena peluquería de señores / señoras / niños / peluquería unisex?

Can you recommend me a good barber / hairdresser?
Pots recomanar-me un bon perruquer / una bona perruquera?
¿Puedes recomendarme un buen peluquero / una buena peluquera?

There is an excellent hairdresser's near here. I usually go there also.
Prop d'aquí hi ha una perruqueria excel.lent. Jo també acostumo anar-hi.
Aquí cerca hay una peluquería excelente. Yo también suelo ir allá.

Hello. This is Mrs. Puig.
Escolti'm. Sóc la senyora Puig.
Oiga. Soy la señora Puig.

I would like to make an appointment for tomorrow.
Voldria demanar una hora per demà.
Quisiera pedir una hora para mañana.

Fine. Tomorrow morning at ten o'clock.
Està bé. Demà a les deu del matí.
Está bien. Mañana a las diez de la mañana.

Thank you. See you tomorrow.
Gràcies. Fins demà.
Gracias. Hasta mañana.

11.22 **Men's hairdresser's / barber's**
Perruqueria masculina
Peluquería masculina

What would you like, sir?
Què desitja el senyor?
¿Qué desea el señor?

A haircut and a shave.
Un tallat de cabells i afaitat.
Un corte de pelo y afeitado.

Wash my hair.
Renti'm els cabells.
Láveme el pelo.

Give me a shave, please.
Afaiti'm, sisplau.
Aféiteme, por favor.

Shall I cut your hair a bit?
Li tallo una mica els cabells?
¿Le corto un poco el pelo?

Yes please, but not too short.
Si, però no molt curts, sisplau.
Sí, por favor, pero no muy corto.

You can leave it longer up front / in the back.
Al davant / Al darrere pot quedar més llarg.
Delante / Detrás puede quedar más largo.

Leave it longer in the back.
Al darrere deixi'ls més llargs.
Detrás déjelo más largo.

Cut the sides more.
Talli més pels costats.
Corte más por los lados.

How shall I comb your hair?
Com li pentino els cabells?
¿Cómo le peino el pelo?

Towards the back or to the side?
Cap endarrere o al costat?
¿Hacia atrás o al / de lado?

Towards the back, without a part / parting.
Cap endarrere, sense ratlla.
Hacia atrás, sin raya.

Do you want hair lotion?
Li poso loció?
¿Le pongo loción?

Don't wet it.
No els mulli.
No lo moje.

Is it all right like this?
Està bé, així?
¿Está bien, así?

Perfect, thank you.
Perfecte, gràcies.
Perfecto, gracias.

How much do I owe you?
Què li dec?
¿Cuánto le debo?

11.23 **Women's hairdresser's**
Perruqueria de senyores
Peluquería de señoras

What would you like, Madam?
Quin servei desitja, senyora?
¿Qué servicio desea, señora?

A wash and setting, please.
Rentar i marcar, sisplau.
Lavar y marcar, por favor.

A haircut / a permanent / a manicure.
Un tallat de cabells / una permanent / una manicura.
Un corte de pelo / una permanente / una manicura.

I'd like a different hairstyle.
Voldria un pentinat diferent.
Quisiera un peinado diferente.

Do you want hairspray?
Li poso laca?
¿Le pongo laca?

Could you dye my hair?
Podria tenyir-me els cabells?
¿Podría teñirme em pelo?

Would you like the same color?
Desitja el mateix color?
¿Desea el mismo color?

A bit lighter / darker.
Una mica més clar / fosc.
Un poco más claro / oscuro.

Ow!, the water is very hot.
Ai, l'aigua és molt calenta.
¡Ay! El agua está muy caliente.

The water is too cold.
L'aigua és massa freda.
El agua está demasiado fría.

My eyes are stinging.
Em piquen els ulls.
Me pican los ojos.

Pluck my eyebrows.
Depili'm les celles.
Depíleme las cejas.

Do you do depilations?
Fan depilació?
¿Hacen depilación?

Would you like a manicure?
Desitja manicura?
¿Desea manicura?

Yes, and paint my nails also.
Sí, i posi esmalt també.
Sí, y ponga esmalte también.

Thank you, how much do I owe you for everything?
Gràcies, quant li dec per tot?
Gracias, ¿cuánto le debo por todo?

Could you recommend me a good chiropodist?
Pot recomanar-me un bon callista?
¿Puede recomendarme un buen callista?

11.24 **Exchanging money. Bank**
Canvi de diner. Banc
Cambio de dinero. Banco

Where can I exchange money?
On puc canviar (diner)?
¿Dónde puedo cambiar (dinero)?

Where is there a bank, a bank branch near here?
On hi ha per aquí un banc, una sucursal de banc?
¿Dónde hay por aquí un banco, una sucursal de banco?

What's the exchange rate for the U.S.A. dollar, German mark, French franc?
Com és el canvi del dòlar EUA, marc alemany, franc francès?
¿Cómo es el cambio del dólar USA, marco alemán, franco francés?

How many pesetas do I get for a pound sterling?
Quantes pessetes em donen per una lliura esterlina?
¿Cuántas pesetas me dan por una libra esterlina?

I'd like to change one hundred dollars into pesetas.
Voldria canviar cent dòlars a pessetes.
Quisiera cambiar cien dólares a pesetas.

Could you change five thousand pesetas into Swiss francs for me?
Podria canviar-me cinc mil pessetes en francs suïssos?
¿Podría cambiarme cinco mil pesetas en francos suizos?

This bill / note is false.
Aquest bitllet és fals.
Este billete es falso.

Go ahead to the cashier's window / till,
Passi a caixa,
Pase a caja,

to window number three.
a la finestreta número tres.
a la ventanilla número tres.

Could you change this ten thousand peseta bill / note?
Podria canviar-me aquest bitllet de deu mil pessetes?
¿Podría cambiarme este billete de diez mil pesetas?

Give me small notes / bills please.
Doni'm bitllets petits, sisplau.
Déme billetes pequeños, por favor.

Give me loose change.
Doni'm també canvi / moneda fraccionària.
Déme también suelto / moneda fraccionaria.

I'd like to cash this traveller's check.
Voldria cobrar / canviar aquest xec de viatge.
Quisiera cobrar / cambiar este cheque de viaje.

I'd like to cash a check to bearer.
Voldria cobrar un xec al portador.
Quisiera cobrar un cheque al portador

Has money, a bank transfer arrived for me?
Ha arribat diner, una transferència per a mi?
¿Ha llegado dinero, una transferencia para mí?

In who's name?
A nom de qui?
¿A nombre de quién?

Your passport,
El seu passaport,
Su pasaporte,

your papers **please.**
els seus documents, sisplau.
sus documentos, *por favor.*

Sign here.
Firmi / Signi aquí
Firme aquí.

11.25 **Post office. Generalities.**
Correus. Generalitats.
Correos. Generalidades.

Where is there a post office around here?
On hi ha per aquí una oficina de correus?
¿Dónde hay por aquí un oficina de correos?

How do I get to the central post office?
Com puc anar a la central de correus?
¿Cómo puedo ir a la central de correos?

Is there a mailbox / letter box near here?
Hi ha aquí a la vora una bústia?
¿Hay cerca de aquí un buzón?

Where can I buy
On puc comprar
¿Dónde puedo comprar

stamps, **envelopes,**
segells, sobres,
sellos, *sobres,*

postcards, **writing paper?**
postals, paper de cartes?
postals, *papel de cartas?*

You can also find them at the cigar store / tobacconist's.
En pot trobar també a l'estanc.
Los puede encontrar también en el estanco.

Have they picked up the letters yet?
Han recollit ja les cartes?
¿Han recogido ya las cartas?

Do I have any mail?
Tinc correspondència?
¿Tengo correspondencia?

Yes, there is a letter for you.
Sí, té una carta.
Sí, tiene una carta.

Please send my mail to this address.
Remeteu, sisplau, la meva correspondència a aquesta adreça.
Remitan, por favor, mi correspondencia a esta dirección.

At the post office.
A correus. A l'oficina de correus.
En correos. En la oficina de correos.

Excuse me, where do they sell stamps?
Perdoni, on venen segells?
Perdone, ¿dónde venden sellos?

At window number five.
A la finestreta número cinc.
En la ventanilla número cinco.

I would like to send
Voldria enviar
Quisiera enviar

a registered letter,
una carta certificada,
una carta certificada,

a parcel,
un paquet,
un paquete,

money,
diners,
dinero,

a telegram,
un telegrama,
un telegrama,

a telex,
un tèlex,
un télex,

a telefax / fax to the United States / England.
un telefax / fax als Estats Units / a Anglaterra.
un telefax / fax a los Estados Unidos / a Inglaterra.

Please give me a form for registered mail.
Doni'm, sisplau, un imprès per a correu certificat.
Déme, por favor, un impreso para correo certificado.

How much is the postage to the United States / England for these
Quant costa el franqueig als Estats Units / Anglaterra d'aquestes cartes per correu
¿Cuánto cuesta el franqueo a los Estados Unidos / Inglaterra de estas cartas por correo

airmail,
aeri,
aéreo,

registered,
certificat,
certificado,

urgent registered letters?
urgent certificat?
urgente certificado?

Please write the return address.
Posi el remitent, sisplau.
Ponga, por favor, el remitente.

The address isn't right.
L'adreça no és exacta.
La dirección no es exacta.

The zip / post code is missing.
Manca el codi postal.
Falta el código postal.

Please check and see if I have letters on the mail list.
Mireu, sisplau, si tinc cartes a la llista de correus.
Mire, por favor, si tengo cartas en la lista de correos.

I have received notice of a parcel for me.
He rebut un avís d'un paquet.
He recibido un aviso de un paquete.

What papers do I need to pick it up?
Quin document necessito per a retirar-lo / recollir-lo?
¿Qué documento necesito para retirarlo / recogerlo?

I don't have my passport with me.
No porto el meu passaport.
No llevo mi pasaporte.

I'd like to send a telegram,
Voldria enviar un telegrama
Quisiera enviar un telegrama

a telex to the United States / England.
un tèlex als Estats Units / Anglaterra.
un télex a los Estados Unidos / Inglaterra.

Which form must I fill out?
Quin imprès he d'omplir?
¿Qué impreso tengo que rellenar?

How much is it per word?
Quant costa una paraula?
¿Cuánto cuesta una palabra?

When will it reach New York?
Quan arribarà a Nova York?
¿Cuándo llegará a Nueva York?

Will they receive it today?
El rebran avui?
¿Lo recibirán hoy?

11.26 Telephone. Telephone call
Telèfon. Telefonada
Teléfono. Llamada telefónica

How do I telephone from my room?
Com puc trucar des de la meva habitació?
¿Cómo puedo llamar de mi habitación?

To call between rooms, dial the number of the desired room.
Per comunicar entre habitacions marqui el número de l'habitació que desitja.
Para comunicar entre habitaciones marque el número de la habitación deseada.

You will find the most important telephone numbers (outside / direct line; reception; the time; information) in your room.
Els més importants números de telèfon (línia exterior / directa; recepció; hora exacta; informació) els trobarà a la seva habitació.
Los más importantes números de teléfono (línea exterior / directa; recepción; hora exacta; información) los encontrará en su habitación.

Here are the telephone directories.
Aquí té les guies telefòniques.
Aquí tiene las guías telefónicas.

Where is there a public telephone / a telephone booth?
On hi ha un telèfon públic / una cabina telefònica?
¿Dónde hay un teléfono público / una cabina telefónica?

I'd like to telephone abroad / England.
Voldria fer una telefonada a l'estranger / a Anglaterra.
Quisiera hacer una llamada al extranjero / a Inglaterra.

How much does it cost per minute to the United States?
Quant val un minut als Estats Units?
¿Cuánto cuesta un minuto a los Estados Unidos?

What time do the night rates begin?
Des de quina hora hi ha tarifa nocturna?
¿A partir de qué hora hay tarifa nocturna?

A collect / reverse charge telephone call, please.
Una telefonada amb cobrament revertit, sisplau.
Por favor, una conferencia a cobro revertido.

This is the number of the person I wish to speak to.
Aquest és el número de la persona amb qui vull parlar.
Este es el número de la persona con quien quiero hablar.

There is no answer.
No contesten.
No contestan.

It's engaged.
Està comunicant.
Está comunicando.

The line is engaged.
La línia està ocupada.
La línea está ocupada.

The call has been cut off.
S'ha interromput la telefonada.
Se ha interrumpido la conferencia / llamada.

Please call back later.
Truqui-li més tard, sisplau.
Vuelva a llamarlo más tarde, por favor.

Cancel the call, please.
Anuli, sisplau, la telefonada.
Anule, por favor, la llamada / conferencia.

Hello? (when you call)
Escolti'm.
¡Oigame!

Hello? (when you answer)
Digui'm.
¡Dígame!

Is that you, Maria?
Ets tu, Maria?
¿Eres tú , María?

Yes, it's me.
Sí, sóc jo.
Sí, soy yo.

Is John there?
Hi és, en Joan?
¿Está Juan?

Excuse me, but I think you've dialed the wrong number.
Perdoni, però em sembla que s'equivoca.
Perdone, pero me parece que se equivoca.

Isn't this 234 5678?
No és el 234 56 78?
¿No es el 234 56 78?

Is this Mister Puig's house?
És la casa del senyor Puig?
¿Es la casa del señor Puig?

No. You've dialed the wrong number.
No. S'ha equivocat.
No. Se ha equivocado.

You've dialed the wrong number.
Ha marcat malament.
Ha marcado mal.

Excuse me, I've dialed the wrong number.
Perdoni, m'he equivocat.
Perdone, me he equivocado.

Dial the number 274-7326
Marqui el número 274 73 26.
Marque el número 274 73 26.

Thank you.
Gràcies.
Gracias.

Hello, is this the university?
Escolti'm, és la universitat?
Oiga, ¿es la universidad?

Extension one hundred and twenty, please.
L'extensió cent vint, sisplau.
La extensión ciento veinte, por favor.

Please wait a moment.
Esperi, sisplau.
Espere, por favor.

I would like to speak with Mister Puig.
Voldria parlar amb el senyor Puig.
Quisiera hablar con el señor Puig.

Who's calling please?
De part de qui?
¿De parte de quién?

A friend.
D'un amic.
De un amigo.

Just a moment, hold the line.
Un moment, no pengi.
Un momento, no cuelgue.

He'll be right with you. I'll put you through to him.
Ara s'hi posa. Ara li passo.
En seguida se pone. Ahora se lo paso.

He's speaking on another line.
Està parlant per un altre telèfon.
Está hablando por otro teléfono.

He has left his office.
Ha sortit del seu despatx.
Ha salido de su despacho.

Call him back in ten minutes.
Truqui-li de nou al cap de deu minuts.
Llámelo de nuevo dentro de diez minutos.

He's not in right now. Call him back later.
Ara no hi és. Truqui-li més tard.
Ahora no está. Llámele más tarde.

Excuse me, with whom am I speaking?
Perdoni, amb qui parlo?
Perdone, ¿con quién hablo?

Your name, please.
El seu nom, sisplau.
Su nombre, por favor.

Be kind enough to speak
Tingui la bondat de parlar
Tenga la bondad de hablar

louder,
més alt,
más alto,

slower.
més lentament.
más despacio.

Do you wish to leave him a message?
Vol deixar-li un encàrrec?
¿Quiere dejarle un recado?

The line is very bad.
Se sent molt malament.
Se oye (escucha) muy mal.

Tell him that an American / English friend called.
Digui-li que ha trucat un amic americà / anglès.
Dígale que ha llamado un amigo americano / inglés.

What number can he reach you at?
A quin número pot trucar-li?
¿A qué número puede llamarle?

Call me at the number 321-5476
Truqui'm al número 321 54 76
Llámeme al número 321 54 76

National trunk calls
Telefonades interurbanes nacionals
Llamadas interurbanas nacionales

If the number with which you which to speak is in the same province, you dial the number directly.
Si el telèfon amb què vol parlar és de la mateixa província, pot marcar el número directament.
Si el teléfono con el que quiere hablar es de la misma provincia, puede marcar el número directamente.

If it is in another province, dial the area code first.
Si és d'una altra província marqui primer l'indicatiu / el codi territorial.
Si es de otra provincia, marque primero el indicativo / el código territorial.

Automatic international calls
Telefonades internacionals automàtiques
Llamadas internacionales automáticas.

Example: subscriber number 123-4567 in New York
Exemple: abonat 123 45 67 de Nova York.
Ejemplo: abonado 123 45 67 de Nueva York.

07 access to the international network.
07 accés al servei internacional.
07 acceso a la red internacional.

(wait for second tone)
(esperar el segon to)
(esperar el segundo tono)

dial 1, area code for U.S.A.
1 indicatiu d'EUA
1 indicativo de U.S.A.

dial 212, area code for New York.
212 indicatiu de Nova York.
212 indicativo de Nueva York.

123-4567 subscriber number.
123 45 67 número de l'abonat.
123 45 67 número del abonado.

12 **HEALTH**. SALUT. *SALUD*

21.1 **Drug store; Chemist's.** Farmàcia. *Farmacia*

Where is there a
On hi ha aquí una
¿Dónde hay aquí una

drug store / chemist's,
farmàcia,
farmacia,

24 hour drug store / chemist's near here?
farmàcia de guàrdia?
farmacia de guardia?

Please let me have something for
Doni'm, sisplau, una cosa contra
Por favor, déme algo contra

insomnia,
l'insomni,
el insomnio,

a headache,
el mal de cap,
el dolor de cabeza,

a toothache,
el mal de queixal,
el dolor de muelas,

diarrhoea,
la diarrea,
la diarrea,

a (head) cold,
el refredat,
el resfriado,

a (nose) cold,
el constipat,
el constipado,

nausea.
el mareig.
el mareo.

Let me have a cough syrup.
Doni'm algun xarop contra la tos.
Déme algún jarabe contra la tos.

Give me
Doni'm algun
Déme algún

some sleeping pills,
somnífer,
somnífero / dormitivo,

a sedative,
calmant / antineuràlgic,
calmante / antineurálgico,

a disinfectant,
desinfectant,
desinfectante,

a laxative,
laxant,
laxante,

an antipyretic,
antipirètic,
antipirético,

a sedative.
calmant / sedant.
calmante / sedante.

Could you recommend me an ointment
Pot aconsellar-me una pomada
¿Puede aconsejarme una pomada

for burns,
per a les cremades,
para las quemaduras,

for sunburn?
per a les cremades de sol?
para las quemaduras de sol?

Do you have condoms,
Teniu preservatius,
Tienen preservativos,

tooth paste?
dentifrici?
dentífrico?

Please give me
Doni'm, si us plau,
Déme, por favor,

a box of aspirin with vitamin C,
una capsa d'aspirina amb vitamina C,
una cajita de aspirina con vitamina C,

a packet of cotton,
un paquet de cotó,
un paquete de algodón,

a roll of gauze,
un rotlle de gasa,
un rollo de gasa,

a bottle / a small bottle of distilled water,
una ampolla / ampolleta d'aigua destil·lada,
una botella / un frasco de agua destilada,

a tube of ointment,
un tub de pomada,
un tubo de pomada,

a thermometer.
un termòmetre,
un termómetro,

You need a prescription for this medicine.
Es necessita recepta per a aquest medicament.
Se necesita receta para este medicamento.

It is an antibiotic.
És un antibiòtic.
Es un antibiótico.

Could you prepare this prescription for me?
Pot preparar-me aquesta recepta?
¿Puede prepararme esta receta?

When will it be ready?
Quan estarà llesta?
¿Cuándo estará lista?

May I wait for it here?
Puc esperar-la aquí?
¿Puedo esperarla aquí?

It should be taken three times a day before / after meals.
Cal prendre-la tres vegades al dia abans / després dels àpats.
Hay que tomarla tres veces al día antes / después de las comidas.

On an empty stomach.
En dejú.
En ayunas.

Without chewing.
Sense mastegar.
Sin masticar.

Allow it to dissolve in your mouth.
Deixar dissoldre a la boca.
Dejar disolver en la boca.

For internal / external use only.
Per a ús intern / extern.
Para uso interno / externo.

Shake before using.
Agitar abans d'usar.
Agitar antes de usar.

Dissolve in water.
Dissoldre en aigua.
Disolver en agua.

Poison.
Metzina.
Veneno.

12.2 **Dentist**. Dentista. Dentista

My teeth hurt.
Em fan mal les dents.
Me duelen los dientes / las muelas.

I have a terrible toothache.
Tinc un terrible mal de queixal.
Tengo un terrible dolor de muelas.

I have to go see a dentist.
He d'anar a veure un dentista.
Tengo que ir a ver a un dentista.

Where can I find a good dentist near here?
On trobo un dentista prop d'aquí?
¿Dónde puedo encontrar un dentista en la cercanía?

Open your mouth.
Obri la boca.
Abra la boca.

Open it wide.
Obri-la bé.
Abrala bien.

Where does it hurt, below / above?
On li fa mal, a baix / a dalt?
¿Dónde le duele, abajo / arriba?

Which tooth hurts you?
Quina de les dents li fa mal?
¿Cuál de los dientes le duele?

This tooth hurts.
Em fa mal aquesta dent / aquest caixal.
Me duele este diente / esta muela.

It's very sensitive to the cold.
És molt sensible al fred.
Es muy sensible al frío.

Its filling has fallen out.
Li ha caigut l'empastament.
Se le ha caído el empaste.

A piece of it has broken off.
Se li ha trencat un tros.
Se le ha roto un trozo.

Do you have to extract / pull it?
Cal treure-la / arrencar-la / extraer-la?
¿Hay que sacarlo / arrancarlo / extraerlo?

Don't extract / pull it!
No me l'extregui!
¡No me lo extraiga!

Can you put in a temporary filling?
Pot empastar-la / obturar-la (provisionalment)?
¿Puede empastarlo (provisionalmente)?

I have to give you an X-ray.
He de fer-li una radiografia.
Tengo que hacerle una radiografía.

There's really nothing wrong with it.
No té res d'especial.
No tiene nada especial.

This isn't going to hurt.
No li farà mal.
No le va a doler.

I'm going to give you an anesthetic injection.
Li posaré una injecció anestèsica.
Voy a ponerle un inyección anestésica.

My prosthesis is broken.
S'ha trencat la meva pròtesi.
Se me ha roto la prótesis.

Where can I have it repaired?
On la repararan?
¿Dónde la arreglan / reparan?

Must I come back another day?
He de tornar un altre dia?
¿Tengo que volver otro día?

Only if your tooth begins to hurt again.
Només si li fara mal de nou la dent.
Solo si le duele de nuevo el diente.

12.3 **At the doctor's office.**
Al consultori mèdic
En el consultorio médico

I feel very bad / ill.
Em trobo molt malament.
Me siento muy mal.

He / She feels very bad /ill.
Es troba molt malament.
Se encuentra muy mal.

I'm sick / ill.
Estic malalt / malalta.
Estoy enfermo / enferma.

My daughter has a fever.
La meva filla té febre.
Mi hija tiene fiebre.

Please help me, my husband feels very ill / sick / bad.
Ajudi'm, sisplau, el meu marit es troba molt malament.
Ayúdeme, por favor, mi marido se encuentra muy mal.

I think he has something very serious.
Crec que té alguna cosa molt greu.
Creo que tiene algo muy grave.

Call a doctor, please.
Cridi un metge, sisplau.
Llame a un médico, por favor.

He / She / You should go see a doctor.
Hauria d'anar a veure un metge.
Tendría que ir a ver a un médico.

Where is there a
On hi ha per aquí
¿Dónde hay por aquí

doctor's office,
un consultori mèdic,
un consultorio médico,

hospital,
hospital,
hospital,

first aid station near here?
lloc de primers auxilis?
puesto de primeros auxilios?

Is there a doctor in the / this hotel?
Hi ha un metge a l'hotel?
¿Hay un médico en el hotel?

What are the doctor's visiting hours?
A quina hora té consulta el metge?
¿A qué hora tiene consulta el médico?

Make an appointment for me this afternoon.
Demani'm una hora per aquesta tarda.
Pídame una hora para esta tarde.

Please call an ambulance.
Avisi l'ambulància, sisplau.
Avise, por favor, a la ambulancia.

What's the problem? What's wrong?
Què té?
¿Qué tiene?

Where does it hurt?
Què li fa mal?
¿Qué le duele?

I haven't been feeling well for a few days.
Des de fa uns dies no em trobo bé.
Desde hace unos días no me encuentro bien.

It hurts here; I have a pain here.
Em fa mal aquí.
Me duele aquí.

My head
Em fa mal el cap
Me duele la cabeza

throat
la gola
la garganta

right arm hurts.
el braç dret.
el brazo derecho.

ears hurt.
les orelles.
los oídos.

It hurts here.
Em fa mal aquí.
Me duele aquí.

I have indigestion.
Tinc una indigestió.
Tengo una indigestión.

stomach
l'estómac
el estómago

left foot,
el peu esquerre
el pie izquierdo

My eyes
Em fan mal els ulls
Me duelen los ojos

I have very strong pains.
Tinc dolors forts.
Tengo dolores fuertes.

I can't sleep at night.
No puc dormir a les nits.
No puedo dormir por las noches.

I cough a lot.
Tusso molt.
Toso mucho.

I get tired easily.
Em canso fàcilment.
Me canso fácilmente.

I vomited.
He vomitat.
He vomitado.

I have a fever.
Tinc febre.
Tengo fiebre.

I sweat a lot.
Suo molt.
Sudo mucho.

I have no appetite.
No tinc gana.
No tengo apetito.

I'm dizzy.
Em marejo.
Me mareo.

I feel sick.
Tinc nàusees.
Tengo náuseas.

I have diarrhoea.
Tinc diarrea.
Tengo diarrea.

I'm very nervous.
Estic molt nerviós.
Estoy muy nervioso.

I have a cold.
Estic constipat.
Estoy constipado.

I'm shivering.
Tinc calfreds.
Tengo escalofríos.

I'm constipated.
Tinc estrenyiment.
Tengo estreñimiento.

I'm pregnant. I'm expecting a child.
Estic prenyada. Espero un nen.
Estoy embarazada. Espero un niño.

I've been out in the sun for a long time.
He estat molt de temps al sol.
He estado mucho tiempo al sol.

I'm very sunburned.
M'he cremat molt.
Me he quemado mucho.

I might have sunstroke.
És possible que tingui una insolació.
Es posible que tenga una insolación.

The food didn't agree with me.
M'ha fet mal el menjar.
Me ha hecho daño la comida.

I fell (down).
He caigut.
Me he caído.

I received a strong blow.
M'he donat un cop fort.
Me he dado un golpe fuerte.

I've dislocated my foot.
M'he torçat el peu.
Me he dislocado el pie.

I'm afraid I've broken my arm.
Tinc por que m'hagi trencat el braç.
Temo que me haya roto el brazo.

I stepped on a sea urchin.
He trepitjat un eriçó de mar.
He pisado un erizo de mar.

Do you have a fever?
Té febre?
¿Tiene fiebre?

This morning I had a temperature of thirty-eight point five C.
Al matí tenia trenta-vuit coma cinc.
Por la mañana tenía treinta y ocho coma cinco.

We're going to take your temperature again now.
Ara mateix la hi prendrem de nou.
Ahora mismo vamos a medírsela de nuevo.

Put the thermometer in place.
Posi's el termòmetre.
Póngase el termómetro.

You don't have a fever now.
Ara no té febre.
Ahora no tiene fiebre.

Your temperature is still high.
Continua tenint febre alta.
Continúa teniendo fiebre alta.

Shall I give you checkup?
Li faig una visita / un reconeixement?
¿Le hago una visita / un reconocimiento?

Where does it hurt?
On li fa mal?
¿Dónde le duele?

Remove your clothes.
Tregui's la roba.
Quítese la ropa.

Exhale deeply.
Expiri fort.
Espire fuerte.

Inhale more deeply.
Respiri més profundament.
Respire más profundamente.

Stick out your tongue.
Tregui la llengua.
Saque la lengua.

Cough.
Tussi.
Tosa.

Hold your breath.
Aguanti's la respiració.
Contenga la respiración.

That's enough.
Prou.
Basta.

Let's check your pulse.
Vejam el pols.
Veamos el pulso.

I'm going to check your pressure.
Li prendré la pressió.
Voy a tomarle la presión.

You have to have a
S'ha de fer una anàlisi
Tiene que hacer un análisis

blood,
de sang,
de sangre,

urine analysis.
d'orina.
de orina.

The laboratories are on the first floor.
Els laboratoris són al primer pis.
Los laboratorios se encuentran en el primer piso.

You have to have an X-ray taken of your arm.
Cal fer una radiografia del seu braç.
Hay que hacer una radiografía de su brazo.

How long have you been feeling ill?
Des de quan no es troba bé?
¿Desde cuándo no se encuentra bien?

What have you eaten?
Què ha menjat?
¿Qué ha comido?

Are you taking any medication?
Pren algun medicament?
¿Toma algún medicamento?

Are you alergic to penicillin?
No és al·lèrgic a la penicil·lina?
¿No es alérgico a la penicilina?

Do you have any alergies?
Té alguna al·lèrgia?
¿Tiene alguna alergia?

Have you been given a tetanus shot?
Li han posat ja l'antitetànica?
¿Le pusieron ya la antitetánica?

Were you vaccinated before coming here?
Ha estat vacunat abans de venir aquí?
¿Ha sido vacunado antes de venir aquí?

Against what?
Contra què?
¿Contra qué?

Do you smoke?
Fuma?
¿Fuma?

Do you have any chronic / serious disease?
Té alguna malaltia crònica / greu?
¿Tiene alguna enfermedad crónica / grave?

Are you diabetic?
No és diabètic?
¿No es diabético?

When were you operated on?
Quan el van operar?
¿Cuándo le operaron?

How long have you used a pacemaker?
Des de quan porta marcapassos?
¿Desde cuándo lleva marcapasos?

Don't worry. You don't have anything serious.
No es preocupi. No té res de greu.
No se preocupe. No tiene nada grave.

I'm sorry, but you have pneumonia.
Ho sento, però té una pulmonia.
Lo lamento, pero tiene una pulmonía.

You have appendicitis.
Té una apendicitis.
Tiene una apendicitis.

I must hospitalize you.
He d'hospitalitzar-lo.
Tengo que hospitalizarlo.

You must be operated on.
Cal sotmetre'l a una operació.
Hay que someterle a una operación.

I'm going to give you an injection.
Li posaré una injecció.
Voy a ponerle una inyección.

I'm going to prescribe you a very effective medicine.
Li receptaré un medicament molt eficaç.
Voy a recetarle un medicamento muy eficaz.

Here is the prescription.
Aquí té la recepta.
Aquí tiene la receta.

You need a complete rest.
Necessita repòs absolut.
Necesita reposo absoluto.

You must go on a diet.
Ha de fer dieta.
Tiene que guardar dieta.

You must stay in bed for a few days.
Ha de fer llit uns dies.
Tiene que guardar cama unos días.

You have to rest.
Ha de descansar.
Tiene que descansar.

Do not smoke.
No fumi.
No fume.

Do not consume alcoholic beverages.
No prengui begudes alcohòliques.
No tome bebidas alcohólicas.

Do not sunbathe.
No prengui el sol.
No tome el sol.

Do not bathe / swim.
No es banyi.
No se bañe.

Come back in
Torni d'aquí a
Vuelva de aquí a

	three days	**eight / fifteen days.**
	tres dies	vuit / quinze dies.
	tres días	*ocho / quince días.*

Are you insured?
Té assegurança?
¿Tiene seguro?

I'm not insured.
No estic assegurat, -ada.
No estoy asegurado, -a.

I have an American / British / international health insurance policy.
Tinc una assegurança de salut americana / anglesa internacional.
Tengo un seguro de salud americano / inglés / internacional.

I'm sorry, but I can't accept it.
Em sap greu, però no puc acceptar aquesta.
Lo lamento, pero no puedo aceptarlo.

How much do I owe you?
Quant li dec?
¿Cuánto le debo?

13. **SPORTS.** ESPORT. *DEPORTE*

13.1 **Sports. Generalities.**
Esport. Generalitats.
Deporte. Generalidades.

Are you a sportsman / sportswoman / an athlete?
Vostè és esportista?
¿Usted es deportista?

What sport does he / she play?; What sport do you play?
Quin esport practica?
¿Qué deporte practica?

What sport do you play?
Quin esport practiques?
¿Qué deporte practicas?

I'm a boxer.
Sóc boxador.
Soy boxeador.

When I was young I used to go in for athletics.
A la meva joventut practicava l'atletisme.
En mi juventud practicaba el atletismo.

What's your favorite sport?
Quin és el seu esport favorit?
¿Cuál es su deporte favorito?

Who is your favorite sportswoman / athlete?
Quina és la seva esportista favorita?
¿Cuál es su deportista favorita?

When is the television going to broadcast the swimming events?
Quan transmet la televisió les proves de natació?
¿Cuándo transmite la televisión las pruebas de natación?

Are the individual events over yet?
Han acabat ja les proves individuals?
¿Han acabado ya las pruebas individuales?

Have the team competitions begun yet?
Han començat ja les competicions per equips?
¿Han comenzado ya las competiciones por equipos?

When do the finals begin?
Quan comencen les finals?
¿Cuándo comienzan las finales?

When does the match / game end?
Quan acaba el partit?
¿Cuándo acaba el partido?

It's a very interesting match / game.
És un partit molt interessant.
Es un partido muy interesante.

What place did the American / British / Spanish team finish in?
En quin lloc ha quedat l'equip americà / anglès espanyol?
¿En qué lugar ha finalizado el equipo americano / inglés español?

Who was first / second / third?
Qui és el primer / segon / tercer?
¿Quién es el primero / segundo / tercero?

Who won the gold medal?
Qui ha guanyat la medalla d'or?
¿Quién ganó la medalla de oro?

Did we lose / win?
Hem perdut / guanyat?
¿Hemos perdido / ganado?

What's the final score?
Quin és el resultat final?
¿Cuál es el resultado final?

Who's winning?
Qui guanya?
¿Quién gana?

Who won?
Qui ha guanyat?
¿Quién ha ganado?

What was the score at half time?
Quin ha estat el resultat del primer temps?
¿Cuál ha sido el resultado del primer tiempo?

A nil-nil draw / tie.
Empat a zero.
Empate a cero.

The Spanish team won two - one.
L'equip espanyol ha guanyat per dos a u.
El equipo español ha ganado por dos a uno.

They lost two - nil.
Ha perdut per dos a zero.
Ha perdido por dos a cero.

They tied.
Han empatat.
Han empatado.

That's a new Olympic record.
Això és nou rècord olímpic.
Esto es nuevo récord olímpico.

He / She has set a new European record.
Ha establert un nou rècord d'Europa.
Ha establecido un nuevo récord de Europa.

He / She has tied / broken the world record for one thousand five hundred meters.
Ha igualat / millorat el rècord mundial dels mil cinc-cents metres.
Ha igualado / mejorado la plusmarca mundial de los mil quinientos metros.

He / She has broken the world record.
Ha batut el rècord mundial.
Ha batido el récord mundial.

13.2 **Olympics**. Olimpíada. *Olimpiada*

I'm a member of the American / British team.
Sóc membre de la delegació americana / anglesa.
Soy miembro de la delegación americana / inglesa.

I'm an American / British athlete / journalist.
Sóc esportista / periodista / americà / americana / anglès / anglesa.
Soy deportista / periodista / americano / americana / inglés / inglesa.

Excuse me, where is the press center?
Perdoni, on és el centre de premsa?
Perdone, ¿dónde está el centro de prensa?

Where is the press conference going to be held?
On tindrà lloc la conferència de premsa?
¿Dónde tendrá lugar la conferencia / rueda de prensa?

Can tickets still be obtained
Es poden aconseguir encara entrades
¿Se puede conseguir todavía entradas

for the opening
per a la inauguració
para la inauguración

for the closing cerimonies?
per a la clausura?
para la clausura?

I'm going to watch the opening ceremony on television.
Jo miraré per la televisió la cerimònia inaugural.
Yo veré / miraré la ceremonia inaugural en la televisión.

Is the Olympic Village far from here?
La vila olímpica és / queda lluny?
¿La villa olímpica está / queda lejos?

How does one get to the Olympic stadium?
Com anar a l'estadi olímpic?
¿Cómo ir al estadio olímpico?

Please point it out to me on the map.
Mostri-m'ho al mapa, sisplau.
Muéstremelo en el mapa, por favor.

Where is the firing range, the swimming pool?
On és el camp de tir, la piscina?
Donde está el campo de tiro, la piscina?

Where are the canoeing events going to be held?
On tindran lloc les proves de piragüisme?
¿Dónde tendrán lugar las pruebas de piragüismo?

Where is the Spanish team playing?
On juga l'equip espanyol?
¿Dónde juega el equipo español?

Who is playing for the Spanish team?
Qui juga a l'equip espanyol?
¿Quiénes juegan en el equipo español?

Who is the team's coach?
Qui és l'entrenador de l'equip?
¿Quién es el entrenador del equipo?

Our team
El nostre equip, la nostra selecció,
Nuestro equipo, nuestra selección,

is in first place.
ocupa el primer lloc.
ocupa el primer lugar.

Our best player, our favorite (player),
El nostre millor jugador, el nostre favorit,
Nuestro mejor jugador, nuestro favorito,

is injured.
està lesionat.
está lesionado.

He / She is in shape.
Està en forma.
Está en forma.

He / She isn't in (good) shape.
No està en (bona) forma.
No está en (buena) forma.

13.3 **Summer Olympic Games**
Esports olímpics d'Estiu
Deportes olímpicos de verano

table tennis; ping-pong
tennis de taula; ping-pong
tenis de mesa; ping-pong

athletics
atletisme
atletismo

baseball
beisbol
beisbol

wrestling
lluita
lucha

rowing
rem
remo

field hockey
hoquei sobre herba
hockey sobre hierba

archery
tir amb arc
tiro con arco

canoeing (flatwater)
Piragüisme (en aigues tranquilles)
Piragüismo (en aguas tranquilas)

cycling
ciclisme
ciclismo

handball
handbol
balonmano

basketball
basquetbol; bàsquet
baloncesto

football / soccer
futbol
fútbol; balompié

equestrian
hípica
hípica

shooting
tir (esportiu); tir olímpic
tiro (deportivo); tiro olímpico

springboard diving
salt(s) de trampolí i de palanca
salto(s) de trampolín y de palanca

tennis
tennis
tenis

synchronized swimming
natació sincronitzada
natación sincronizada

boxing
boxa; pugilisme
boxeo; pugilismo

pentathlon
pentatló modern
pentatlón moderno

volleyball
voleibol
voleibol; balonboleo

weight-lifting
halterofília
halterofilia; levantamiento de pesos

badminton
bàdminton
bádminton

gymnastics
gimnàstica
gimnasia

swimming
natació
natación

sailing
vela; esport de vela
vela; deporte de vela

fencing
esgrima
esgrima

waterpolo
waterpolo
waterpolo; polo acuático

demonstration sports
esports de demonstració
deportes de demonstración

roller hockey
hoquei sobre patins
hockey sobre patines

(Basque) pelota
pilota (basca)
pelota (vasca)

tae-kwondo
tae-kwondo
tae-kwondo

13.4 **Athletics**. Atletisme. *Atletismo*

straight race
cursa plana / llisa
carrera plana / lisa

steeple chase
cursa d'obstacles
carrera de / con obstáculos

hurdle race
cursa de tanques
carrera de vallas

relay race
cursa de relleus
carrera de relevos

marathon
marató f
maratón

walking race
marxa
marcha

high jump
salt d'alçada
salto de altura

pole vault
salt amb perxa
salto de pertiga

long jump
salt de llargada
salto de longitud

hop, step and jump
triple salt
triple salto

shot put
llançament de pes
lanzamiento de peso

discus throwing
llançament de disc
lanzamiento de disco

hammer throwing
llançament de martell
lanzamiento de martillo

javelin throwing
llançament de javelina
lanzamiento de jabalina

decathlon
decatló
decatlón

heptathlon
heptatló
heptatlón

14. VOCABULARY. VOCABULARI. *VOCABULARIO*

abdomen; womb	ventre	*vientre*
above; on	sobre	*encima de*
accelerate [v.]	accelerar	*acelerar*
accelerator	(pedal de l') accelerador	*(pedal del) acelerador*
access	accés	*acceso*
accessory, -ies	accesori(s)	*accesorio(s)*
accident	accident	*accidente*
accompaniments and sauces	acompanyaments i salses	*guarniciones y salsas*
account	compte	*cuenta*
a couple of	un parell de	*un par de*
act	acte	*acto*
actor	actor	*actor*
actress	actriu f	*actriz f*
address	adreça	*dirección f; señas*
addressee	destinatari, -ària	*destinatario, -a*
adhesive tape	esparadrap	*esparadrapo*
advance ticket sales	venda anticipada de bitllets	*venta anticipada de billetes*
adventure film	pel·lícula d'aventures	*película de aventuras*
a few	uns, -unes	*unos, -as*
after	després	*después*
afternoon	tarda	*tarde f*
afternoon, in the	a la tarda	*por la tarde*
afternoon snack	berenar	*merienda*
age	edat f	*edad f*
ahead; forward	endavant	*adelante*
AIDS	SIDA; sida	*SIDA m; sida m*
air [adj)	aeri, aèria	*aéreo, -a*
air conditioning	aire condicionat	*aire acondicionado*
air filter	filtre de l'aire	*filtro de aire*
airmail	correu aeri	*correo aéreo*
airmail, by	per correu aeri	*por correo aéreo*
airplane; plane	avió	*avión*
airplane modeling	modelisme; aeromodelisme	*modelismo; aeromodelismo*

airport	aeroport	*aeropuerto*
air shuttle	pont aeri	*puente aéreo*
alcohol	alcohol	*alcohol*
(a)live	viu, viva	*vivo, -a*
all	tot, -a	*todo, -a*
all-purpose opener	obridor universal	*abretodo*
allergic to penicillin	al·lèrgic, -a a la penicil·lina	*alérgico, -a a la penicilina*
allergic; to be allergic	al·lèrgic, -a; tenir al·lèrgia	*alérgico, -a; tener alergia*
allergy	al·lèrgia	*alergia*
almond	ametlla	*almendra*
aloud / out loud	en veu alta	*en voz alta; alto*
already	ja	*ya*
also	també	*también*
although	encara que	*aunque*
aluminium	alumini	*aluminio*
ambulance	ambulància	*ambulancia*
American football	futbol americà	*fútbol americano*
amusement park	parc d'atraccions; atraccions f pl	*parque de atracciones; atracciones f pl*
anchor, to weigh	salpar; llevar àncores	*zarpar; levar anclas*
anchovy	anxova	*anchoa*
ancient; old	antic, -iga; vell, -a	*antiguo, -a; viejo, -a*
and	i	*y*
anesthetic injection	injecció anestèsica	*inyección anestésica*
angina; inflamed throat	angina; inflamació de la gola/faringe	*angina; inflamación de la garganta/ faringe*
announcement	avís	*aviso*
announcer	anunciador, -a	*anunciador, -a*
answer	resposta	*respuesta*
answer the telephone	contestar el telèfon	*contestar el teléfono*
antibiotic	antibiòtic	*antibiótico*
antipyretic	antipirètic	*antipirético*
antiques; antique shop	antiguitats; botiga d'antiguitats	*antigüedades; tienda de antigüedades*
anus	anus	*ano*
anywhere	en qualsevol lloc	*en cualquier parte*
apartment	apartament	*apartamento*
apholsterer	tapisser, -a	*tapicero, -a*

appendicitis	apendicitis f	*apendicitis f*
appetite, to not have an	no tenir gana	*no tener apetito*
appetizer	aperitiu	*aperitivo*
apple	poma	*manzana*
apple juice	suc de poma	*zumo de manzana*
apricot	albercoc	*albaricoque*
April	abril	*abril*
archery	tir amb arc	*tiro con arco*
architect	arquitecte	*arquitecto*
arm(s)	braç(os)	*brazo(s)*
armchair	butaca	*butaca; sillón*
arrival	arribada	*llegada*
arrive; get to [v.]	arribar	*llegar*
art gallery	sala d'art; galeria	*sala de arte; galería*
artery, -ries	artèria, -ries	*arteria(s)*
artist	artista	*artista*
artistic gymnastics	gimnàstica artística	*gimnasia artística*
as much ... as	tant, -a ... quant, -a	*tanto, -a ... cuanto*
a short time ago	fa poc	*hace poco*
as soon as possible	com més aviat millor	*lo antes posible*
ashtray	cendrer	*cenicero*
asparagus	espàrrec	*espárrago*
asparagus with mayonnaise	espàrrecs amb maionesa	*espárragos con mayonesa*
aspirin	aspirina	*aspirina*
aspirin with vitamin C	aspirina amb vitamina C	*aspirina con vitamina C*
assorted cheeses	safata de formatges	*surtido de quesos*
assorted cold cuts/meats	assortiment de carn freda	*surtido de fiambres*
assorted grilled fish	graellada de peix	*parrillada de pescado*
assorted pastries	rebosteria	*repostería*
asthma	asma	*asma*
asymmetric bars	barres assimètriques	*barras asimétricas*
at	en	*en*
at an untimely moment	a deshora	*a deshora*
at dawn/daybreak	a la matinada	*en la madrugada*
at (hour)	a	*a*
at midnight	a mitjanit	*a medianoche*

at night	de nit	*de noche*
at noon	al migdia	*a(l) mediodía*
at once	de seguida; tot seguit	*enseguida*
at the same time	al mateix temps; alhora	*al mismo tiempo*
athletics	atletisme	*atletismo*
atmospheric pressure	pressió atmosfèrica	*presión atmosférica*
audience; public	públic	*público*
August	agost	*agosto*
aunt	tia	*tía*
aunt and uncle	oncles	*tíos*
authorization	autorización f; poders m pl	*autorización f; poder*
authorize [v.]	autoritzar	*autorizar*
auto repair shop	taller de reparació d'automòbil; auto-taller	*taller de reparación de automóviles*
automatic call	trucada automàtica	*llamada automática*
automobile; car	automòbil; coche	*automóvil; coche*
autumn, fall	tardor f	*otoño*
autumn, this	aquest tardor	*este otoño*
avenue	avinguda	*avenida*
avocado	alvocat	*aguacate*
axle	eix	*eje*
bachelor	solter	*soltero*
back [anat.]	esquena	*espalda*
back; backwards	endarrere; enrere	*atrás*
backstroke	esquena; estil d'esquena	*espalda; estilo de espalda*
bacon	bacó; cansalada	*bacón; tocino*
bad	dolent, -a	*malo, -a*
badly	mal; malament	*mal;*
badminton	bàdminton	*bádminton*
bag	bossa	*bolsa*
baggage claim	recollida d'equipatges	*recogida de equipajes*
baggage excess	excès d'equipatge	*exceso de equipaje*
baked	al forn	*al horno*
baker	flequer; forner	*panadero*
bakery	fleca; forn (de pa)	*panadería; horno; tahona*
balcony	balcó	*balcón*

bald	calb, -a	*calvo, -a*
ball; football	pilota	*pelota; balón*
banana	plàtan; banana	*plátano; banana*
bandage	bena	*venda*
bandaid; plaster	tireta	*tirita*
bank	banc	*banco*
bank book	llibreta d'estalvis	*libreta de ahorros*
bank statement	estat de compte	*estado de cuenta*
bar	bar; taulell/barra	*bar; barra*
bar car	vagó-bar	*coche bar*
barbecued meat	rostit	*asado*
barbecued meats	graellada de carn	*parrillada de carne*
barber; hairdresser	perruquer	*peluquero*
barber's shop	barber	*barbería*
baseball	beisbol	*beisbol*
basketball	basquetbol; bàsquet	*baloncesto*
bathing slippers	sabatilles de bany	*zapatillas de baño*
bathing suit/trunks	vestit de bany	*traje de baño; bañador*
bathing/swimming cap	gorra de bany	*gorro de baño*
bathrobe	barnús	*albornoz*
bathroom	(cambra de) bany	*(cuarto de) baño*
bathtub	banyera	*bañera*
battery	pila	*pila*
battery [auto.]	bateria	*batería*
battery-powered car	cotxe de piles	*coche de pilas*
battery recharge	recàrrega de la bateria	*recarga de la batería*
beard	barba	*barba*
bearer, to the	al portador	*al portador*
beautician	esteticista	*esteticista*
beauty parlor	saló de bellesa	*salón de belleza*
because	perquè	*porque*
bed	llit	*cama*
bed linen	roba de llit	*ropa de cama*
bedspread	cobrellit	*colcha*
beef	carn de bou	*carne de res*
beer; ale	cervesa	*cerveza*
before	abans	*antes*
behind	darrere	*detrás*
bell	timbre	*timbre*

bellboy	grum	*botones*
below	sota	*bajo; debajo*
belt	cinturó; cinyell	*cinturón*
berth	llitera	*litera*
biathlon	biatló; prova combinada	*biatlón; prueba combinada*
bicarbonate of soda	bicarbonat sòdic	*bicarbonato sódico*
bicycle	bicicleta	*bicicleta*
big; large	gran	*grande; gran*
bile; gall	bilis f; fel	*bilis f; hiel f*
bill	compte	*cuenta*
bill; note	bitllet	*billete*
bill; invoice	factura	*factura*
bill of fare	menú; carta (de plats)	*menú; carta (de platos)*
birthday	aniversari (del naixement)	*cumpleaños*
bitter	amarg, -a	*amargo, -a*
black	negre, -a	*negro, -a*
black/strong cigarettes	cigarretes negres/ fortes	*cigarrillos negros/ fuertes*
black and white film	pel·lícula en blanc i negre	*película en blanco y negro*
black coffee	cafè sol; sol	*café solo; solo*
blanket	manta; flassada	*manta*
bleach	lleixiu	*lejía*
bleed; bleeding, to be	sagnar; estar sagnant	*sangrar; estar sangrando*
blinker; indicator	indicador intermitent	*intermitente*
blond	ros, -ossa	*rubio, -a*
blood	sang	*sangre*
blood, to take/draw	prendre(-li) sang	*sacar(le) sangre*
blood analysis	anàlisi de sang	*análisis de sangre*
blood pressure	pressió arterial; tensió f	*presión arterial; tensión f*
blood transfusion; tranfusion	transfusió de sang; transfusió f	*transfusión de sangre; transfusión f*
blood type	tipus de sang	*tipo de sangre*
blouse	brusa; camisa de dona	*blusa; camisa de mujer*
blue	blau, -ava	*azul*
boarding gate	porta d'embarcament	*puerta de embarque*

boarding pass	targeta d'embarcament	*tarjeta de embarque*
boat	vaixell; bot	*barco; bote*
bobsleigh	bobsleigh; bob	*bobsleigh; bob*
body	cos	*cuerpo*
body; bodywork [auto.]	carrosseria	*carrocería*
boiled	bullit, -ida	*hervido, -a*
boiled eggs	ous passats per aigua	*huevos pasados por agua*
bone(s)	os; ossos	*hueso(s)*
bonfire	foguera	*hoguera*
book	llibre	*libro*
bookstore	llibreria	*librería*
boots	botes f pl	*botas f pl*
born, to be [v.]	néixer	*nacer*
borrow [v.]	manllevar	*pedir prestado*
bosom(s); chest	pit(s)	*pecho(s)*
bottle	ampolla	*botella*
boulevard; promenade	passeig; rambla	*paseo*
bowling	joc de bitlles	*juego de bolos*
box office	taquilla	*taquilla*
box [theat.]	llotja	*palco*
boxing	boxa; pugilisme	*boxeo; pugilismo*
boy	noi; nen	*niño; muchacho; chico*
boyfriend; fiancé	nuvi; promès	*novio*
brassière	sostenidors m pl	*sostén; sujetador*
bracelet	polsera; braçalet	*pulsera; brazalete*
brain	cervell	*seso*
braised	a la brasa	*a la brasa*
brake	fre	*freno*
brake [v.]	frenar	*frenar*
brake fluid	líquid de frens	*líquido de frenos*
braking lights	llum de fre	*luz de "pare"*
brass	llautó	*latón*
bread	pa	*pan*
bread toaster	torradora de pa	*tostador de pan*
bread with tomato	pa amb tomàquet	*pan con tomate*
breadcrumbs	pa ratllat	*pan rallado*
break [v.]	trencar	*romper*
break (a record) [v.]	batre (un rècord)	*batir (un récord)*

break down [v.]	avariar-se	*averiarse*
break one's arm/leg, to	trencar-se-li el braç/ la cama	*rompérsele el brazo pierna*
breakfast	esmorzar	*desayuno*
breakfast, to have	esmorzar	*desayunar*
breast [of fowl]	pit	*pechuga*
breast/s	tita, tites; mamella	*seno/s; teta/s*
breaststroke	braça; estil braça	*braza; estilo braza*
breeze	brisa	*brisa*
bridge [game]	bridge	*bridge*
bridge	pont	*puente*
bridge [mar.]	pont de comandament	*puente de mando*
brief; short	breu	*breve*
brilliant; diamond	brillant	*brillante*
bring alongside [v.]	atracar	*atracar*
broad bean	fava	*haba*
broken down	averiat	*averiado*
bronchitis	bronquitis f	*bronquitis f*
bronze	bronze	*bronce*
bronze medal	medalla de bronze	*medalla de bronce*
broom	escombra	*escoba*
broth; stock	brou	*caldo*
brother	germà	*hermano*
brother-in-law	cunyat	*cuñado*
brothers and sisters	germans	*hermanos*
brown	marró	*marrón*
browned	ofegat, -ada	*rehogado, -a*
brush	raspall	*cepillo*
buffet lunch	bufet	*bufet*
building	edifici	*edificio*
bulb; lamp	làmpada; llum	*lámpara*
bull	toro; brau	*toro*
bull ring	plaça de toros	*plaza de toros*
bulls; bull fight	toros m pl	*toros m pl; corrida de toros*
bungalow	bungalow	*bungalow*
bunk car	vagó-llitera	*coche litera*
bunk; berth	llitera	*litera*
burn	cremada	*quemadura*
burn [v.]	cremar-se	*quemarse*
burn oneself [v.]	cremar-se	*quemarse*

bus; coach	autobús; bus; autocar	*autobús; bus; autocar*
business class (air)	classe f preferent	*clase f preferente*
business trip	viatge de negocis	*viaje de negocios*
but	però	*pero*
but (with "not")	sinó	*sino*
butcher's	carnisseria	*carnicería*
butter	mantega	*mantequilla*
butterfly [swimming]	papallona; estil de papallona	*mariposa; estilo de mariposa*
button(s)	botó; botons	*botón; botones*
buy; purchase [v.]	comprar	*comprar*
by	por	*por*
cabbage	col f	*col f; berza; repollo*
cabin [mar.]	cabina	*camarote*
cabin; cockpit	cabina de comandament	*cabina de mando*
cable	cable	*cable*
cable car	telefèric	*teleférico*
cacao	cacau	*cacao*
cactus	cactus	*cacto*
caecum	cec; intestí cec	*ciego; intestino ciego*
cake	pastís	*pastel; tarta*
cake, a piece of	un tall de pastís	*un corte de pastel*
calculator	calculadora	*calculadora*
calendar	calendari	*calendario*
calf; veal	vedella; carn de vedella	*ternera; carne de ternera*
call; phone [v.]	trucar	*llamar*
call a doctor [v.]	cridar un metge	*llamar a un médico*
calm	tranquil, -il·la	*tranquilo, -a*
calmly	tranquil·lament	*tranquilamente*
camera	màquina/cambra fotogràfica	*máquina/cámara fotográfica*
camp (out) [v.]	acampar	*acampar*
camper	autocaravana	*autocaravana*
camping site	càmping	*cámping*
can opener	obrellaunes	*abrelatas*
cancel [v.]	anul·lar	*anular*
cancer	càncer	*cáncer*
candied	confitat, -ada	*confitado, -a*

canneloni	canelons	*canelones*
canoeing (flatwater)	piragüisme (en aigües tranquil·les)	*piragüismo (en aguas tranquilas)*
canvas shoes	sabates de tela; espardenyes	*zapatos de tela; alpargatas*
cap	gorra	*gorro; gorra*
captain	capità	*capitán*
car; auto	cotxe	*coche; auto*
car repair shop	taller de reparació d'automòbils; auto-taller	*taller de reparación de automóviles*
car [train]	vagó; cotxe	*coche; vagón*
caramel custard	crema cremada	*crema caramelo*
caravan; trailer	caravana; remolc	*caravana; remolque*
carburator	carburador	*carburador*
card	targeta	*tarjeta*
cardan joint	arbre del cardan	*árbol del cardán*
cards (game)	cartes	*cartas; naipes; barajas*
cards, to play	jugar a les cartes	*jugar a las cartas*
carnation	clavell; clavellina	*clavel*
carp	carpa	*carpa*
carpenter	fuster	*carpintero*
carrot	pastanaga	*zanahoria*
cartoon	dibuixos animats	*dibujos animados*
cash	(diner) efectiu / metàl·lic	*(dinero) efectivo / metálico*
cash, in	al comptat; en efectiu / metàl·lic	*al contado; en efectivo / metálico*
cash (a check) [v.]	cobrar (un xec)	*cobrar (un cheque)*
cash on delivery; C.O.D.	contra reemborsament	*contra reembolso*
cashier	caixer, -a	*cajero, -a*
cashier's desk	caixa	*caja*
casino	casino (de joc)	*casino (de juego)*
casserole; pan	cassola	*cazuela*
cassette	cassette f	*casete; cassette f*
castle	castell	*castillo*
Catalan sausage	botifarra	*butifarra*
cathedral	catedral f	*catedral f*
cauliflower	col-i-flor	*coliflor*

"cava" (sparkling wine)	cava m; xampany	*cava m; champaña m*
caviar	caviar	*caviar*
celery	api	*apio*
Celsius	grau Celsius	*grado Celsius*
cementery	cementiri	*cementerio*
center	centre	*centro*
center/middle, in the	al centre	*en el centro*
centigrade	grau centígrad	*grado centígrado*
central post office	central de correus	*central de correos*
century	segle	*siglo*
ceramics; porcelain	ceràmica; porcellana; cristalleria	*cerámica; porcelana; cristalería*
certificate	certificat	*certificado*
chain	cadena	*cadena*
chair	cadira	*silla*
chamber maid	cambrera	*camarera*
champion	campió, -ona	*campeón, -ona*
championship	campionat	*Campeonato*
change [money]	canvi; moneda fraccionària	*suelto; moneda fraccionaria*
change [v.]	canviar	*cambiar*
changing room(s)	vestidor(s)	*vestuario(s)*
chapel	capella	*capilla*
charter flight	vol xàrter	*vuelo chárter*
chauffeur; driver	xofer	*chófer*
cheap	barat, -a	*barato, -a*
check; cheque	xec; taló	*cheque; talón*
check; overhaul	revisió	*revisión*
check [v.] in the luggage	facturar el equipatge	*facturar el equipaje*
check-room; left luggage office	consigna	*consigna*
checkbook	talonari	*talonario*
checking/current account	compte corrent	*cuenta corriente*
checking account, to open a	obrir un compte corrent	*abrir una cuenta corriente*
checkroom; cloakroom	guarda-roba m	*guardarropa*
checks and credit cards and cheques/ are not accepted	no s'admeten talons i targetes de crèdit	*no se admiten talones y cartas de crédito*

cheek/s	galta; galtes	*mejilla/s*
cheese	formatge	*queso*
chemist; chemical engineer	químic, -a; enginyer químic	*químico, -a; ingeniero químico*
chemist's; farmacy	farmàcia	*farmacia*
cherry	cirera	*cereza*
chess [game]	escacs m pl	*ajedrez*
chess, to play [v.]	jugar als escacs	*jugar al ajedrez*
chestnut-colored	castany, -a	*castaño, -a*
chewing-gum	xiclet	*chicle; goma de mascar*
chicken	pollastre	*pollo*
chickpea	cigró	*garbanzo*
chicken pox	varicel·la	*varicela*
child	nen	*niño*
children [in general]	nens	*niños*
children [one's own]	fills	*hijos*
children's disease	malaltia infantil	*enfermedad infantil*
children's film	pel·lícula infantil	*película infantil*
children's storybook	llibre de contes infantils	*libro de cuentos infantiles*
chills	calfreds m pl	*escalofríos m pl*
Chinese restaurant	restaurant xinès	*restaurante chino*
chocolate	xocolata	*chocolate*
chocolate, a bar of	una rajola de xocolata	*una tableta de chocolate*
chocolate cake	pastís de xocolata	*pastel de chocolate*
chocolate ice cream	gelat de xocolata	*helado de chocolate*
chocolate mousse	mousse de xocolata	*mousse de chocolate*
chocolate with almonds/ halzenuts	xocolata amb ametlles/ avellanes	*chocolate con almendras / avellanas*
chocolates; sweets	bombons	*bombones*
chronic disease	malaltia crònica	*enfermedad crónica*
church	església	*iglesia*
cigar/s	cigar/s	*puro/s; cigarro/s*
cigarette(s)	cigarreta; cigarretes	*cigarillo(s)*
cinema; movie theater	cine; cinema m	*cine; cinema m*
circus	circ	*circo*
citadel	ciutadella	*ciudadela*
city	ciutat f	*ciudad f*

city map	plànol de la ciutat	*plano de la ciudad*
civil servant	funcionari. -ària	*funcionario, -a*
civil guard/ policeman	guàrdia civil	*guardia civil*
claim; demand [v.]	reclamar	*reclamar*
clam; mussel	musclo; cloïssa; copinya	*almeja; mejillón*
class	classe f	*clase f*
classes, to take	seguir cursos (de)	*seguir cursos (de)*
clean	net, -a	*limpio, -a*
cleaning	neteja	*limpieza*
cleaning products	articles de neteja	*artículos de limpieza*
cleaning woman; charlady	dona de fer feines	*asistenta*
clear	clar, -a	*claro, -a*
clear; cloudless	clar	*despejado*
clearance sale	liquidació f;	*liquidación f;*
clever	llest, -a; eixerit, -ida	*listo, -a*
client	client, -a	*cliente*
clinic	clínica	*clínica*
cloakroom; checkroom	guarda-roba m	*guardarropa m*
closet; cupboard	armari	*armario*
closing; closure	clausura	*clausura*
clothes pin/s	agulla/agulles d'estendre	*pinza/s de ropa*
cloud	núvol	*nube f*
cloudy	ennuvolat	*nuboso*
club; sports club	club; club esportiu	*club; club deportivo*
clutch [auto.]	embragatge	*embrague*
coast	costa	*costa*
cocktail; mixed drink	còctel; combinat	*cóctel; combinado*
cod(fish)	bacallà	*bacalao*
coffee	cafè	*café*
coffeepot	cafetera	*cafetera*
cognac; brandy	conyac	*coñac*
coin	moneda	*moneda*
coin purse	portamonedes; cartereta	*portamonedas; monedero*

cold	fred	*frío*
cold [sickness]	refredat; constipat	*resfriado; constipado*
cold [adj.]	fred, -a	*frío, -a*
cold, to have a	constipat, -a; estar constipat, -ada	*constipado, -a; estar constipado, -a*
cold cut(s)	embotit(s)	*embutido(s)*
colic	còlic	*cólico*
collect [v.]	retirar; recollir	*retirar; recoger*
collect [v.] stamps	col·leccionar segells	*coleccionar sellos*
collect call; reverse charge call	telefonada amb cobrament revertit	*conferencia a cobro revertido*
college, to go to	anar a la universitat	*ir a la universidad*
collide; run into [v.]	xocar	*chocar; colisionar*
color	color	*color*
color, in	de color	*de color*
comb	pinta	*peine*
comb [v.)	pentinar	*peinar*
combined medley	estil combinat	*estilo combinado*
comedy	comèdia	*comedia*
comedy film	pel·lícula còmica	*película cómica; película de risa*
commercial establishments and services	establiments comercials i serveis	*establecimientos comerciales y servicios*
commission	comissió f	*comisión f*
commuter train	tren de rodalies	*tren de cercanías*
compact disc	disc compacte; compact disc	*disco compacto; compact disc*
compartment	compartiment	*departamento*
competition	competició f; prova	*competición f; prueba*
competition swimming	competició de natació	*competición de natación*
complete competition	concurs complet	*concurso completo*
completely	completament	*completamente*
complexion; skin	cutis	*cutis*
complicated	complicat, -ada	*complicado, -a*
composer	compositor, -a	*compositor, -a*
compress, sanitary towel	compresa	*compresa*
compressed air gun	pistola d'aire comprimit	*pistola de aire comprimido*

compressed air rifle	carrabina/fusell d'aire comprimit	*carabina/fusil de aire comprimido*
computer	ordinador	*ordenador*
computer advising	assessorament d'informàtica	*asesoramiento de informática*
computer programs	programes per a ordinador	*programas para ordenador*
computer science	informàtica	*informática*
conceited	presumit	*presumido*
concert	concert	*concierto*
conductor; inspector	cobrador; revisor	*cobrador; revisor*
congratulatory telegram	telegrama de felicitació	*telegrama de felicitación*
connect; plug in [v.]	connectar	*conectar*
connection	connexió	*conexión*
connection [train]	enllaç; correspondència	*enlace; correspondencia*
consommé	consomé	*consomé*
constipation	estrenyiment	*estreñimiento*
consulate	consulat	*consulado*
consulting room; surgery	consulta	*consulta*
consulting hours	hores de consulta	*horas de consulta*
contagious disease	malaltia contagiosa	*enfermedad contagiosa*
continuous line	línia contínua	*línea continua*
continuous session	sessió f contínua	*sesión f continua*
conversation guide	guia de conversa	*guía de conversación*
cook	cuiner, -a	*cocinero, -a*
cook [v.]	coure; cuinar; guisar	*cocer; cocinar; guisar*
cooked	cuit, -a	*cocido, -a*
cookies; biscuits	galetes pl	*galletas pl*
cool	fresc	*fresco*
coolant	líquid de refrigeració	*líquido de refrigeración*
copper	coure	*cobre*
cops-and-robbers film	pel.lícula de lladres i serenos; pel.lícula policíaca	*película policíaca*
copy	còpia	*copia*
copy, to make a	fer una còpia	*hacer una copia*

corn; maize	blat de moro	*maíz*
corner [street]	cantonada	*esquina*
corpulent; stout	corpulent, -a	*corpulento, -a*
corridor; passage	passadís	*pasillo*
cotton	cotó (fluix)	*algodón*
cough	tos f	*tos f*
cough [v.]	tossir	*toser*
cough syrup	calmant de la tos	*calmante de la tos*
count [v.]	comptar	*contar*
counter	taulell	*mostrador*
country	país	*país*
course	curs	*curso*
course; direction	rumb	*rumbo*
cousin f	cosina	*prima*
cousin(s)	cosí; cosins	*primo(s)*
cove; inlet	cala	*cala*
cover; case; slip	funda	*funda*
covered/fried in batter	arrebossat, -ada	*rebozado, -a*
crab	cranc	*cangrejo*
crash; smash [car]	xoc; topada; col·lisió	*choque; colisión f*
cream	nata; crema; crema de llet	*nata; crema; crema de leche*
cream caramel	flam	*flan*
cream of vegetable soup	crema de llegums/ verdures	*crema de legumbres/ verduras*
creamery; milk shop	lleteria; granja; productes làctics	*lechería; granja; productos lacteos*
creamy soup	crema	*crema*
credit	crèdit	*crédito*
credit, on	a crèdit	*a crédito*
credit card	targeta de crèdit	*tarjeta de crédito*
crêpes	creps	*creps*
crew	tripulació f	*tripulación f*
cricket	criquet; cricket	*criquet; cricket*
croissant	croissant	*croissant*
croquettes	croquetes	*croquetas*
cross-country skiing	esquí nòrdic/de fons	*esquí nórdico/de fondo*
crossword puzzle	mots encreuats m pl	*crucigrama m*
crullers	xurros	*churros*
cucumber	cogombre	*pepino*

cufflinks	botons m pl de puny	*gemelos m pl*
cup [trophy]	copa	*copa*
cup	tassa	*taza*
cup of ice cream	copa de gelat	*copa de helado*
curious	curiós, -osa	*curioso, -a*
curly	arrissat, -ada; cresp, -a	*rizado, -a; crespo, -a*
currency	divisa	*divisa*
current (electrical)	corrent (elèctric)	*corriente f eléctrica*
curtain	cortina	*cortina*
curve; bend	revolt	*curva*
custard	crema	*crema*
customs	duana	*aduana*
customs declaration	declaració de duana	*declaración de aduana*
customs officer	duaner, -a	*aduanero, -a*
cut; wound	tall; ferida	*corte; herida*
cut [v.]	tallar	*cortar*
cutlery; silverware	cobert	*cubiertos*
cutlets	llonzes; costelles	*chuletas*
cuttlefish	sípia; sèpia	*sepia; jibia*
cycling	ciclisme	*ciclismo*
cylinder	cilindre	*cilindro*
cylinder head	culata	*culata*
daddy; papa	papa	*papá*
daily	diàriament	*diariamente*
damage	dany; desperfecte	*daño; desperfecto*
dance hall	sala de festa/ball	*sala de baile*
daring	atrevit, -ida	*atrevido, -a*
dark	fosc, -a	*oscuro, -a*
dark beer	cervesa negra	*cerveza negra*
date	data	*fecha*
date of birth	data de naixement	*fecha de nacimiento*
daughter	filla	*hija*
dawn	matinada	*madrugada; amanecer*
day	dia m	*día m*
day, by	de dia	*de día*
day after, the	l'endemà	*al día siguiente*
day after tomorrow, the	demà passat	*pasado mañana*
day before yesterday, the	abans d'ahir	*antes de ayer*

day, the other	l'altre dia	*el otro día*
debut; opening	estrena	*estreno*
decade	dècada; decenni	*década; decenio*
decaffeinated coffee	cafè descafeinat	*café descafeinado*
decathlon	decatló	*decatlón*
December	desembre	*diciembre*
deck [mar.]	coberta	*cubierta*
deck/lawn chair	gandula; cadira plegable	*hamaca; silla plegable*
deep	fondo	*profundo; hondo*
deer; venison	cérvol	*ciervo; venado*
defeat	derrota	*derrota*
defeat; beat [v.]	derrotar	*derrotar*
deflate [v.]	desinflar-se	*desinflarse*
degree	grau	*grado*
delay	retard	*retraso*
delayed, to be [v.]	portar retard	*llevar retraso*
delicatessen	xarcuteria; cansaladeria	*charcutería; tocinería*
demonstration sports	esports de demostració	*deportes de demos tración*
dentist	dentista; odontòleg, -òloga	*dentista; odontólogo, -a*
deodorant	desodorant	*desodorante*
depart [v.]	sortir	*salir*
department store	magatzem; gran magatzem	*almacén; gran almacén*
departure	sortida	*salida*
depilation	depilació f	*depilación f*
depilation cream/wax	crema/cera depilatòria	*crema/cera depilatoria*
dessert	postres f pl	*postre*
desserts and sweets	postres i plats dolços	*postres y platos dulces*
destination	destí; destinació f	*destino*
detective novel	novel.la policíaca	*novela policíaca*
detergent	detergent	*detergente*
diabetes	diabetis f	*diabetes f*
diabetic	diabètic, -a	*diabético, -a*
dial [v.] (the number)	marcar (el número)	*marcar (el número)*
diamond	diamant	*diamante*
diarrhoea	diarrea	*diarrea*

dictionary	diccionari	*diccionario*
die [v.]	morir	*morir*
difficult	difícil	*difícil*
difficulty, with	difícilment	*difícilmente*
dining room	menjador	*comedor*
dinner; supper	sopar	*cena*
dinner/supper, to have	sopar	*cenar*
diphtheria	difteria	*difteria*
diploma	diploma m	*diploma m*
dipped headlights	llum f d'encreuament	*luz F de cruce*
direct flight	vol directe	*vuelo directo*
direct/exterior line	línia directa/exterior	*línea directa/exterior*
directly	directament	*directamente*
director	director; directora	*director; directora*
dirty	brut, -a	*sucio, -a*
disconnect: unplug [v.]	desconnectar	*desconectar*
discothèque	discoteca	*discoteca*
discount	descompte	*descuento*
discus throwing	llançament de disc	*lanzamiento de disco*
disease; sickness	malaltia	*enfermedad f*
disembark [v.]	desembarcar	*desembarcar*
dish(es)	plat(s)	*plato(s)*
dish-washing powder/ liquid	(pólvores/detergent) rentavaixelles	*(polvos/detergente) lavavajillas*
dishwasher	rentaplats; rentavaixella	*lavaplatos; lavavajillas*
dislocate [v.]	torcer; dislocar; dislocar-se; desllorigar; desllorigar-se	*dislocar; dislocarse*
dismantle; strip [v.]	desmuntar	*desmontar*
display case	aparador	*escaparate; aparador*
distilled water	aigua destil·lada	*agua destilada*
district	districte	*distrito*
divorce [v.]	divorciar-se	*divorciarse*
divorced	divorciat, -ada	*divorciado, -a*
dock; wharf	moll	*muelle*
doctor	doctor, -a; metge,-essa	*doctor, -a; médico*
doctor, to go see a	anar a veure un metge; consultar un metge	*ir a ver a un médico; consultar a un médico*

documentary	documental	*documental*
doll	nina	*muñeca*
domestic flight	vol nacional/interior	*vuelo nacional*
domestic items	articles per a la llar	*artículos domésticos; artículos para el hogar*
door	porta	*puerta; portezuela*
doorkeeper; concierge	porter, -a; conserge	*portero, -a; conserje*
doorman	porter	*portero*
double bed	llit de matrimoni	*cama de matrimonio*
double room	habitació doble; habitació per a dues persones	*habitación doble; habitación para dos personas*
double sculls	doble scull	*doble scull*
double-deck motorboat	golondrina	*golondrina*
doubles	dobles	*dobles*
doughnuts	bunyols	*buñuelos*
down	a baix	*abajo*
downhill race	descens	*descenso*
downwards; down	avall	*hacia abajo*
drama	drama m	*drama m*
draught beer	cervesa de barril	*cerveza de barril*
draught beer, a glass of	una canya	*una caña*
draw; tie	empat	*empate*
draw; tie [v.]	empatar	*empatar*
dress	vestit	*vestido*
dressing gown; housecoat	bata	*bata*
drink; beverage	beguda	*bebida*
drink [v.]	beure; prendre	*beber; tomar*
drinking water	aigua potable	*agua potable*
drive [v.]	conduir	*conducir*
driver	conductor (de l'automòbil	*conductor (del automóvil)*
driver's license	permís de conducció	*carné/permiso de conducir*
driving licence	permís de circulació	*permiso de circulación*
drug store	farmàcia	*farmacia*

drumstick; leg	cuixa	*muslo*
dry	sec, -a	*seco, -a*
dry oneself [v.]	eixugar-se	secarse
dry cleaner's	tintoreria	*tintorería*
dry cleaning	neteja en sec; rentat en sec	*limpieza en seco; lavado en seco*
dry wine	vi sec	*vino seco*
drysaltery; drug-store	drogueria	*droguería*
dubbed	doblat	*doblado*
duck	ànec	*pato*
during	durant	*durante*
dusk	vesprada	*anochecer*
duty-free shop	botiga lliure d'impostos	*tienda libre de impuestos*
dye [v.]	tenyir	*teñir*
dyer	tintorer, -a	*tintorero, -a*
dynamo	dinamo f	*dinamo f*
dysentery	disenteria	*disentería*
each	cada	*cada*
each/every day	cada dia	*cada día*
each/every hour	cada hora	*cada hora*
ear/s	orella; orelles	*oreja/s*
earache	otitis f	*otitis f*
early	d'hora	*temprano*
earn [v.]	cobrar	*cobrar*
earring(s)	arracada; arracades	*pendiente(s); arracada(s)*
easily	fàcilment	*fácilmente*
east	est	*este*
easy	fàcil	*fácil*
eat [v.]	menjar	*comer*
Eau de Cologne	colònia; aigua de Colònia	*colonia; agua de Colonia*
eau-de-vie; brandy	aiguardent	*aguardiente*
education	educació f	*educación f*
eel	anguil(l)a	*anguila*
egg	ou	*huevo*
egg dishes	plats d'ous	*platos de huevos*
eggplant	albergínia	*berenjena*
eiderdown	edredó	*edredón*

eight oared	de vuit rems	*de ocho remos*
electric appliances	electrodomèstics	*electrodomésticos*
electrical appliance repair	reparació d'electrodomèstics	*reparación de electrodomésticos*
electrical current	corrent (elèctric)	*corriente f (eléctrica)*
electrical items	articles d'electricitat	*artículos de electricidad*
electric shaver	maquineta (d'afaitar) elèctrica	*maquinilla (de afeitar) eléctrica*
electric train	electrotren	*electrotrén*
electrician	electricista; lampista	*electricista*
electricity	electricitat f	*electricidad f*
electronic games	jocs electrònics	*juegos electrónicos*
elevator; lift	ascensor	*ascensor*
embark; board [v.]	embarcar	*embarcar*
embassy	ambaixada	*embajada*
emergency ward	urgències	*urgencias*
employee	empleat, -ada	*empleado, -a*
employer; manager	empresari, -ària	*empresario, -a*
empty	buit, -ida	*vacío*
engaged [telephone]	ocupat, -ada; comunica	*ocupado, -a; comunica*
engine; motor	motor	*motor*
engineer	enginyer, -a	*ingeniero, -a*
engraving of objects	gravat d'objectes	*grabado de objetos*
enlarge [v.]	ampliar	*ampliar*
enlargement	ampliació f	*ampliación f*
enough	bastant; prou	*bastante*
entertainment section	cartellera	*cartelera*
envelope	sobre	*sobre*
épée fencing	esgrima d'espasa	*esgrima de espada*
epidemic	epidèmia	*epidemia*
equalize [v.]	igualar	*igualar*
equestrian	hípica	*hípica*
eraser	goma; goma d'esborrar	*goma; goma de borrar*
escalator	escala mecànica	*escalera mecánica*
escalope	escalopa	*escalope*
"escudella" stew	escudella	*"escudella"*
European champion	campió, -ona d'Europa	*campeón, -ona de Europa*

European championship	campionat d'Europa	*campeonato de Europa*
European record	rècord d'Europa	*récord de Europa*
evening	vespre; nit f	*noche f*
every	tots, totes	*todos, -as*
everyone	tots, totes	*todos, -as*
everywhere	arreu; pertot; pertot arreu	*en/por todas partes*
exact time	hora exacta	*hora exacta*
exam; test	examen; prova	*examen; prueba*
examine [v.]; give an check-up [v.]	examinar; fer(-li) una visita/un reconeixement	*examinar; hacer(le) una visita / un reconocimiento*
excellent	excel·lent	*excelente*
exchange; change [v.]	canviar	*cambiar*
exchange rate	tipus de canvi; cotització	*tipo de cambio; cotización*
exchange; change	canvi	*cambio*
exhaust pipe	tub d'escapament	*tubo de escape*
exhibition	exposició f	*exposición f*
expecting a baby, to be	esperar un nen	*esperar un niño*
expensive	car, -a	*caro, -a*
express (train)	(tren) exprés	*(tren) expreso*
extension	extensió f	*extensión f*
extraction	extracció f	*extracción f*
eyebrow/s	cella; celles	*ceja/s*
eyebrow pencil	llapis per a les celles	*lápiz para cejas*
eye drops	gotes per als ulls; col·liri	*gotas para los ojos; colirio*
eyelash/es	pestanya; pestanyes	*pestaña/s*
eye shadow	ombra d'ulls; ombrejador	*sombra de ojos*
"fabada" (Asturian dish made of beans, sausage and bacon)	mongetes estofades; cassola de faves	*fabada; cazuela de habas*
face	cara; rostre	*cara; rostro*
face powder	pólvores facials	*polvos faciales*
factory	fàbrica	*fábrica*

fail [v.] [auto.]	fallar	*fallar*
faint [v.]	desmaiar-se	*desmayarse*
fair [adj.]	just, -a	*justo, -a*
fair; market	fira	*feria*
false	fals, -a	*falso, -a*
family	família	*familia*
fan [hand-held]	ventall	*abanico*
fan; supporter	aficionat, -ada; seguidor, -a	*aficionado, -a; seguidor, -a; hincha*
fare; tariff	tarifa	*tarifa*
farm worker	treballador agrícola	*trabajador agrícola*
fashion patterns	patrons de moda	*patrones de moda*
fashion shop	botiga de confeccions; botiga/casa de modes	*tienda de confecciones; tienda/casa de modas*
fast	ràpid, -a	*rápido, -a*
fast, to be [a watch]	avançar-se; anar avançat	*adelantar; ir adelantado*
fast/express train	(tren) ràpid	*(tren) rápido*
fat	gras, -assa	*gordo, -a*
father	pare	*padre*
father-in-law	sogre	*suegro*
feast day; holiday	(dia m.) festiu	*(día m.) festivo*
feature film	llarg-metratge	*largometraje*
February	febrer	*febrero*
feel [v.] bad/sick	trobar-se/sentir-se malament	*encontrarse/sentirse mal*
feel [v.] sick/dizzy	marejar-se	*marearse*
feel [v.] sick/ nauseated	sentir nàusees	*tener ganas de vomitar; sentir nauseas*
feminine; women's	femení, -ina; de dones	*femenino, -ina; de mujeres*
fencing	esgrima	*esgrima*
fender; bumper	para-xocs	*parachoques*
fever; temperature	febre f; temperatura	*fiebre f; temperatura; calentura*
field	camp	*campo*
field hockey	hoquei sobre herba	*hockey sobre hierba*
fig	figa	*higo*
figure skating	patinatge artístic	*patinaje artístico*
file	llima	*lima*

fill [v.]	omplir	*llenar*
fill in/out [v.]	omplir; emplenar	*rellenar*
fillet; sirloin	filet	*filete*
filling [tooth]	empastament	*empaste*
filling, to put in a	empastar; obturar	*empastar*
film	pel·lícula	*película*
film for slides	pel·lícula per a diapositives	*película para diapositivas*
film for color slides	pel·lícula en color per a diapositives	*película en color para diapositivas*
film library	filmoteca	*filmoteca*
filter [cigarette]	filtre; broquet	*boquilla; filtro*
filter	filtre	*filtro*
final [n.]; finals	final f; finals	*final f; finales*
final score	resultat final	*resultado final*
fine; ticket	multa	*multa*
finger(s)	dit(s)	*dedo(s)*
fingernail polish	laca; esmalt	*laca; esmalte*
fingernail polish remover	dissolvent per a les ungles	*quitaesmalte; disolvente para las uñas*
fingernail(s)	ungla; ungles	*uña(s)*
finn	finn	*finn*
fire extinguisher	extintor	*extintor*
firing ranges	camps de tir	*campos de tiro*
first-aid	primers socors; primers auxilis m pl	*primeros auxilios*
first-aid kit	farmaciola	*botiquín*
first-aid post	lloc de socors	*puesto de socorro*
first-aid station	lloc de primers auxilis	*puesto de primeros auxilios*
first-class car	vagó de primera (classe)	*coche de primera (clase)*
first-run cinema	sala/cine d'estrena	*sala/cine de estreno*
fish	peix	*pez; pescado*
fish and seafood stew	sarsuela de peix i marisc	*zarzuela de pescado y marisco*
fish shop	peixateria	*pescadería*
fish soup	sopa de peix	*sopa de pescado*
fishing	pesca	*pesca*
five minutes ago	fa cinc minuts	*hace cinco minutos*
five peseta coin	duro	*duro*

fixed price	preu únic	*precio único*
flabby	tou, -ova	*blando, -a*
flambé	flamejat, -ada	*flameado, -a*
flash	flash	*flash*
flashlight	llanterna	*linterna*
flat tire	rebentada; punxada	*pinchazo*
flavor(s)	sabor(s)	*sabor(es)*
flight	vol	*vuelo*
floor; storey	pis; planta	*piso; planta*
floor; floor exercises	terra; exercicis a terra	*suelo; ejercicios en el suelo*
florist	florista	*florista*
flour	farina	*harina*
flower shop	floreria	*floristería*
flowers	flors	*flores*
flu	grip	*gripe f*
fly [v.]	volar	*volar*
Flying Dutchman	flying dutchman	*flying dutchman*
fog	boira	*niebla*
foie gras	foie gras	*foie gras*
foil fencing	esgrima de floret	*esgrima de florete*
food	menjar	*comida*
foolish	ximple	*tonto, -a*
foot; feet	peu/s	*pie/s*
football/soccer field	camp de futbol	*campo de fútbol*
football; soccer	futbol	*fútbol; balonpié*
footwear	calçat	*calzado*
footwear/umbrella repair	reparació de calçat	*reparación de calzado/ paraguas*
for now	ara per ara	*por el momento*
for a long time	(des de) fa molt	*(desde) hace mucho*
forehead	front f	*frente f*
fork	forquilla	*tenedor*
fork; junction	bifurcació	*bifurcación*
form; printed paper	imprès	*impreso*
formerly	antigament	*antiguamente*
fountain	font f; brollador	*fuente f; surtidor*
four rowers with coxswain	quatre (remers) amb timoner	*cuatro (remeros) con timonero*
four sculls	quadruple scull	*cuadruple scull*
four-seater	quatre places	*cuatro plazas*

fowl	aviram	*aves*
fragile	fràgil	*frágil*
frames and glasses	vidres i marcos	*vidrios y marcos*
frank; stamp [v.]	franquejar	*franquear*
frankfurter	salsitxes de Frankfurt	*salchichas de Frank-furt*
freestyle	estil lliure	*estilo libre*
freestyle relay	relleus d'estil lliure	*relevos de estilo libre*
freestyle wrestling	lluita lliure	*lucha libre*
freeway; motorway	autopista	*autopista*
freezer	congelador	*congelador*
freight train	(tren de) mercaderies	*m (tren de) mercan-cías m*
French franc(s)	franc francès; francs francesos	*franco francés; fran cos franceses*
French omelette	truita (a la) francesa	*tortilla (a la) francesa*
fresh fruit	fruita del temps	*fruta del tiempo*
fresh water fish	peixos d'aigua dolça	*peces de agua dulce*
Friday	divendres	*viernes*
fried	fregit, -ida	*frito, -a*
fried eggs	ous ferrats	*huevos fritos*
from	de	*de*
from here	des d'aquí	*desde aquí*
from there	des d'allí	*desde allí*
from today on	des d'avui	*de hoy en adelante*
from tomorrow on	a partir de demà	*a partir de mañana*
frost; freeze	glaçada	*helada*
fruit juice	suc de fruita	*zumo de fruta*
fruit cocktail	macedònia de fruites	*macedonia de frutas*
fruit and vegetable shop	botiga de verdures; fruiteria	*tienda de verduras; frutería*
fruit shop	fruiteria	*frutería*
fruits	fruitas	*frutas*
fuel	combustible	*combustible*
full	ple, -ena	*lleno, -a*
full board	pensió completa	*pensión completa*
funicular	funicular	*funicular*
funny	divertit, -ida	*divertido, -a*
fur shop; furrier's	pelleteria	*peletería*
furniture	moble(s)	*mueble(s)*
furniture shop	botiga de mobles	*mueblería*

fuse	fusible	*fusible*
gallstone(s)	càlcul(s) biliar(s)	*cálculo(s) biliar(es)*
game [animal]	caça	*caza*
game; match	partit	*partido*
gangway; gangplank	passarel·la	*pasarela*
garage	garatge	*garaje*
garage; repair shop	taller	*taller*
garden produce	hortalissa; hortalisses	*hortalizas*
garlic	all	*ajo*
garlic mayonnaise	allioli	*alioli*
gas/petrol station	gasolinera	*gasolinera*
gas lighter	encenedor de gas	*encendedor de gas*
gas cylinder	bombona de gas	*bombona de gas*
gas/diesel oil	gas-oil	*gasóleo; gasoil*
gas/petrol tank	dipòsit (de gasolina)	*depósito (de gasolina)*
gasoline; petrol	gasolina	*gasolina*
gastric ulcer	úlcera gàstrica; úlcera de l'estómac	*úlcera gástrica, úlcera del estómago*
gastroenteritis	gastro-enteritis f	*gastroenteritis f*
gate [airport]	porta	*puerta*
"gazpacho" (cold tomato and garlic soup)	gaspatxo	*gazpacho*
gear stick	palanca del canvi de marxes	*palanca de cambio*
gear; speed	marxa	*marcha*
gearshift; gear change	canvi de marxes	*cambio de marchas*
General Delivery (Poste Restante)	llista de correus	*lista de correos*
general malaise	malestar general	*malestar general*
German measles	rubèola	*rubeola; rubéola*
German mark(s)	marc(s) alemany(s)	*marco alemán; marcos alemanes*
get off, to	baixar	*bajar; apearse*
get out/off, to (vehicle)	baixar (d'un vehicle)	*bajar (de un vehícu-lo)*
giant slalom	eslalom gegant	*eslalon/slalom gigante*
gin	ginebra	*ginebra*
girl	nena; noia	*niña; muchacha; chica*

girlfriend; fiancée	núvia; promesa	*novia*
gladiolus	gladiol	*gladiolo*
glass	got; copa	*vaso; copa*
gliding [aviat.]	planatge; vol sense motor	*planeo; vuelo sin motor*
give way (auto)	cedir el pas	*ceder el paso*
gloves	guants	*guantes*
glue	cola; goma d'enganxar	*cola; pegamento; goma de pegar/ enganchar*
glue [v.]	enganxar	*pegar*
goat	cabra	*cabra*
gold	or	*oro*
gold chain	cadena d'or	*cadena de oro*
gold medal	medalla d'or	*medalla de oro*
golden	dorat, -ada	*dorado, -a*
goldsmith's articles	articles d'orfebreria	*artículos de orfebreria*
golf	golf	*golf*
good	bo, -ona	*bueno, -a*
goose	oca	*ganso; oca*
grade	nota	*nota*
grammar	gramàtica	*gramática*
grammar/secondary school	institut (de batxillerat)	*instituto (de bachillerato)*
grandchildren	néts	*nietos*
granddaughter	néta	*nieta*
grandfather	avi	*abuelo*
grandmother	àvia	*abuela*
grandparents	avis	*abuelos*
grandson	nét	*nieto*
grape	raïm	*uva*
grapefruit	aranja; poncem	*pomelo; toronja*
gratin	gratinat, -ada	*gratinado, -a*
grave; serious	greu	*grave*
Greco-Roman wrestling	lluita grecorromana	*lucha grecorromana*
green	verd, -a	*verde*
green beans	mongetes tendres	*judías verdes; vainas*
green pepper	pebrot	*pimiento*
grey-haired; grey	gris, -a	*canoso, -a; gris*
greyhounds	llebrers	*galgos*

grilled	a la graella/planxa	*a la parrilla/plancha*
ground [adj.]	picat, -ada	*picado, -a*
ground beef	carn capolada/picada	*carne picada*
ground floor	planta baixa; baixos m pl	*planta baja*
guarantee	garantia	*garantía*
guest house	pensió	*pensión*
guide (book)	guia	*guía*
gun; pistol	pistola (lliure)	*pistola (libre)*
gymnastics	gimnàstica	*gimnasia*
haberdashery; notions store	merceria; vetes-i-fils	*mercería*
half board	mitja pensió	*media pensión*
hail; hailstones	calamarsa; pedra	*granizo; piedra*
hair	cabells m pl	*pelo; cabellos m pl*
haircut	tallat de cabells	*corte de pelo*
hairdresser	perruquera	*peluquera*
hairdresser's	perruqueria	*peluquería*
hair dryer	assecador (de cabells); eixuga-cabells	*secador (de pelo)*
hair drying	assecat de cabells	*secado de pelo*
hair dying	tint de cabells	*teñido de pelo*
hairspray	laca (per als cabells)	*laca (para el pelo)*
hairstyle	pentinat	*peinado*
hair washing	rentat de cabells	*lavado de cabeza*
hake	lluç	*merluza*
half an hour	mitja hora	*media hora*
hall; classroom	sala; aula	*sala; aula*
halt; wayside station	baixador	*apeadero*
ham	pernil	*jamón*
ham omelette	truita de pernil	*tortilla de jamón*
hammer	martell	*martillo*
hammer throwing	llançament de martell	*lanzamiento de martillo*
handbag	bossa (de mà)	*bolso (de mano)*
handball	handbol	*balonmano*
hand brake	fre de mà	*freno de mano*
hand(s)	mà; mans	*mano(s)*
hand luggage	equipatge de mà	*equipaje de mano*
handicrafts	artesania popular	*artesanía popular*

English	Català	Español
handkerchief	mocador (de butxaca)	*pañuelo (de bolsillo)*
handsome; good-looking	maco, -a	*guapo, -a*
hang up [v.]	penjar	*colgar*
hanger	penjador	*colgador*
happy	alegre; feliç	*alegre; feliz*
harbor	port; estació marítima	*puerto; estación marítima*
hard	dur, -a	*duro, -a*
hard-boiled eggs	ous durs	*huevos duros*
hardly	difícilment	*difícilmente*
hardware store	ferreteria	*ferretería*
hare	llebre; conill de bosc	*liebre*
haricot bean	fesol; mongetes seques	*alubia*
hat	barret; capell	*sombrero*
hazel nut	avellana	*avellana*
head	cap	*cabeza*
headache	mal de cap	*dolor de cabeza*
headache, to have a	fer-li mal el cap; tenir mal de cap	*dolerle la cabeza; tener dolor de cabeza*
headache tablets	comprimits contra el mal de cap	*comprimidos para el dolor de cabeza*
headband [head phones]	casc	*casco*
headlamp; headlight	far	*faro*
headphone	auricular	*auricular*
health	salut f	*salud f*
healthy	sa, sana	*sano, -a*
heart	cor	*corazón*
heart attack	atac cardíac; atac de cor	*ataque cardíaco; ataque de corazón*
heartburn	ardor; cremor a l'estómac	*ardor de estómago*
heat; hot	calor f; calent	*calor; caliente*
heat up [v.]	escalfar-se	*calentarse*
heater	estufa	*estufa*
heating	calefacció f	*calefacción f*
heavy	pesant; pesat, -ada	*pesado, -a*
heavy/ sultry weather	xafogor f	*bochorno*
heel	taló; tacó	*tacón*

hello? Yes?	escolti'm; digui'm	*óigame; dígame*
hemorrhoid	hemorroide f	*hemorroide f*
hen	gallina	*gallina*
hepatitis	hepatitis f	*hepatitis f*
heptathlon	heptatló	*heptatlón*
here	aquí; ací	*aquí; acá*
hernia	hèrnia	*hernia*
herring	areng	*arenque*
high	alt, -a	*alto, -a*
high-fidelity equipment	equip d'alta fidelitat	*equipo de alta fidelidad*
high jump	salt d'alçada	*salto de altura*
highway headlights	llum f de carretera	*luz de carretera*
highway; turnpike	autovia	*autovía*
hiking	excursionisme	*excursionismo*
homework	deures	*deberes*
honest	honest, -a	*honesto, -a*
honey	mel f	*miel f*
hood; bonnet [auto.]	capot; capota	*capó; capota*
hop, step and jump	triple salt	*triple salto*
horizontal bar	barra fixa	*barra fija*
horn [auto.]	botzina; clàxon	*bocina; claxon*
hors d'oeuvres	entremesos	*entremeses*
horse; horsemeat	cavall; carn de cavall	*caballo; carne de caballo*
hospital	hospital	*hospital*
to hospitalize	hospitalitzar	*hospitalizar*
hostel; boarding house	hostal; pensió f	*hostal; pensión f*
hot	calent, -a	*caliente*
hot and cold water	aigua freda i calenta	*agua fría y caliente*
hot water	aigua calenta	*agua caliente*
hot and spicy	picant	*picante*
hotel	hotel	*hotel*
hour	hora	*hora*
hour from now, an	d'aquí a una hora	*dentro de una hora*
house painter	pintor (de parets)	*pintor (de brocha gorda)*
housewife	mestressa de casa	*ama de casa*
house wine	vi de la casa	*vino de la casa*
housing development	urbanizació f	*urbanitzación f*

how?	com?	*¿cómo?*
how much	quant, -a?	*¿cuánto, -a?*
human body	el cos humà	*el cuerpo humano*
humid	humit, -ida	*húmedo, -a*
humidity	humitat f	*humedad f*
Hungarian goulash	goulash a l'hongare-sa	*goulash a la húngara*
hungry, to be (very)	tenir (molta) gana	*tener (mucha) hambre*
hunting	caça	*caza*
hurdle race	cursa de tanques	*carrera de vallas*
hurt; to have a pain [v.]	fer mal; fer-li mal	*doler; dolerle*
husband	marit	*marido*
hut; cabin	caseta	*caseta*
I need to buy:	He de comprar:	*He de comprar:*
ice	gel	*hielo*
ice cream	gelat	*helado*
ice cream parlour	gelateria	*heladería*
ice cubes	glaçons	*cubitos de hielo*
ice hockey	hokei sobre gel	*hockey sobre hielo*
identity card number	número de DNI (document nacional d'identitat = carnet d'identitat)	*número de D.N.I. (documento nacional de identidad = carné de identidad)*
identity card photo	foto-carnet f	*foto-carné f; foto-carnet*
ignition	encesa	*encendido*
ignition key	clau de l'encesa	*llave del encendido*
ill, to fall	emmalaltir-se; posar-se malalt	*enfermarse; caer enfermo*
illumination	enllumenat	*alumbrado*
in	a; en	*en*
in a week's time	d'avui en vuit	*de aquí a ocho días*
inflate [v.]	inflar	*hinchar*
injure/ hurt oneself (v.)	ferir-se; quedar ferit	*herirse; resultar herido*
injured person	ferit, -ida	*herido, -a*
insure [v.]	assegurar	*asegurar*
in front; ahead	davant	*delante*
incomplete/incorrect address	adreça incompleta/ insuficient	*dirección incompleta insuficiente*

indigestion	indigestió f	*indigestión f*
indigestion, to suffer from	tenir una indigestió	*tener una indigestión*
individual	individual	*individual*
infarct	infart (de miocardi)	*infarto (de miocardio)*
infection	infecció f	*infección f*
inflammation	inflamació f	*inflamación f*
inflatable mattress	matalàs pneumàtic; matalàs inflable	*colchón neumático; colchón inflable*
inflatable raft	bot pneumàtic	*bote neumático*
injection	injecció f	*inyección f*
injection, to give an	posar(-li) una injecció	*poner(le) una inyección*
ink	tinta	*tinta*
inn	parador	*parador*
inner room	habitació interior	*habitación interior*
insipid; tasteless	insípid, -a	*insípido, -a*
insoles	plantilles	*plantillas*
insomnia	insomni	*insomnio*
installations	instal·lacions	*instalaciones*
insulating tape	cinta aïllant	*cinta aislante*
insurance	assegurança	*seguro; aseguramiento*
insured	assegurat, -ada	*asegurado, -a*
intelligent	intel·ligent	*inteligente*
interest	interès	*interés*
interest rate	tipus d'interès	*tipo de interés*
interesting	interesant	*interesante*
international flight	vol internacional	*vuelo internacional*
international tournament	torneig internacional	*torneo internacional*
interpreter	intèrpret	*intérprete*
intersection; junction	encreuament; cruïlla	*cruce*
interval	entreacte	*entreacto*
intoxication	intoxicació f	*intoxicación f*
iris	lliri blanc; assutzena	*lirio; azucena*
iron	planxa	*plancha*
iron (metal)	ferro	*hierro*
Is there a supermarket near here?	Hi ha per aquí un supermercat?	*¿Hay por aquí un supermercado?*

it's busy [telephone]	està comunicant	*está comunicando*
Italian lira(s)	lira italiana; lires italianes	*lira(s) italiana(s)*
itch; stinging	picor	*picor; comezón*
I've made a mistake	m'he equivocat	*me he equivocado*
jack (auto)	cric; gat	*gato*
jacket; coat	jaqueta; americana	*chaqueta; americana*
January	gener	*enero*
Japanese yen(s)	ien japonès; iens japonesos	*yen japonés; yenes japoneses*
javelin throwing	llançament de javelina	*lanzamiento de jabalina*
jazmin	gessamí; llessamí	*jazmín*
jeans	pantalons vaquers/ texans	*pantalón (pantalones) vaquero(s)/tejanos*
jewel	joia	*joya*
jeweller	joier, -a	*joyero, -a*
jeweller's	joieria	*joyería*
journalist	periodista	*periodista*
judo	judo	*judo*
July	juliol	*julio*
jump competition	prova de salt	*prueba de salto*
June	juny	*junio*
jury; panel of judges	jurat	*jurado*
ketsup	catsup	*catsup*
key	clau f	*llave f*
key duplication	duplicat de claus	*duplicado de llaves*
kid [animal]	cabrit	*cabrito*
kidney	càlcul(s) renal(s)	*cálculo(s) renal(es)*
kidney/s	ronyó; ronyons	*riñón; riñones*
kidney bean	mongeta	*judía*
kitchen	cuina	*cocina*
kitchen utensils	bateria/estris de cuina	*batería de cocina*
knapsack	motxilla	*mochila*
knee	genoll	*rodilla*
knife	ganivet	*cuchillo*
knock; ping [v.]	picar	*golpear; picar*
knock-out; K.O.	fora de combat;-	*fuera de combate;*
K.O.	knock-out, K.O.	*knockout; K.O.*
label	etiqueta	*etiqueta*
laboratory	laboratori	*laboratorio*

lady; Mrs.	senyora	*señora*
lamb	anyell; bé	*cordero*
lamp	llum	*lámpara*
land [v.] [aviat.]	aterrar	*aterrizar*
landing [aviat.]	aterratge	*aterrizaje*
landing strip	pista d'aterratge	*pista de aterrrizaje*
lane [highway]	via	*carril*
language	idioma m; llengua	*idioma m; lengua*
(language) course	curs (de llengua)	*curso (de lengua)*
language manual	manual (de llengua)	*manual (de lengua)*
lard	llard; sagí	*manteca; grasa*
large	gran	*grande*
large prawn	llagostí	*langostino*
last name(s)	cognom(s)	*apellido(s)*
last week	la setmana passada	*la semana pasada*
last year	l'any passat	*el año pasado*
late	tard	*tarde*
late night session	sessió f de matinada	*sesión f de madrugada*
lately	darrerament; últimament	*últimamente*
later (on)	després; més tard	*después; más tarde*
laundry; laundromat	bugaderia	*lavandería*
lavatory	wàter	*water*
lawyer	advocat, -essa/-ada	*abogado, -a*
laxative	laxant	*laxante*
lazy	peresós, -osa	*perezoso, -a*
league; table	classificació f	*clasificación f*
learn [v.]	aprendre	*aprender*
leather cleaning and dying	neteja i tint de la pell	*limpieza y tinte de cuero*
leather; skin	pell f	*piel f*
left, on/to the	a l'esquerra	*a la izquierda*
leg(s)	cama; cames	*pierna(s)*
lemon	llimona	*limón*
lemon juice	suc de llimona	*zumo de limón*
lemonade	llimonada	*limonada*
lens	objectiu	*objetivo*
lentil	llentia	*lenteja*
lentil stew	cassola de llenties	*cazuela de lentejas*
less	menys	*menos*

letter	carta	*carta*
letter, to write/send a	escriure/enviar una carta	*escribir/enviar una carta*
lettuce	enciam; lletuga	*lechuga*
level/railroad crossing	pas a nivell	*paso a nivel*
level of education	nivell d'instrucció	*nivel de instrucción*
librarian	bibliotecari, -ària	*bibliotecario, -a*
library	biblioteca	*biblioteca*
license/number plate	matrícula	*matrícula*
life	vida	*vida*
life buoy; life belt	salvavides	*salvavidas*
lifeboat	bot salvavides	*bote salvavidas*
light [adj.]	lleuger, -a	*ligero, -a*
light bulb	bombeta	*bombilla*
lighter	encenedor	*encendedor; mechero*
lighter flint	pedres per a l'encenedor	*piedras para mechero*
lights; headlights	els llums; enllumenat	*las luces; alumbrado*
like this	així	*así*
limbs	extremitats f pl; membres m pl	*extremidades f pl; miembros m pl*
line	línia	*línea*
line; queue	caravana; cua	*caravana*
linen	lli; fil; bri	*lino; hilo*
lip(s)	llavi(s)	*labio(s)*
lipstick	llapis de llavis	*lápiz de labios*
liqueur	licor	*licor*
literature	literatura	*literatura*
live [v.]	viure	*vivir*
(live) oysters	ostres (vives)	*ostras (vivas)*
liver	fetge	*hígado*
loan	préstec	*préstamo*
loan; lend [v.]	prestar	*prestar; dar prestado*
lobster	llagosta	*langosta*
locksmith	manyà	*cerrajero*
locomotive; engine	locomotora; màquina	*locomotora; máquina*
lodge/stay (in) [v.]	allotjar-se	*alojarse*
lodgings; accommodation	allotjament	*alojamiento*

loin	llom	*lomo*
long	llarg, -a	*largo, -a*
long distance call	telefonada interurbana	*conferencia interurbana*
long distance train	tren de llarg trajecte; tren interurbà	*tren de largo recorrido; tren interurbano*
long horse vault	salt de cavall	*salto de caballo*
long jump	salt de llargada	*salto de longitud*
long pork sausage	fuet	*longaniza*
lose; be beaten [v.]	perdre; ser vençut	*perder; ser vencido*
loser	perdedor, -a	*perdedor, -a*
lost and found; lost objects office	objectes perduts; oficina d'objectes perduts	*objetos perdidos; oficina de objetos perdidos*
loudly	en veu alta	*en voz alta; alto*
loudspeaker; speaker	altaveu	*altavoz*
lounge	saló	*salón*
low	baix, -a	*bajo, -a*
lubrication; oiling	greixatge	*engrase*
luge	luge	*luge*
luggage	equipatge	*equipaje*
luggage registration	facturació d'equipatges	*factoración de equipajes*
(luggage) trolley	carret (per a l'equipatge)	*carrito (para el equipaje)*
lunch	dinar	*comida; almuerzo*
lunch, to have	dinar	*almorzar; comer*
lung/s	pulmó; pulmons	*pulmón; pulmones*
lustrum	lustre	*lustro*
macaroni	macarrons	*macarrones*
mackintosh; raincoat	gavardina	*gabardina*
magnificent	magnífic, -a	*magnífico, -a*
mail; post; letters	correspondència	*correspondencia*
mailbox; letter box	bústia	*buzón*
mailman; postman	carter	*cartero*
main course	plat fort	*plato fuerte*
main character	protagonista	*protagonista*
make-up	maquillatge	*maquillaje*
male nurse	infermer	*enfermero*
man	home	*hombre*
man; Mr.; sir	senyor	*señor*

manager	director, -a; gerent	*director, -a; gerente*
mandarine	mandarina	*mandarina*
manicure	manicura	*manicura*
map	mapa m; plànol	*mapa m; plano*
marathon	marató	*maratón f*
March	març	*marzo*
margarine	margarina	*margarina*
marital status	estat civil	*estado civil*
market	mercat	*mercado*
market place	plaça	*plaza*
marmelade	melmelada	*mermelada*
marriage; married couple	matrimoni	*matrimonio*
married	casat, -ada	*casado, -a*
marry [v.]	casar-se	*casarse*
marrow	carbassó	*calabacín*
marzipan	massapà	*mazapán*
masculine; men's	masculí, -ina; d'homes	*masculino, -ina; de hombres*
mashed potatoes	puré de patates	*puré de patatas*
masseur; masseuse	massatgista	*masajista*
mat [straw]	estora	*estera*
match; meeting	partit	*encuentro*
matches	mistos; llumins	*cerrillas*
matress	matalàs	*colchón*
maximum (temperature)	(temperatura) màxima	*(temperatura) máxima*
May	maig	*mayo*
mayonnaise	maionesa; salsa maionesa	*mayonesa; salsa mayonesa*
meanwhile	mentrestant	*mientras tanto*
measles	xarampió	*sarampión*
meat	carn f	*carne f*
meat rolls	rotllos de carn	*rollos de carne*
meat stew	estofat	*estofado*
meatball soup	sopa de mandonguilles	*sopa de albóndigas*
meatballs	mandonguilles	*albóndigas*
mechanic; car mechanic	mecànic; mecànic d'automòbils	*mecánico; mecánico de automóviles*
medical consulting room	consultori (mèdic)	*consultorio (médico)*
medicine; remedy	medicament; remei	*medicamento; remedio*
medley race	estils; quatre estils	*estilos; cuatro estilos*
medley relay	relleus d'estils	*relevos de estilos*

melon	meló	*melón*
menstruation; period	regla; menstruació f	*regla, menstruación f*
merchant; shopkeeper	comerciant, -a	*comerciant*
message	encàrrec; missatge	*recado; mensaje*
metal	metall	*metal*
microwave oven	forn microones	*horno microondas*
midnight	mitjanit f	*medianoche f*
migraine	migranya	*jaqueca*
mild	suau	*suave*
milk	llet f	*leche f*
milk shake	batut	*batido*
millennium	mil·lenni	*milenio*
mineral water	aigua mineral	*agua mineral*
minibus	microbús	*microbús*
minimum (temperature)	(temperatura) mínima	*(temperatura) mínima*
minute	minut	*minuto*
mirror	mirall	*espejo*
miss [v.] the train	perdre el tren	*perder el train*
mixed doubles	dobles mixtos; parelles mixtos	*dobles mixtos*
mixed salad	amanida mixta	*ensalada mixta*
mixed vegetables	minestra de verdures	*menestra de verdures*
modality; sport	esport; modalitat f	*deporte; modalidad f*
model	maniquí; model	*maniquí; modelo*
moderate	moderat	*moderado*
modest	modest, -a	*modesto, -a*
moisturizing cream	llet hidratant	*leche hidratante*
molar	queixal	*muela*
mommy; mum	mama	*mamá*
Monday	dilluns	*lunes*
money	diner	*dinero*
money order	gir postal	*giro postal*
monkey wrench	clau anglesa	*llave inglesa*
month	mes	*mes*
monthly	mensualment	*mensualmente*
monthly-ticket	abonament mensual	*abono mensual*
monument	monument	*monumento*
more	més	*más*
morning	matí	*mañana*
morning, in the	al matí	*por la mañana*
morning, this	aquest matí	*esta mañana*

morning session	matinal f	*matinal f*
mother	mare f	*madre f*
mother-in-law	sogra	*suegra*
moto-cross	motocross	*motocross*
motorboat	motora	*motora*
motorcycle	motocicleta; moto f	*motocicleta; moto f*
motorcycling	motorisme;motociclisme	*motorismo;motociclismo*
motorcyclist; driver	motorista; conductor, -a	*motorista; conductor, -a*
motoring; driving	automobilisme	*automovilismo*
motorist; driver	automobilista; conductor	*automovilista; conductor*
mountaineering	muntanyisme; alpinisme	*montañismo; alpinismo*
moustache	bigoti(s)	*bigote(s)*
mouth	boca	*boca*
movie; film	pel·lícula; film	*película; filme*
movie camara	cambra/màquina de filmar	*cámera/máquina de filmadora*
movie theater; cinema	cinema m; cine; sala	*cinema m; cine; sala*
moving target shooting	blanc mòbil; tir al senglar	*blanco móvil; tiro al jabalí*
much	molt, -a	*mucho, -a*
mudguard; fender	parafang	*guardabarros*
muffler; scarf	bufanda	*bufanda*
mumps	galterres	*paperas*
museum	museu	*museo*
mushroom	bolet; xampinyó	*seta; champiñón*
music	música	*música*
music-hall	music-hall; teatre de revista	*music-hall; teatro de revista*
musical instruments	instruments musicals	*instrumentos musicales*
musician	músic, -a	*músico, -a*
mustard	mostassa	*mostaza*
mutton	moltó; xai	*carnero*
name	nom	*nombre*
named/called, to be	dir-se	*llamarse*
napkin	tovalló	*servilleta*
narrow	estret, -a	*estrecho, -a*
national record	rècord nacional	*récord nacional*
nationality	nacionalitat f	*nacionalidad f*
natural	al natural	*al natural*
nausea; dizziness	mareig	*mareo*
neck	coll	*cuello*

necklace	collaret	*collar*
needle	agulla	*aguja*
negative	negatiu	*negativa*
neighborhood	barri	*barrio*
neither	ni; tampoc	*ni; tampoco*
nephew	nebot	*sobrino*
nephritis	nefritis f	*nefritis f*
nervous	nerviós, -osa	*nervioso, -a*
never	mai	*nunca; jamás*
new	nou, -ova	*nuevo, -a*
news-stand	quiosc	*quiosco*
newspaper seller	venedor de periòdics; quiosquer, -a	*vendedor de periódios; quiosquero, -a*
newsreel	noticia	*noticiario*
next week	la setmana que ve	*la semana que viene*
next year	a l'any que ve	*el año que viene*
nice	simpàtic, -a	*simpático, -a*
niece	neboda	*sobrina*
night	nit f	*noche f*
night, by/at	al vespre; a la nit	*por la noche*
night club; bar	night club; club nocturn; bar	*night club; club; bar*
night (bus) line	línia nocturna	*línea nocturna*
night rate	tarifa nocturna	*tarifa nocturna*
night table	tauleta de nit	*mesita de noche*
nightgown	camisa de dormir	*camisa de dormir; camisón*
nominal	nominatiu, -iva	*nominativo, -a*
non-alcoholic beverage	beguda sense alcohol	*bebida sin alcohol*
non-smoker's compartment	compartiment/vagó per a no fumadors	*departamento/coche para no fumadores*
noon	migdia m	*mediodía m*
north	nord	*norte*
nose	nas	*nariz f*
nose drops	gotes per al nas	*gotas para la nariz*
not much; little	poc, -a	*poco, -a*
not yet	encara no	*todavía no*
notary	notari	*notario*
notebook	quadern; llibreta	*cuaderno; libreta*
nothing	res	*nada*

novel	novel·la	*novela*
November	novembre	*noviembre*
now	ara	*ahora*
nowhere	enlloc	*en ninguna parte*
number	número	*número*
numbered ticket	entrada numerada	*entrada numerada*
nurse	infermera	*enfermera*
nursery school	parvulari	*parvulario*
nut [tech.]	femella	*tuerca*
occupation; job	ofici	*oficio*
October	octubre	*octubre*
octopus	pop	*pulpo*
octopus in its own ink	pops amb la tinta	*pulpos en su tinta*
of	de	*de*
official opening	inauguració oficial	*inauguración oficial*
often	sovint	*a menudo*
oil	oli	*aceite*
oil bottle	setrill	*aceitera*
oil change	canvi d'oli	*cambio de aceite*
oil filter	filtre de l'oli	*filtro de aceite*
ointment	pomada; ungüent	*pomada; ungüento*
old	vell, -a	*viejo, -a*
old person	vell, -a	*viejo, -a*
older brother	germà gran	*hermano mayor*
older sister	germana gran	*hermana mayor*
olive	oliva	*aceituna*
olive oil	oli d'oliva	*aceite de oliva*
Olympic champion	campió, -ona olímpic, -a	*campeón, -ona olímpico, -a*
Olympic Games	Jocs Olímpics (JJOO)	*Juegos Olímpicos (JJOO)*
Olympic record	rècord olímpic	*récord olímpico*
Olympic Village	vila olímpica	*villa olímpica*
Olympics	Olimpíada	*Olimpiada*
on	en	*en*
once	una vegada; un cop	*una vez*
once again	una altra vegada	*otra vez más*
once in a while	de tant en tant	*de vez en cuando*
one hundred percent cotton	cotó cent per cent	*algodón ciento por ciento*
one way street	carrer de sentit únic	*calle de dirección única*

onion	ceba	*cebolla*
open-air theater	teatre a l'aire lliure	*teatro al aire libre*
opener; bottle opener	obridor; obreampolles; descapsulador	*abridor; abrebotellas; descapsulador*
opera (theater)	(teatre de l') òpera; Liceu (Barcelona)	*(teatro de la) ópera*
opera	òpera	*ópera*
operate (on) [v.]	operar; sometre a una operació	*operar; someter a una operación*
operation	operació f	*operación f*
opportunely	oportunament	*oportunamente*
optician (shop)	òptic; òptica	*óptico; óptica*
or	o	*o*
orange [adj.]	ataronjat, -ada	*(a)naranjado, -a*
orange	taronja	*naranja*
orange juice	suc de taronja	*zumo de naranja*
orangeade	taronjada	*naranjada*
orchestra	orquestra	*orquesta*
orchestra conductor	director d'orquestra	*director de orquesta*
orchestra pit; stalls	platea; pati de butaques	*platea; patio de butacas*
orchid	orquídia	*orquidea*
organizer	organitzador, -a	*organizador, -a*
orgeat	orxata d'ametlles	*horchata de almendras*
original version	versió f original; V.O.	*versión f original; V.O.*
other sports	altres esports	*otros deportes*
outward journey; one-way	anada	*ida*
overcast	tapat	*cubierto*
overcoat; coat	abric	*abrigo*
overhaul; checking	reglatge	*puesta a punto; reglaje*
overpass	pas superior	*paso superior*
overtake [v.] [a car]	avançar	*adelantar*
overturn [v.]	bolcar	*volcar(se)*
ox	bou	*buey*
oyster	ostra	*ostra*
pack; knapsack	motxilla	*mochila*
paddle boat	patí (de pedals)	*patín (de pedales)*
"paella" (rice dish)	paella; arròs a la cassola	*paella*
pain; ache	dolor m/f	*dolor*

paint	pintura	*pintura*
painter	pintor	*pintor*
pairs with coxswain	dos (remers) amb timoner	*dos (remeros) con timonel*
pajamas	pijama m	*pijama m*
palace	palau	*palacio*
palm (of the hand)	palmell	*palma (de la mano)*
pan	paella	*sartén*
panties; knickers	calces; bragues f pl	*bragas f pl*
pants; trousers	pantalons m pl	*pantalón; pantalones m pl*
paper	paper	*papel*
paprika	pebre vermell	*pimentón*
parachuting	paracaigudisme	*paracaidismo*
parade	desfilada	*desfile*
parallel bars	paral·leles; barres paral·leles	*paralelas; barras paralelas*
parasol; sunshade	para-sol	*parasol; sombrilla*
parcel; box	paquet; capsa	*paquete; bulto; caja*
parcels	paquets	*paquetes*
parents	pares	*padres*
parents-in-law	sogre(s)	*suegros*
park	jardí (públic); parc	*jardín (público); parque*
park [v.]	aparcar	*aparcar*
parking lot	aparcament; pàrking	*aparcamiento; parking*
parliament	parlament	*parlamento*
parsley	julivert	*perejil*
part; parting [hair]	ratlla	*raya*
passage; ticket	passatge	*pasaje*
passenger	passatger	*pasajero*
passport	passaport	*pasaporte*
passport control	control de passaports	*control de pasaportes*
passport number (no.)	número (núm.) de passaport	*número (no.) de pasaporte*
pastas	pastes	*pastas*
pastas and rices	pastes i arrossos	*pastas y arroces*
pastries and cakes	pastes i pastissos	*pastas y pasteles*
pastry	pasta	*pasta*
pastry shop	pastisseria	*pastelería*
patés	patés	*patés*

pavilion	pavelló	*pabellón*
pay [v.]	pagar	*pagar*
pay [v.] in cash	pagar en efectiu	*pagar en efectivo*
pay [v.] in instalments	a terminis	*a plazos*
pea	pèsol	*guisante*
peach	préssec	*melocotón; (albérchigo)*
pear	pera	*pera*
pebble; stone	còdol	*guijarro*
pedal	pedal	*pedal*
pedestrian	vianant	*peatón*
pedestrian crossing	pas de vianants	*paso de cebra*
pedicure	pedicura	*pedicura*
pelota	pilota (basca)	*pelota (vasca)*
pen	bolígraf	*bolígrafo*
pencil	llapis	*lápiz*
pencil lead	mina; recanvi	*mina; repuesto*
pendant	penjoll	*colgante*
pensioner; retired person	jubilat, -ada; pensionat, -ada; pensionista	*jubilado, -a; pensionado,*
pentathlon	pentatló modern	*pentatlón moderna*
pepper	pebre	*pimienta*
perfume	perfum	*perfume*
perfumery	perfumeria	*perfumería*
permanent	permanent f	*permanente f*
personal details	dades personals	*señas personales*
pharmacist; chemist	farmacèutic, -a;	*farmacéutico, -a*
pharmacy; drugstore	farmàcia f	*faramcia*
(phone) call	trucada; telefonada	*llamada (telefónica)*
photo, to take a	fer/tirar una foto	*sacar una foto*
photocopies	fotocòpies; copisteria	*fotocopias; copistería*
photograph; photo	fotografia; foto f	*fotografía; foto f*
photograph [v.]	fotografiar	*fotografiar*
photograph album	àlbum de fotografies	*álbum de fotografías*
	fotògraf, -a	*fotógrafo, -a*
photographic paper	paper fotogràfic	*papel fotográfico*
pick up [v.] [telephone]	descolgar	*descolgar*
pickled	en escabetx	*en escabeche*
pig; pork	porc	*cerdo*
pill; tablet	pastilla; comprimit	*pastilla; comprimido*
pillow	coixí	*almohada*
pin (sewing)	agulla de cap	*alfiler*

pineapple (tropical/ American)	pinya (tropical/ americana)	*piña (tropical/ americana)*
pink	rosat, -ada	*rosado, -a*
pipe tabacco	tabac de pipa	*tabaco de pipa*
pistol; gun	pistola	*pistola*
pitch [v.] the tent	parar la tenda	*armar la tienda*
pizza	pizza	*pizza*
pizzeria	pizzeria	*pizzería*
place of birth	lloc de naixement	*lugar de nacimiento*
(plastic) bag	bossa (de plàstic)	*bolsa (de plástico)*
plate	plat	*plato*
platform [station]	andana	*andén*
play [v.] [game, sport]	jugar	*jugar*
play [v.] a (musical) instrument	tocar un instrument (musical)	*tocar un instrumento (musical)*
play (theatre)	peça (teatral)	*pieza (teatral); obra*
player	jugador, -a	*jugador, -a*
pliers	alicates f pl	*alicates m pl; tenazas*
plug	endoll	*enchufe*
plumber	fontaner	*fontanero*
pneumonia	pulmonia	*pulmonía*
pocket	butxaca	*bosillo*
pocket dictionary	diccionari de butxaca	*diccionario de bolsillo*
poet	poeta, poetessa	*poeta, poetisa*
poetry	poesia	*poesía*
point	punt	*punto*
poison	metzina; verí	*veneno*
pole vault	salt amb perxa	*salto de pertiga*
policeman	policia; guàrdia	*policía; guardia*
polite	cortès, -esa	*cortés; educado, a-*
polo	polo	*polo*
polyclinic; dispensary	policlínica; dispensari	*policlínica; dispensario*
pomegranate	magrana	*granada*
pool; billiards	billar	*billar*
poor	pobre, -a	*pobre*
porcelain/china shop	botiga de porcellana	*tienda de porcelana*
pork loin	llom de porc	*lomo de cerdo*
pork rib/chop	costella de porc	*costilla de cerdo*
"porrón" glass wine jar	porró	*porrón*

port; harbor	port	*puerto*
porter	mosso (d'equipatge)	*mozo (de equipaje)*
post	càrrec	*cargo*
post/mail [v.] a letter	tirar una carta	*echar/tirar una carta*
post office	correus	*correo*
post-office box	apartat de correus	*apartado de correos*
postage	franqueig	*franqueo*
postcard	targeta postal; postal f	*tarjeta postal; postal f*
postmark	matasegells	*matasellos*
pot	olla	*olla*
potato	patata	*patata*
potato chips/crisps	patates fregides	*patatas fritas*
potato/Russian salad	ensalada russa	*ensalada rusa*
potatoes	patates	*patatas*
poultry shop	polleria	*pollería; aves*
prawn	gamba	*gamba*
precious stone	pedra preciosa	*piedra preciosa*
preference	preferència	*preferencia*
pregnant, to be	estar prenyada	*estar embarazada*
preliminary/ qualifying round	eliminatòria; elimina-tòries	*eliminatoria; elimina-torias*
prawn cocktail	còctel de gambes	*cóctel de gambas*
prepare oneself [v.]	preparar-se	*prepararse*
prescription	recepta	*receta*
present world record holder	l'actual detentor del rècord mundial	*el actual plusmarquista mundial*
presently	actualment	*actualmente*
president	president, -a	*presidente, -a*
pressure, to have low/ high	tenir la pressió baixa/ alta	*tener la presión baja/ alta*
pressure, to take one's	prendre(-li) la pressió	*tomar(le) la presión*
pretty	bonic, -a	*hermoso, -a*
price	preu	*precio*
price list	llista de preus	*lista de precios*
printer	impressora	*impresora*
printing (house)	imprempta (ràpida)	*imprenta (rápida)*
private car	automòbil; turisme	*automóvil; turismo*
private room	habitació privada	*habitación privada*
profession	professió f	*profesión*

professor; teacher	professor, -a	*profesor, -a*
program	programa m	*programa m*
pronounce [v.]	pronunciar	*pronunciar*
pronunciation	pronúncia	*pronunciación f*
prophylactic; condom	preservatiu	*preservativo*
prosthesis	pròtesi f	*prótesis f*
prow; bow [mar.]	proa	*proa*
prune	pruna	*ciruela*
pub; tavern; bar	taverna	*tasca; taberna; bar*
public house; bar	cerveseria	*cervecería*
public telephone	telèfon públic	*teléfono público*
public transport	transport públic	*transporte público*
pudding	púding	*puding; pudín; budín*
pullover; sweater	pul·lòver; jersei	*pull-over; jersey*
pulse, to take one's	prendre(-li)/veure(-li) el pols	*tomar(le)/ver(le) el pulso*
pump	bomba d'aire; bomba d'inflar	*bomba de aire; bomba de hinchar*
punctual; on time	puntual	*puntual*
pupil; student	escolar; estudiant	*escolar; estudiante, -a*
purchase; buy	compra	*compra*
purchases; shopping	compres	*compras*
pure virgin wool	pura llana verge	*pura lana virgen*
pursuit race; time trial (cycling)	cursa de persecució; persecució/cursa contra rellotge	*carrera de persecución; persecución/carrera contra reloj*
quail	guatlla	*cordoniz*
qualify [v.] (for the finals)	classificar-se (per a finals)	*clasificarse (para las finales)*
quarter of an hour	quart d'hora	*cuarto de hora*
quartz watch	rellotge de quars	*reloj de cuarzo*
quickly	ràpidament; de pressa	*rápido; rápidamente*
quietly	en veu baixa	*en voz baja; bajo*
quill; pen	ploma	*pluma*
rabbit	conill	*conejo*
radiator	radiador	*radiador*
radio	ràdio f	*radio f*
radish	rave	*rábano*
ragout	ragout	*ragout*
railroad; railway	ferrocarril	*ferrocarril*
railway line/track	via	*vía*

rain	pluja	*lluvia*
rainy	plujós	*lluvioso*
raisin	pansa	*pasa; uva pasa*
rapid-fire gun	pistola de tir ràpid	*pistola de tiro rápido*
rasberry	gerd; gerdó	*frambuesa*
raw vegetable salad	crudités	*crudités*
read [v.]	llegir	*leer*
reading room	sala de lectura	*sala de lectura*
rearview mirror	(mirall) retrovisor	*(espejo) retrovisor*
receipt; voucher	comprovant	*comprobante*
reception (desk)	recepció f	*recepción f*
reception hall	sala de festes	*sala de fiestas*
reception notice	avís de recepció	*aviso de recibo*
receive [v.]	rebre	*recibir*
record (police)	fitxa (de policia)	*ficha (de policía)*
record (music)	disc	*disco*
record (sport)	rècord	*récord; marca; plusmarca*
record card	fitxa	*ficha*
record store; records and cassettes	botiga de discos; discos i cassettes	*tienda de discos; discos y casetes*
recreational parlour	sala de jocs; saló recreatiu	*sala de juegos; salón recreativo*
red	vermell, -a; roig, -oja	*rojo, -a*
Red Cross	Creu Roja	*Cruz Roja*
red wine	vi negre	*vino tinto*
reduction	reducció f	*reducción f*
refrigerator; ice-box	frigorífic; nevera	*frigorífico; nevera*
refuge	refugi	*refugio*
registered	certificat	*certificado*
registered letter	carta certificada	*carta certificada*
registered mailform	imprès per a correu certificat	*impreso para correo certificado*
registered special	urgent certificat	*urgente certificado*
registration; enrolment	matrícula	*matrícula*
rehearsal	assaig	*ensayo*
relative(s)	familiar(s)	*familiar(es)*
relay	relleus	*relevos*
relay race	cursa de relleus	*carrera de relevos*
remit [v.]	remetre	*remitir*
remove; pull out [v.]	treure; arrencar	*sacar; arrancar; extraer*

rent; hiring	lloguer	*alquiler*
rent; hire out [v.]	llogar	*alquilar*
repair [v.]	reparar	*reparar*
repair shop	reparacions; taller de reparacions	*reparaciones; taller de reparaciones*
re-run (of film)	restrena	*reestreno*
residence	residència; domicili	*residencia; domicilio*
restaurant	restaurant	*restaurante*
restaurant car	vagó-restaurant	*coche restaurante*
return journey	tornada	*vuelta*
reverse (gear)	marxa enrere	*marcha atrás*
rheumatism	reumatisme; reuma m	*reumatismo; reuma/ reúma m*
rhythmic gymnastics	gimnàstica rítmica	*gimnasia rítmica*
rice	arròs	*arroz*
rice pudding	arròs amb llet	*arroz con leche*
rich	ric, -a	*rico, -a*
right, on/to the	a la dreta	*a la derecha*
ring	anell	*anillo*
ring road	ronda	*ronda*
road	carretera	*carretera*
road races	proves/curses de ruta	*pruebas/carreras de ruta*
roadway	calçada	*calzada*
roast meat	rostit	*rostido*
roastbeef	rosbif	*rosbif*
roasted	rostit, -ida	*asado, -a*
rock	roca	*roca*
rod-fishing	pescar amb canya	*pescar con caña*
role	paper	*papel*
roll	rodet	*rollo*
roll of film	rodet de pel·lícula	*rollo de película*
roller hockey	hoquei sobre patins	*hockey sobre patines*
roof; luggage rack	baca	*baca*
room	habitació	*habitación*
rose	rosa	*rosa*
rosé wine	vi rosat	*vino rosado*
round [adj.]	rodó, -ona	*redondo, -a*
row	fila	*fila*
rowing	rem	*remo*
rug	catifa	*alfombra*

rugby	rugby	*rugby*
ruler	regle	*regla*
rum	rom	*ron*
run over [v.]	atropellar	*atropellar*
running over [by a car]	atropellament	*atropello*
running water	aigua corrent	*agua corriente*
runway	pista	*pista*
rush hour	hores f pl punta	*horas f pl punta*
sabre fencing	esgrima de sabre	*esgrima de sable*
sąd	trist, -a	*triste*
safety belt	cinturó de seguretat	*cinturón de seguridad*
sailboat	barca de vela	*barca de vela*
sailing	vela; esport de vela	*vela; deporte de vela*
sailor	mariner	*marinero*
saint's day	onomàstic; el sant	*onomástico; el santo*
salad	amanida	*ensalada*
salami-type sausage	llonganissa	*longaniza; salchichón*
sales	saldos	*saldos*
sale; reduction	rebaixa	*rebaja*
sale; sales	venda	*vent*
salesman	depenent; venedor	*dependiente; vendedor*
saleswoman	depenenta; venedora	*dependienta; vendedora*
salmon	salmó	*salmón*
salt	sal	*sal f*
salt, to add	posar-hi sal	*ponerle sal*
salt shaker	saler	*salero*
salt water fish	peixos de mar	*peces de mar*
salted	saltat, -ada	*salteado, -a*
salty	salat, -ada	*salado, -a*
sanatorium	sanatori	*sanatorio*
sand	sorra	*arena*
sandals	sandàlies	*sandalias*
sandwich	entrepà m	*bocadillo*
Saturday	dissabte	*sábado*
sausage	salsitxa; xoriç; xoriço	*salchicha; chorizo*
savings bank	caixa d'estalvis	*caja de ahorros*
say [v.]	dir	*decir*
scales; balance	balança; balances	*balanza; balances*
scarlet fever	escarlatina	*escarlatina*
scheduled flight	vol regular	*vuelo regular*

school; high school	escola; col·legi	*escuela; colegio*
school, to go to	anar a l'escola	*ir a la escuela*
(school) teacher	mestre (d'escola)	*maestro, -a (de escuela)*
scissors	tisores f pl	*tijeras f pl*
scooter	scooter	*escúter*
score; result	resultat	*resultado*
scoreboard	marcador	*marcador; tanteador*
scoring races	cursa de puntuació	*carrera de puntuación*
scrambled eggs	ous remenats	*huevos revueltos*
screw [tech.]	cargol	*tornillo*
screwdriver	tornavís	*destornillador*
seafood	marisc	*marisco*
seafood salad/cocktail	amanida/còctel de marisc	*ensalada/cóctel de marisco*
seafood soup	sopa de marisc	*sopa de marisco*
seal [v.] [with wax]	acrar; enlacrar	*lacrar*
seasickness	mareig; mal de mar	*mareo*
season	estació f	*estación f*
season; spice [v.]	condimentar	*condimentar*
season-ticket	abonament temporal;	*abono temporal; pase*
seat	passi seient; plaça	*asiento; plaza*
seat reservation	reserva de plaça	*reserva de plaza*
second	segon	*segundo*
second class car	vagó de segona (classe)	*coche de segunda (clase)*
secretary	secretari, -ària	*secretario, -a*
security control	control de seguretat	*control de seguridad*
sedative	calmant; antineuràlgic	*calmante; antineurálgico*
selection	selecció f	*selección f*
self-service store	autoservei	*autoservicio*
sell [v.]	vendre	*vender*
semester	semestre	*semestre*
semi-direct train	(tren) semidirecte	*(tren) semidirecto*
semolina	sèmola	*sémola*
send; mail [v.]	enviar; remetre;	*enviar; remitir/*
send [v.] by ordinary post	trametre / enviar per correu ordinari	*enviar por correo ordinario*
sender	remitent; remet	*remitente; remite*
separated	separat, -ada	*separado, -a*
September	setembre	*septiembre*
serious; grave	greu	*grave*

service charge included	servei inclòs	*servicio incluido*
service station	estació de servei	*estación de servicio*
session; showing	sessió f	*sesión f*
set [v.] (a record)	establir (un rècord)	*establecer (un récord)*
set [v.] [hair]	marcar	*marcar*
sew [v.]	cosir	*coser*
sewing machine	màquina de cosir	*máquina de coser*
shade	ombra	*sombra*
shake; jerk [v.] [auto.]	sotraguejar; fer sotragades	*dar sacudidas*
shampoo	xampú	*champú*
shave [v.]	afaitar	*afeitar*
shaving cream	crema/escuma d'afaitar	*crema/espuma de afeitar*
shaving lotion	loció per l'afaitat	*loción (para el afeitado)*
sheep	ovella; xai	*oveja*
sheet	llençol	*sábana*
ship; boat	vaixell	*barco*
shipment; parcel	tramesa	*envío*
shirt; men's shirt	camisa; camisa d'home	*camisa; camisa de hombre*
shock absorber	amortidor	*amortiguador*
shoe brush	raspall per a les sabates	*cepillo de/para los zapatos*
shoehorn	calçador	*calzador*
shoe laces	cordons	*cordones*
shoe polish	betum; crema	*betún; crema*
shoe store	sabateria	*zapatería*
shoes; footwear	sabates; calçat	*zapatos; calzado*
shoes, a pair of	un parell de sabates	*un par de zapatos*
shooting	tir (esportiu); tir olímpic	*tiro (deportivo); tiro olímpico*
shopping mal	centre comercial	*centro comercial*
shopping, to go	fer les compres; anar a comprar	*hacer las compras; ir de compras*
shore; bank	vora	*orilla*
short film	curt-metratge	*cortometraje*
short [person]	baix, -a	*bajo, -a*
short [thing]	curt, -a	*corto, -a*
shortly; soon	d'aquí a poc temps	*dentro de poco*

shot put	llançament de pes	*lanzamiento de peso*
shoulder	espatlla	*hombro*
shoulder [meat]	espatlla	*paletilla*
show; performance	funció f; espectacle; representació f	*función f; espectáculo; representación f*
shower	dutxa	*ducha*
shower [v.]; to take a shower	dutxar-se; prendre una dutxa	*ducharse*
shrimp	gambeta	*camarón*
shy	tímid, -a	*tímido, -a*
sick; to be sick	malalt, -a; estar malalt, -a	*enfermo, -a; estar enfermo, -a*
sick person; patient	malalt, -a; pacient	*enfermo, -a; pacient*
sickness; nausea	mareig	*mareo*
side dish; entrée	entremès; entrant	*entremés; entrante*
side horse	cavall amb arcs	*caballo con arcos*
sidewalk; pavement	vorera	*acera*
sign; notice	rètol	*letrero; rótulo*
sign [v.]	firmar; signar	*firmar*
signature	firma; signatura	*firma; signatura*
silk	seda	*seda*
silver	argent; plata	*plata*
silver medal	medalla d'argent	*medalla de plata*
silver-plated	argentat, -ada	*plateado, -a*
simple	senzill, -a	*sencillo, -a*
sincerely	sincerament	*sinceramente*
singer	cantant	*cantante*
single	solter, -a	*soltero, -a*
single room	habitació individual	*habitación sencilla*
single-seater	monoplaça	*monoplaza*
single woman	soltera	*soltera*
sister	germana	*hermana*
sister-in-law	cunyada	*cuñada*
skeet-shooting	skeet	*skeet*
skid; slip [v.]	patinar; relliscar	*patinar; resbalar*
skiff	esquif	*esquife*
skiing	esquí	*esquí*
skilled worker	obrer especialitzat	*obrero especializado*
skin	pell f	*piel f*
skin diving	natació subaquàtica	*buceo (deportivo); natación subacuática*

skirt	faldilla	*falda*
sky	cel	*cielo*
slalom	eslalom	*eslalon; slalom*
sleeping bag	sac de dormir	*saco de dormir*
sleeping car	vagó-llit	*coche cama*
sleeping pill	somnífer	*somnífero*
slender	prim, -a	*delgado, -a; fino, -a*
slide [photo.]	diapositiva	*diapositiva*
slim; slender	esvelt, -a	*esbelto, -a*
slippers	sabatilles	*zapatillas; chinelas;*
slope; gradient	pendent m	*pendiente f*
slow	lent, -a	*lento, -a*
slow, to be [a watch]	anar retardat/endarrerit	*ir atrasado*
slow/stopping train	(tren) òmnibus	*(tren) ómnibus*
slow down	reduir la velocitat	*reducir la velocidad*
slowly	a poc a poc	*despacio*
small; small child	petit, -a	*pequeño, -a*
small bill(s)/note(s)	bitllet(s) petit(s)	*billete(s) pequeño(s)*
small package	petit paquet	*pequeño paquete*
smoke [v.]	fumar	*fumar*
smoke [v.] a cigarette	fumar una cigarreta	*fumar un cigarrillo*
smoke a pipe	fumar pipa	*fumar pipa*
smoked	fumat, -ada	*ahumado, -a*
smoker's compartment	compartiment/vagó per a fumadors	*departamento/coche para fumadores*
smoking paper	paper de fumar	*papel de fumar*
snail	cargol	*caracol (comestible)*
snatch [weight-lifting]	arrencada	*arrancada*
snow	neu f	*nieve f*
so	així	*así*
soap	(pastilla de) sabó	*(pastilla de) jabón*
sock(s)	mitjó; mitjons m pl	*calcetín; calcetines m pl*
socket	endoll	*enchufe*
soda water	soda; aigua de sifó	*doda; agua seltz/de sifón*
soft	tou, -ova	*blando, -a*
soft drink	refresc	*refresco*
softly; in a low voice	en veu baixa	*en voz baja; bajo*
soldier	militar; soldat	*militar; soldado*
sole (of shoe)	sola	*suela*

sole (of the foot)	planta del peu	*planta (del pie)*
sole (fish)	llenguado	*lenguado*
soling	soling	*soling*
some	alguns, algunes	*algunos, -as*
sometimes	a/de vegades	*a veces*
son	fill	*hijo*
soon	aviat	*pronto*
soothe; go numb [v.]	adormir-se	*adormecerse*
sore throat	mal de coll	*dolor de garganta*
soup concentrate	pastes de sopa	*pastas de sopa*
soups	sopes	*sopas*
sour	agre, -a; àcid, -a	*agrio, -a; ácido, -a*
sour cream	nata/crema agra	*crema agria*
south	sud	*sur*
souvenirs	objectes de regal; records	*objetos de regalo; recuerdos*
spaghetti	espaguetis	*espaguetis*
Spanish omelette	truita (a l') espanyola	*tortilla (a la) española*
Spanish peseta(s)	pesseta espanyola; pessetes espanyoles	*peseta(s) española(s)*
RENFE Spanish railway line	RENFE f	*RENFE f*
spare part	peça de recanvi	*pieza de repuesto*
spare tire	roda de recanvi	*rueda de repuesto; rueda de recambio*
spark plug	bugia	*bujía*
speak [v.]	parlar	*hablar*
special branch; field	especialitat f	*especialidad f*
special delivery	urgent	*urgente*
specialist	especialista	*especialista*
spectator	espectador, -a	*espectador, -a*
speed	velocitat	*velocidad*
speed limit	límit de velocitat	*límite de velocidad*
speed race	cursa de velocitat	*carrera de velocidad*
speed skating	patinatge de velocitat	*patinaje de velocidad*
speeding	excés de velocitat	*exceso de velocidad*
speedometer	velocímetre	*velocímetro*
spend [v.] the night	pernoctar	*pernoctar*
spices	espècies; condiments	*especias; condimentos*
spinach	espinac	*espinaca*
spleen	melsa	*bazo*

English	Catalan	Spanish
spoon	cullera	*cuchara*
sport	esport	*deporte*
sport, to play a; go in for sports	practicar un esport; fer esport	*practicar los deportes; practicar un deporte; hacer deporte*
sporting goods	articles d'esports	*artículos de deporte*
sports [adj.]; sporty	esportiu, -iva	*deportivo, -a*
sports hall	palau d'esports	*palacio de deportes*
sports pavilion	pavelló d'esports	*pabellón de deportes; polideportivo*
sports shoes	sabates esportives	*zapatos deportivos*
sportsman; sportswoman	esportista	*deportista*
spring [season]	primavera	*primavera*
spring, in	a la primavera	*en primavera*
springboard dive(s)	salt(s) de trampolí i de palanca	*salto(s) de trampolín y de palanca*
squall; downpour	xàfec	*chubasco*
square [adj.]	quadrat, -ada	*cuadrado, -a*
square; public square	plaça	*plaza*
squid	calamar(s)	*calamar*
stadium	estadi	*estadio*
box; presidential box	llotja; llotja presidencial	*palco, palco presidencial*
bleachers; tiers	grades	*gradas*
standing room	localitats de peu	*localidades de (a) pie*
staff; teachers	professorat	*profesorado*
stage	escenari	*escenario*
stain	taca	*mancha*
stain remover	llevataques	*quitamanchas*
stall [theat.]	butaca	*butaca*
stall [v.] [tech.]	calar-se	*calarse*
stamp	segell	*sello*
stamp (for documents)	pòlissa	*póliza*
stamp sales	venda de segells	*venta de sellos*
stamp vendor	venedor/expenedor de segells	*expendedor de sellos*
standard gun/pistol	pistola estàndard; (pistola esportiva)	*pistola estándar; (pistola deportiva)*
standard rifle	carrabina/fusell estàndard	*carabina/fusil estándar*
star [boat]	star	*star*

.... star [hotel]	de .... estrelles	*de .... estrellas*
start [v.] [a car]	engegar	*arrancar*
starting motor	motor d'engegada	*motor de arranque*
station	estació f	*estación f*
stationer's; school material	papereria; material escolar	*papelería; material escolar*
statue	estàtua	*estatua*
steak	bistec	*bistec; bisté*
steak tartare	bistec tàrtar	*bistéc tártar*
steel	acer	*acero*
steeplechase	cursa d'obstacles	*carrera de/con obstáculos*
steering wheel	volant	*volante*
sterilized gauze	gasa (esterilitzada)	*gasa (esterilizada)*
sterling pound(s)	lliura esterlina; lliures esterlines	*libra(s) esterlina(s)*
stern [mar.]	popa	*popa*
stewardess	assistenta de vol; hostessa d'avió	*azafata*
stock exchange	borsa	*bolsa*
stockings	mitges f pl	*medias f pl*
stomach	estòmac	*estómago*
stomach ache, to have a	tenir mal d'estómac	*dolerle el estómago*
stop [v.]	parar; aturar-se	*parar*
stop in [v.]	fer escala	*hacer escala*
stopover	escala	*escala*
stopped, to be	estar parat	*estar parado*
store; shop	comerç; botiga	*comercio; tienda*
storm	tempesta; tempestat f	*tormenta*
story; tale	conte	*cuento*
stove; cooker	cuina	*cocina*
straight [hair]	llis, -a	*liso, -a*
straight ahead/on	(tot) recte	*(todo) derecho*
straight race	cursa plana/llisa	*carrera plana/lisa*
strange	estrany, -a; rar, -a	*extraño, -a; raro, -a*
strawberry	maduixa; maduixot	*fresa; fresón*
street	carrer	*calle*
streetcar; tram	tramvia m	*tranvía m*
stroll; walk	passeig; passejada	*paseo*
strong	fort, -a	*fuerte*

student; university student	estudiant, -a; universitari, -ària	*estudiante; universitario, -a*
student; pupil	alumne, -a	*alumno, -a*
studious	aplicat, -ada	*aplicado, -a*
study, studies	estudi(s)	*estudio(s)*
study [v.]	estudiar	*estudiar*
stuffed	farcit, -ida	*relleno, -a*
stuffed pepper	pebrot farcit	*pimiento relleno*
sub-director	vice-director, -a	*vicedirector, -a*
subtitled	subtitulat; versió original subtitulada; V.O.	*subtitulado; versión original subtitulada; V.O.*
suburban train railway	ferrocarrils de rodalies	*ferrocarriles de cercanías*
subway; underpass	pas subterrani	*paso subterráneo*
suckling pig	porcell; garrí	*lechón; cochinillo*
sudden braking	frenada brusca	*frenazo*
sugar	sucre	*azúcar*
sugar bowl	sucrera	*azucarero; azucarera*
suit	tern; vestit	*traje*
suitcase	maleta	*maleta*
summer	estiu	*verano*
summer, in	a l'estiu	*en verano*
sunbathe [v.]	prendre el sol	*tomar el sol*
Sunday	diumenge	*domingo*
sunglasses	ulleres de sol	*gafas de sol*
sunstroke	insolació f	*insolación f*
super (4-star) (gasoline/petrol)	gasolina súper	*gasolina súper*
super-eight film	pel·lícula super vuit	*película super ocho*
supermarket	supermercat	*supermercado*
supplement	suplement	*suplemento*
supplementary bed	llit adicional; llit supletori	*cama adicional; cama supletoria*
suppository	supositori	*supositorio*
surname(s)	cognom(s)	*apellido(s)*
suture; stitch up [v.]	suturar; posar(-li) punts	*suturar; poner(le) puntos*
sweat [v.]	suar; transpirar	*sudar; transpira*
sweet [adj.]	dolç, -a	*dulce*
sweet wine	vi dolç	*vino dulce*

sweets	dolços	*dulces*
swim [v.]	nedar	*nadar*
swimming	natació	*natación*
swimming pool	piscina	*piscina*
Swiss franc(s)	franc suís; francs suïssos	*franco(s) suizo(s)*
switch	interruptor	*interruptor*
switchboard	centraleta	*centraleta*
swollen; distended	inflat, -ada	*hinchado, -a*
symptom	símptoma m	*síntoma m*
synchronized swimming	natació sincronitzada	*natación sincronizada*
synthetic fiber	de fibra artificial	*de fibra artificial*
syrup	xarop	*jarabe*
t-shirt	camiseta; samarreta	*camiseta*
table	taula	*mesa*
tablecloth	(es)tovalles f pl	*mantel*
tack(s)	xinxeta; xinxetes	*chinche f; chinches; chincheta(s)*
tack [v.] [mar.]	virar	*virar*
tae-kwondo	tae-kwondo	*tae-kwondo*
tailer	sastre	*sastre*
tailor's shop	sastreria; sastreria a mida	*sastrería; sastrería a medida*
take [v.]; to get on	agafar; prendre; pujar	*tomar; subir*
take [v.] (a vehicle)	agafar/prendre (un vehicle)	*tomar (un vehículo)*
takeoff [aviat.]	envol	*despegue*
take off [v.] [aviat.]	envolar-se	*despegar*
talcum powder	talco; pólvores de talco	*talco; polvos de talco*
talk [v.]	parlar	*hablar*
tall	alt, -a	*alto, -a*
tampon	tampó	*tampón*
tan [v.]	bronzejar-se	*broncearse*
tanned	moreno, -a	*moreno, -a*
tanning cream	crema bronzejadora	*crema bronceadora*
tanning lotion	bronzejador; loció bronzejadora	*bronceador; loción bronceadora*
tape	cinta	*cinta*
tape-recorder	magnetòfon	*magnetófono; grabador, -a*

tariff; rate; fee	tarifa	*tarifa*
taste [v.]	tastar	*probar*
tasty	gustós, -osa	*gustoso, -a*
tauten [v.]	tibar	*tensar*
tavern; boarding house	fonda; posada	*fonda; posada*
taxi	taxi	*taxi*
taxi driver	taxista	*taxista*
taxi stop	parada de taxis	*parada de taxis*
tea	te	*té*
tea pastries	pastes seques	*pastas de té; pastas secas*
teacher	mestre; mestra	*maestro; maestra*
team	equip	*equipo*
team competition	competició per equips	*competición de equipos*
teaspoon	cullereta	*cucharilla*
technical K.O; inferiority	K.O. tècnic; inferioritat f	*K.O. técnico; inferioridad f*
technician	tècnic	*técnico*
teddy bear	osset de peluix	*osito de peluche*
teeth; set of teeth	dentadura	*dentadura*
telefax; fax	telefax; fax; burofax	*telefax; fax; burofax*
telegraph [v.]	telegrafiar	*telegrafiar*
telegraph, by	telegràficament	*telegráficamente*
telegram	telegrama m	*telegrama m*
telegram, to send a	enviar/posar un tele-	*enviar/poner un tele-*
telegrams by telephone	telegrames per telèfon	*grama telegramas por teléfono*
telephone	telèfon	*teléfono*
telephone; phone [v.]	telefonar; trucar per telèfon; fer una trucada	*telefonear; llamar por teléfono; hacer una llamada*
telephone book	guia telefònica	*guía telefónica*
telephone booth	cabina telefònica	*cabina telefónica*
telephone call	telefonada; trucada	*llamada telefónica*
telephone number	número telefònica	*número telefónica*
telephone token	fitxa (telefònica)	*ficha (telefónica)*
television, TV	televisor; TV	*televisor; TV*
television; t.v.	televisió f; tele f	*televisión f; tele f*
telex	tèlex	*télex*
telex, to send a	enviar un tèlex	*enviar un télex*

telfer; telpher	funicular/transbordador	*funicular/transbordador*
tell [v.]	dir	*decir*
temperature	temperatura	*temperatura*
temperature, to take one's	prendre(-li) la temperatura	*tomar(le) la temperatura*
ten thousand peseta bill	bitllet de deu mil pessetes	*billete de diez mil pesetas*
tennis	tennis	*tenis*
tennis shoes	sabates de tennis	*zapatos de tenis*
tent	tenda (de campanya)	*tienda (de campaña)*
tent, to take down a	desmuntar la tenda	*levantar la tienda*
terminal f	terminal f	*terminal f*
terrace	terrassa	*terraza*
terrible	terrible	*terrible*
test, to take a; to take tests	fer un examen; fer exàmens	*hacer un examen; hacer exámenes*
tetanus shot	antitetànica	*antitetánica*
text book	llibre de text	*libro de texto*
that is	o sigui	*o sea*
that is why	per això	*por eso*
the chef suggests/ recommends	el xef us suggereix/ recomana	*el chef le sugiere/ recomienda*
theater	teatre	*teatro*
then	llavors; aleshores	*entonces*
there	allí; allà	*allí; allá*
there is no answer	no contesten	*no contestan*
thermometer	termòmetre	*termómetro*
thick	gruixut, -uda	*grueso, -a*
thin	prim, -a	*delgado, -a*
thirsty, to be (very)	tenir (molta) set f	*tener (mucha) sed f*
thread	fil	*hilo*
three-scoop cup	copa de tres boles	*copa de tres bolas*
3-star gas/petrol	gasolina normal	*gasolina normal*
throat	gola	*garganta*
through train	(tren) directe	*(tren) directo*
Thursday	dijous	*jueves*
ticket	bitllet	*billete*
ticket office	taquilla; despatx de bitllets	*taquilla; despacho de billetes*
ticket/booking clerk	taquiller, -a	*taquillero, -a*

tie	corbata	*corbata*
till	caixa	*caja*
time, a long	molt (de) temps	*mucho tiempo*
time, in	a temps	*a tiempo*
time, on	puntual	*puntual*
tip	propina	*propina*
tire	pneumàtic	*neumático; cubierta*
tired	cansat, -ada	*cansado, -a*
to	a;	*a*
toast	torrades	*tostadas*
tobacco	tabac	*tabaco*
tobacconist's	estanc; tabacs	*estanco; tabacos*
today	avui	*hoy*
toffees; sweets	caramels; confits	*caramelos; confites*
toilet paper	paper higiènic	*papel higiénico*
toilet(s); restroom(s)	lavabo(s)	*aseo(s);servicio(s); lavabo(s)*
men	homes	*caballeros*
women	dones	*señoras*
toll [adj.]	de peatge; de pagament	*de peaje; de pago*
tomato	tomàquet	*tomate*
tomato juice	suc de tomàquet	*zumo de tomate*
tomato soup	sopa de tomàquet	*sopa de tomate*
tomato salad	amanida de tomàquet	*ensalada de tomate*
tomato sauce	salsa de tomàquet	*salsa de tomate*
tomorrow	demà	*mañana*
tomorrow morning	demà al matí	*mañana por la mañana*
tongue	llengua	*lengua*
tonic water	aigua tònica	*agua tónica*
tonsil	amígdala	*amígdala*
tonsillitis	amigdalitis f; inflamació de les amígdales	*amigdalitis f; inflamación de las amígdalas*
too much	massa	*demasiado, -a*
tool	eina	*herramienta*
tooth	dent f	*diente*
toothache	mal de queixal	*dolor de muelas*
toothache, to have	fer-li mal les dents; tenir mal de queixal	*dolerle los dientes/las muelas; tener dolor*
toothbrush	raspallet de dents	*cepillo de dientes*
toothpaste	pasta dentifrícia; pasta de dents	*dentrífico; pasta dentrífica*

toothpicks	escuradents	*palillos*
top gallery	galliner	*gallinero*
tornado	tornado	*tornado*
total	total	*total*
touch up [v.]	retocar	*retocar*
tourism office	oficina de turisme	*oficina de turismo*
tourist class	classe turista	*clase turista*
tourist dictionary	diccionari turístic	*diccionario turístico*
tourist guide	guia turístic, -a	*guía turístico, -a*
tow-truck; derrick	grua	*grúa*
towards	cap a	*hacia*
towards noon	cap al migdia	*hacia (el) mediodía*
towards here	cap aquí	*hacia aquí*
towel	tovallola	*toalla*
town/city hall	ajuntament	*ayuntamiento*
toy	joguina	*juguete*
toy shop	botiga de joguines; joguines	*juguetería*
track events	proves/curses de pista	*pruebas/carreras de pista*
tractor	tractor	*tractor*
traffic jam	embussament	*atasco*
traffic light ;	semàfor	*semáforo*
red light ;	llum vermella	*luz roja*
yellow light ;	llum groga	*luz amarilla*
green light	llum verd	*luz verde*
traffic police	policia de trànsit	*policía de tráfico*
traffic signal	senyal de circulació	*señal f de tráfico*
tragedy	tragèdia	*tragedia*
train	tren	*tren*
	entrenar(-se)	*entrenar(se)*
train schedule	guia de ferrocarrils; horari (de trens)	*guía de ferrocarriles; horario (de trenes)*
trainer; coach	entrenador, -a	*entrenador, -a*
training; coaching	entrenament	*entrenamiento*
transfer	transferència	*transferencia*
transfer; change [v.]	fer transbord; transbordar	*hacer transbordo; transbordar*
translate [v.]	traduir	*traducir*
trap-shooting	trap; tir de fossa olímpica	*trap; tiro de fosa olímpica*

trash/garbage bag	bossa d'escombraries	*bolsa de basura*
trash; garbage	escombraries f pl	*basura*
travel [v.]	viatjar	*viajar*
travel by train, to	viatjar amb tren	*viajar en tren*
travel bag	bossa de viatge	*bolsa de viaje*
traveller; passenger	viatger	*viajero*
traveller's check	xec de viatge	*cheque de viaje*
tray	plàtera; plata; safata	*bandeja*
trimester	trimestre	*trimestre*
trip	excursió	*excursión*
tripes	tripes	*callos/tripas*
trollybus	troleibús	*trolebús*
trophy	trofeu	*trofeo*
trout	truita	*trucha*
truck; lorry	camió	*camión*
trunk; boot [auto.]	maleter	*maletero*
trunk call	telefonada interurbana	*conferencia interurbana*
tube (tyre)	cambra (d'aire)	*cámara (de aire)*
tube wrench	clau de tub	*llave tubular*
tuberculosis	tuberculosi f	*tuberculosis f*
Tuesday	dimarts	*martes*
tulip	tulipa	*tulipán*
tuna(fish)	tonyina	*atún*
tuning; tune-up [auto.]	reglatge	*puesta a punto; reglaje*
turkey	gall dindi	*pavo*
turn [v.]	girar; tombar	*girar; torcer*
turntable	tocadiscos; giradiscos	*tocadiscos*
twenty-four hour cashpoint	caixer automàtic	*cajero automático*
two halves/periods	dos temps	*dos tiempos*
two weeks ago	fa dues setmanes; dues setmanes endarrera	*hace dos semanas; dos semanas atrás*
two-seater	biplaça	*biplaza*
typical Catalan/ Spanish cooking	cuina típica catalana/ espanyola	*cocina típica catalana/ española*
ugly	lleig, lletja	*feo, -a*
umbrella	paraigua	*paraguas*
umpire; referee	àrbitre, -a; jutge, -essa	*árbitro, -a; juez, -a*
uncle	oncle	*tío*

unconscious, to be	perdre el coneixement	*perder el conocimiento*
underground;	sota	*debajo*
subway	metro	*metro*
underpants	calçotets f pl; eslip	*calzoncillos m pl; slip*
underpass	pas inferior	*paso inferior*
understand [v.]	comprendre	*comprender*
unfair	injust, -a	*injusto, -a*
university classroom	aula universitària	*aula universitaria*
university; college	universitat f	*universidad f*
unknown addressee	destinatari desconegut	*destinatario desconocido*
unleaded gas/petrol	gasolina sense plom	*gasolina sin plomo*
unpleasant	antipàtic, -a	*antipático, -a*
unscrew [v.]	descargolar	*destornillar*
until now	fins ara	*hasta ahora*
until; up to	fins a	*hasta*
up	(a) dalt	*arriba*
upwards; up	amunt	*hacia arriba*
U-rated film (suitable for all)	apta; tots els públics	*apta; todos los públicos*
urgent	urgent	*urgente*
urine analysis	anàlisi d'orina	*análisis de orina*
U.S.A. dollar(s)	dòlar(s) EUA	*dólar(es) USA*
usher	acomodador	*acomodador*
vaccinate [v.]	vacunar	*vacunar*
vacuum cleaner	aspirador(a)	*aspirador*
value	valor	*valor*
valve	vàlvula	*válvula*
van	furgoneta	*furgoneta*
vanilla ice cream	gelat de vainilla	*helado de vainilla*
variable	variable	*variable*
VAT included	IVA inclòs	*I.V.A. incluido*
veal rolls	rotllos de vedella	*revueltos de ternera*
veal pats	medallons de vedella	*medallones de ternera*
vegetable(s)	verdura; verdures	*verdura(s)*
vegetable soup	sopa de verdures	*sopa de verduras*
vegetable dishes	plats de verdura	*platos de verdura*
vehicle	vehicle	*vehículos*
vein/s	vena; venes	*vena/s*
velodrome; cycle track	velòdrom	*velódromo*
venereal disease	malaltia venèria	*enfermedad venérea*

very	molt	*muy*
very much	moltíssim, -a	*muchísimo, -a*
very well	molt bé	*muy bien*
vestibule; lobby	vestíbul	*vestíbulo*
victory	victòria	*victoria*
video	vídeo	*vídeo*
video camara	cambra de vídeo	*cámera de vídeo*
Viennese-style escalope	escalopa a la vienesa	*escalope a la vienesa*
vinegar	vinagre	*vinagre*
violet	violeta	*violeta*
Virginia cigarrettes	cigarretes rosses/suaus	*cigarrillos rubios/suaves*
visa	visat	*visado*
vitamin	vitamina	*vitamina*
volleyball	voleibol	*voleibol; balonvola*
voltage	voltatge	*voltaje*
volume [of a book]	volum; tom	*tomo; volumen*
vomit [v.]	vomitar	*vomitar*
voyage; crossing	travessia	*travesía*
waist	cintura	*cintura*
waiter	cambrer	*camarero*
waiting list	llista d'espera	*lista de espera*
waiting room	sala d'espera	*sala de espera*
waitress	cambrera	*camarera*
walking race	marxa	*marcha*
wall paper	paper pintat	*papel pintado*
wallet	cartera	*cartera*
walnut	nou f	*nuez f*
warm-up exercises	escalfament	*calentamiento*
warning	avís	*aviso*
wash [v.]	rentar	*lavar*
washbasin; washroom	lavabo	*lavabo*
washing machine	rentadora	*lavadora*
washroom(s)	lavabo(s)	*lavabo(s)*
watch	rellotge	*reloj*
watch repair	reparació de rellotges	*reparación de relojes*
watchmaker; clockmaker	rellotger	*relojero*
watchmaker's	rellotgeria	*relojería*
water	aigua	*agua*

water, gas, electrical - instalations	aigua, gas, electricitat instal·lacions	*agua, gas, electricidad - instalaciones*
repairs	reparacions	*reparaciones*
watermelon	síndria	*sandía*
waterpolo	waterpolo	*waterpolo; polo acuático*
water-skiing	esquí aquàtic	*esquí acuático*
wave	ona	*ola*
wax museum	museu de cera	*museo de cera*
weak	feble	*débil*
wedding	boda; casament	*boda*
wedding ring	aliança; anell de casament	*alianza; anillo de boda*
Wednesday	dimecres	*miércoles*
week	setmana	*semana*
weekly	setmanalment	*semanalmente*
weigh [v.]	pesar	*pesar*
weight-lifting	halterofília	*halterofilia; levantamiento de pesas*
well	bé	*bien*
well [interjec.]	doncs	*pues*
west	oest	*oeste*
western (film)	pel·lícula de l'oest	*película del oeste*
wet	humit, -ida	*húmedo, -a*
what	que	*que*
what?	què?	*¿qué?*
wheel	roda	*rueda*
wheel balancing	equilibrat de pneumàtics	*equilibrado de neumáticos*
when?	Quan?	*¿cuándo?*
where?	on?	*¿dónde?*
which?	quin, -a?	*¿cuál?; ¿qué?*
whisky	whisky	*whisky*
white	blanc, -a	*blanco, -a*
white coffee	cafè amb llet	*café con leche*
white wine	vi blanc	*vino blanco*
who?	qui?	*¿quién?*
whooping cough	tos ferina	*tos ferina*
why?	per què?	*¿por qué?*
wide	ample, -a	*ancho, -a*
widow	vídua; viuda	*viuda*

widower	vidu; viudo	*viudo*
wife	esposa	*esposa*
wild boar	senglar; porc senglar	*jabalí*
wild goose	oca salvatge	*ganso salvage*
wild water slalom	eslàlom en aigües vives	*eslalom en aguas bravas*
win [v.]	triomfar; guanyar; vèncer	*triunfar; ganar; vencer*
wind	vent	*viento*
wind up [v.] (a watch)	donar-li corda (al rellotge)	*darle cuerda (al reloj)*
window	finestra; finestrella; vidre	*ventanilla; ventana; cristal*
windshield; windscreen	parabrisa m	*parabrisas*
windshield wiper	eixugaparabrisa m; netejavidres	*limpiaparabrisas m*
windsurfing	windsurfing; surf de vela	*windsurfing; surf de vela*
wine	vi	*vino*
wine cellar	celler	*bodega*
wine, a bottle/liter of	una ampolla/un litre de vi	*una botella/un litro de vino*
wine, a glass of	un vas/got de vi	*un vaso de vino*
winner	guanyador, -a; vencedor, -a; triomfador, -a	*ganador, -a; vencedor, -a; triunfador, -a*
winter	hivern	*invierno*
winter, in	a l'hivern	*en invierno*
wire [metal]	filferro	*alambre*
with cream	amb crema	*a la crema*
withdraw [v.] (money)	treure (diners)	*sacar (dinero)*
with vinaigrette	a la vinagreta	*a la vinagreta*
without a part [hair]	sense ratlla	*sin raya*
woman	dona; muller	*mujer*
wonderful	meravellós, -osa	*maravilloso, -a*
wool	llana; teixit de llana	*lana; tejido de lana*
word	paraula	*palabra*
work	treball; feina	*trabajo*
work [art]	obra	*obra*
worker	obrer, -a; treballador, -a	*obrero, -a; trabajador, -a*
working day	dia (m.) feiner	*día (m.) laborable*

world champion	campió, -ona del món; campió, -ona mundial	*campeón, -a mundial; campeón, -ona del mundo*
world championship	campionat mundial	*campeonato mundial*
world/national record	rècord mundial/ nacional	*récord mundial/ nacional*
wound	ferida	*herida*
wrap [v.]	embolicar	*envolver*
wrench; spanner	clau f	*llave f*
wrestling	lluita	*lucha*
wrist-watch	rellotge de polsera	*reloj de pulsera*
write [v.]	escriure	*escribir*
writer	escriptor, -a	*escritor, -a*
writing paper	paper de cartes	*papel de cartas*
X-rated cinema	sala X (ics)	*sala X (equis)*
X-ray, to have an	fer(-li) una radiografia	*hacer(le) una radio-grafía*
year	any	*año*
year ago, a	fa un any	*hace un año*
year, this	aquest any; enguany	*este año*
yearly	anualment	*anualmente*
yeast	llevat	*levadura*
yellow	groc, -oga	*amarillo, -a*
yes	sí	*sí*
yesterday	ahir	*ayer*
yogurt	iogurt	*yogur*
you've dialed the wrong number	s'ha equivocat de número	*se ha equivocado de número*
young lady; Miss	senyoreta	*señorita*
young; youth	jove(s)	*joven; jóvenes*
yours (at end of letter)	atentament	*atentamente*
youth hostel	alberg de joventut	*albergue de juventud*
zip/post code	codi postal	*código postal*
zipper	cremallera m	*cremallera m*
zoo	(parc) zoològic; zoo	*(parque) zoológico; zoo*

15. THEMATICAL AND ALPHABETICAL INDEX